In the Skin of the City

A THEORY IN FORMS BOOK

Series Editors: Nancy Rose Hunt and Achille Mbembe

In the Skin of the City

Spatial Transformation in Luanda

ANTÓNIO TOMÁS

DUKE UNIVERSITY PRESS
Durham and London   2022

Printed in the United States of America on acid-free paper ∞
Project editor: Lisa Lawley
Designed by Courtney Leigh Richardson
Typeset in Knockout and Portrait by Westchester Publishing Services

Library of Congress Cataloging-in-Publication Data
Names: Tomás, António, [date] author.
Title: In the skin of the city : spatial transformation in Luanda /
António Tomás.
Other titles: Theory in forms.
Description: Durham : Duke University Press, 2022. | Series: Theory in
forms | Includes bibliographical references and index.
Identifiers: LCCN 2021043750 (print)
LCCN 2021043751 (ebook)
ISBN 9781478015529 (hardcover)
ISBN 9781478018155 (paperback)
ISBN 9781478022763 (ebook)
Subjects: LCSH: Urbanization—Angola—Luanda (Luanda) |
Urbanization—Angola—Luanda (Luanda)—History. | Urban renewal—
Angola—Luanda (Luanda) | Ethnology—Angola—Luanda (Luanda) |
Sociology, Urban—Angola—Luanda (Luanda) | Luanda (Luanda,
Angola)—History. | BISAC: SOCIAL SCIENCE / Sociology / Urban |
HISTORY / Africa / South / General
Classification: LCC HT384.A52 L836 2022 (print) | LCC HT384.A52
(ebook) | DDC 307.7609673/2—dc23/eng/20211130
LC record available at https://lccn.loc.gov/2021043750
LC ebook record available at https://lccn.loc.gov/2021043751

Cover art: Detail of *Township Wall/Margem da Zona Limite* (On the
margins of the borderland), 2004. © António Ole. Courtesy of the
artist, André Cunha, and Nadine Siegert.

To my family

SYLVIA, LUCAS, *and* OSCAR

CONTENTS

MAPS AND FIGURES

Maps

Figures

BNA	Banco Nacional de Angola (National Bank of Angola)
CDA	Companhia de Diamantes de Angola (Angola Diamond Company)
CEICA	Centro de Estudos e Investigação Científica de Arquitectura (Center for the Study and Scientific Research of Architecture)
CFB	Caminho de Ferro de Benguela (Benguela Railway)
CFL	Caminho de Ferro de Luanda (Luanda Railway)
CIF	China International Fund
CUDL	Comissão de Desenvolvimento Urbano de Luanda (Luanda Urban Development Commission)
DNIC	Direcção Nacional de Investigação Criminal (National Directorate for Criminal Investigation)
EDURB	Companhia de Desenvolvimento Urbano (Company for Urban Development)
FNLA	Frente Nacional para a Libertação de Angola (National Front for the Liberation of Angola)
GATEC	Grupo Técnico
GOE	Gabinete de Obras Especiais (Office of Special Works)
GPL	Governo Provincial de Luanda (Provincial Government of Luanda)

GRN	Gabinete de Reconstrução Nacional (Office of National Reconstruction)
GUC	Gabinete de Urbanização Colonial (Office of Colonial Urbanization)
IUUP	Institut d'Urbanisme de l'Université de Paris (Urbanism Institute of Paris University)
MPLA	Movimento Popular de Libertação de Angola (People's Movement for the Liberation of Angola)
OPEC	Organization of Petroleum Exporting Countries
OSEL	Odebrecht Serviços no Exterior (Odebrecht Services Abroad)
PDGML	Plano Director Geral Metropolitano de Luanda (Metropolitan Plan for Luanda)
SONIP	Sonangol Imobiliária e Propriedades (Sonangol Estate Company)
UNESCO	United Nations Educational, Scientific and Cultural Organization
UNITA	União Nacional para a Libertação Total de Angola (National Union for the Total Liberation of Angola)

This book would probably not have been written without the encouragement of Gordon Pirie, who invited me to join the African Centre for Cities as the Ray Pahl Fellow. As such, I am deeply indebted to the generosity of the Ray Pahl Fellowship, which provided me with the luxury to spend an entire year working on this book project, and during which I conducted research in Luanda, wrote two draft chapters, and designed the book's general concept. I am grateful for the opportunity I was given at Columbia University to be instructed, to be mentored, and to work with some of the brightest minds in anthropology and African studies, such as Rosalind Morris, Brian Larkin, Mahmood Mamdani, Beth Povinelli, Michael Taussig, David Scott, John Pemberton, and Partha Chatterjee. Informal conversations with colleagues in coffee shops, at parties, or in seminars on anthropology and the craft of ethnography have also been of consequence for me in finding my own voice. I would like to acknowledge these interlocutors with whom I have had formative exchanges: Jun Mizukawa, Christina Carter, Michael Fisch, Antina Von Schnitzler, Patience Kabemba, Juan Obarrio, Natasha Nsabimana, and Fatima Majaddedi.

Research for this book was completed through various short trips to Luanda, where I have been privileged to count on the help and support of my extended family and many friends, such as Makassamba, Cristina Pinto, Ângela Mingas, Agbessi Cora Neto, Ilídio Daio, and Miguel Dias. I have also benefited from the knowledge of colleagues and friends who have done substantial research in Luanda and elsewhere in Angola—namely, Marissa Moorman, Claudia Gastrow, Ricardo Soares de Oliveira, Jon Schubert, Ricardo Cardoso, Chloé Buire, and Aaron di Grassi.

Chapters of this book and parts were presented in different formats at several events at the University of Cape Town; Columbia University; the University of Michigan; the University of Notre Dame; Emory University; the University of California, Berkeley; Sciences Po; the École des Hautes Études en

Sciences Sociales; the Instituto Universitário de Lisboa; Basel University; the Universidade Nova de Lisboa; the Universidade de Coimbra; and the Center for African Studies at Harvard University. I thank those who attended, asked questions, and made comments. I am particularly grateful to the following colleagues and friends for the invitation to speak at their institutions and, in some cases, for visa arrangements and accommodation: Filip de Boeck, Mariana Cândido, Anne Pitcher, Teresa Caldeira, Ana Catarina Teixeira, Pedro Oliveira, Maria Paula Meneses, Miguel Vale de Almeida, Kenny Cupers, Emmanuelle Kadya Tall, Rémy Bazenguissa-Ganga, Ilana Van Wyk, Étienne Smith and Jean Comaroff.

During the writing of the various versions of this book, I have benefited from the comments and criticism from several colleagues such as Steven Robins, Fazil Moradi, Aaron di Grassi, Deborah Thomas, and Kristin Peterson. Substantial editorial work was done by Caroline Jeannerat and Karen Press. Comments provided by the anonymous reviewers have been of great importance, and errors are entirely my responsibility. At Duke University Press, I would like to thank Elizabeth Ault, who has been the kind of editor authors dream about, with constant engagement and support throughout the various stages the manuscript has been through. Special thanks are also due to Benjamin Kossak; the editors of Theory in Form, Nancy Hunt and Achille Mbembe; the book's designer, Courtney Leigh Richardson; and the project editor, Lisa Lawley, who so patiently guided me through the sometimes exasperating phase of book making.

The last stage for the completion of this book was accomplished through two fellowships in South Africa—namely, at the Stellenbosch Institute for Advanced Study (STIAS) and the Johannesburg Institute for Advanced Study. At both institutions, I would particularly like to acknowledge Edward Kirumira, Christoff Pauw, and Nel-Mari Loock at the former, and Tshilidzi Marwala, Bongani Ngqulunga, and Sivuyile Momoza at the latter. At STIAS, I not only presented the book's coda, where listener comments helped me to come to terms with my theoretical contribution, but also had the chance to spend time and engage in various informal conversations with generous and committed academics such as Anne Pitcher and Martin Murray.

This book was generally written during the least stable period of my life, and a substantial part of it was produced while working multiple jobs. For this, I cannot help but state my eternal gratitude to the various colleagues and friends who facilitated my recruitment to the various positions I have held since the beginning of this project, at institutions such as Stellenbosch University, the University of Cape Town, and the University of Johannesburg.

Thanks are due to Bernard Dubbeld, Thomas Cousins, Edgar Pieterse, Tom Asher, Clara Carvalho, and Lesley Lokko. I would also like to thank my colleagues and students in the African Centre for Cities, University of Cape Town, and the Graduate School of Architecture, University of Johannesburg, particularly Finzi Saidi and Mark Raymond.

Special thanks are due to assistants in various institutions, from countries including Angola, South Africa, and Portugal, as well as, particularly, Adriano Mixinge, who facilitated my access to the documents on the construction of the Memorial Dr. António Agostinho Neto. Being based at African institutions means that bibliographic resources are not always easily accessible. Therefore, I am deeply indebted to the commitment of several librarians at Stellenbosch University, the University of Cape Town, and the University of Johannesburg. At the latter, my special thanks go to Roedina Desai. I would also like to thank those who have helped me locate materials on Luanda, such as old documents and maps, as well as those who allowed me to reproduce, or design, the graphic materials in this book—namely, Gerald Titus, Ngoi Salucombo, Kiluanji Kia Henda, Patricia Hayes, Jessica Liebenberg, Joseph Liebenberg, Indira Mateta, Rui Pinto Afonso, Elsa Peralta, António Ole, Nadine Siegert, André Cunha, Rui Sérgio Afonso, the Ferreira de Almeida Arquitectos, the Arquivo Nacional da Torre do Tombo, and the Arquivo Histórico Ultramarino.

While I was in Johannesburg, where I do not have any close relatives, my family has been a deep source of joy and encouragement. My wife, Sylvia Croese, has not only taken on more responsibilities during the times I needed to keep up with deadlines, but she has also read, commented, and edited substantial parts of this book, in its various versions, and her knowledge of the topics addressed in it have made my life easier. I dedicate this book to her and to our children, Lucas and Oscar, who have learned since a very tender age that Papa is writing a book on Luanda, the place where he was born.

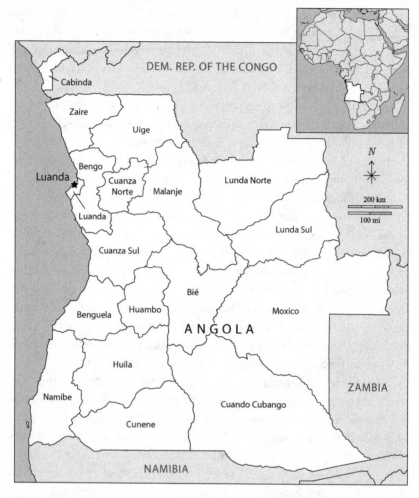

Map Intro.I. Angola.

Hoje muitos edifícios foram construídos. As casas de pau-a-pique e zinco foram substituídas por prédios de ferro e cimento, a areia vermelha coberta pelo asfalto negro e a rua deixou de ser a Rua do Lima. Deram-lhe outro nome.

Today many buildings have been built. Shacks have been replaced by iron and cement buildings, the red sand has been covered by black asphalt, and the street is no longer Lima Street. They have given it another name.—Luandino Vieira, *Cidade e a infância*, 1960

. . .

The substance of this book can easily be grasped through an illustration. Imagine a circle and its different elements, such as the interior and the line that forms the edge. Most writing on cities, from a whole range of disciplines, concerns mostly what is inside the circle.[1] In this book, my interest lies elsewhere, for what constitutes the thrust of this book is less any particular aspect of the city of Luanda than how certain notions of physical and social boundaries, or the lines that denote limits and edges in the city, came into being. It is this set of elements, which figuratively compose the edges of an imaginary circle, that I will be referring to as the skin of the city. I will do so, primarily, by hailing Luanda as a singular city and by bringing back singularity as a fundamental precept to understanding the formation of the modern urban condition.

The concept of skin has a deep currency in architecture, being defined in many ways, particularly as the exterior of a building or, more specifically, its façade. But the way I am using the concept in this book derives from the work of António Ole, himself a student of architecture in Luanda in the late 1960s and early 1970s.[2] It was during these years that he started taking a series of photographs documenting houses, particularly the walls and façades of shacks in the burgeoning urban shantytowns of colonial Luanda, the so-called *musseques*.[3]

Figure Intro.I. António Ole's 1995 installation *Margem de Zona Limite/Edge of the Border Zone* (wood, metal, and glass) from the First Johannesburg Biennale in South Africa. Source: António Ole.

Throughout his long career he used these photographs for different artistic projects, such as the exhibition I saw in Luanda, in 2009, at the Centro Cultural Português, called *In the Skin of the City*.[4]

This exhibition made a huge impression on me, because of Ole's attempt to perform several different things through it. First of all, it is a treatise on form. Although the walls and the façades of the city have been a central topic in his work, *In the Skin of the City* was not simply about this content; it was also, for the most part, a reflection on framing—on how to frame particular gestures of the imagination. Ole has worked on this project for many years, navigating a variety of means of representation. At the core of the project seems to be the assumption that the content of a work of art can be expressed in different artistic media and can inhabit, or be inhabited by, different forms. For instance, a wall in Luanda can be captured in pencil or watercolor, on handmade paper or in acrylic on canvas. The representational trajectory of the exhibition ranged from realistic photographs of walls (in color or in black-and-white) to abstract images (such as in paintings), to elaborate reproductions of whole façades that mimicked the manner in which houses are built on the periphery of the city. Some of the installations were painted in bright colors, reminiscent of pop art, and as such more a revelation of the author's artistic inclinations than an echoing of popular taste, as I will discuss below. As one analyst of Ole's work succinctly put it, these "fragmentos da paisagem urbana de Luanda, designadamente dos bairros pobres (musseques) não poderá (sic) ser encarados apenas na sua dimensão puramente visual mas integram-se numa reflexão mais ampla em torno da história do país e da sociedade que inevitavelmente foram moldando o espaço da cidade, deixando impressos na sua epiderme os vistígios da passage do tempo e da ação humana" (fragments of the urban passage of Luanda, namely the poor neighborhoods [*musseques*], should not be seen in their purely visual dimension, they are part of a larger reflection on the history of the country and the society that inevitably molded the space of the city, leaving on its skin the marks of the passage of time and human actions).[5]

More important, the body of Ole's work I am concerned with is a profound reflection on urban Luanda, particularly one of its main components, the skin, or the set of interior and exterior borders that constitute it. Representing a culmination of more than three decades of work, *In the Skin of the City* had, as its initial impetus, Ole's photographs of houses and shacks in the 1960s and early 1970s, when the city was growing at a rapid pace on account of two interrelated migratory processes: the movement of Portuguese settlers to Luanda from the mother country and the movement of Angolans from the countryside to the capital city in search of better living conditions. These migratory trends were taking place against the backdrop of the anticolonial war that had started in Luanda in February 1961, when a group of nationalists attacked the prisons that held their *campagnons d'armes*.[6] Rather than constructively engaging with the nationalist appeal to negotiate the terms of independence, as other colonial powers were doing, the Portuguese chose instead to deepen colonization through the facilitation of massive migration to Angola. In order to accommodate newcomers to the city, housing had to be built on an unprecedented and massive scale, which was done according to the production techniques championed by the architect Le Corbusier.[7] Behind this urban revolution taking place in Luanda in those years were a handful of colonial architects, trained in architectural schools in Lisbon and Porto, who were proposing sometimes expedient, sometimes more creative and artistic ways to accommodate the waves of migrants and the services and amenities they required. However, an especially relevant feature of this process was that urbanization was taking place through the formal expansion of the urban grid and through the juxtaposition of the new architecture on the setting of previous eras. Very little planning was being done or implemented, nor was housing being built, for the Africans coming to Luanda from the rural areas; they were left to their own creative strategies, to collect materials (pieces of wood, scrap, old tires for the roof, etc.) and resources to build their houses, as Ole documents so well. As a result, the city that was coming into being during these years and up to independence, in 1975, was marked by a stark and sometimes visible line between the planned and the unplanned—between the consolidated core and the *musseques*, the formal and the informal. It is the setup of these borders that divided bodies in the city during colonialism, and how they were overcome or supplemented by the postcolonial state, that I analyze in different registers throughout this book.

This sometimes extremely physical separation between, on the one hand, the built-up and well-serviced historical city stretching toward the ocean and, on the other, the squalor and sprawling shacks of the *musseques* further inland is what at the time was called the *fronteira do asfalto* (the asphalt frontier).[8] This invisible line was manifesting itself through, on the one side, the city per se, extensively reproduced in pictures, postcards, and other forms of colonial propaganda, with its high-rise buildings of glass and concrete, manicured parks, and green spaces, only available for the Portuguese settlers. On the other side were the *musseques*, formed by houses built on sand and inhabited by people coming from the countryside, whose living conditions and stratagems to cope with the urban did not concern the colonial government and the body of professional architects, planners, and urbanists in general. The internal migration of which they were part was for the colonial authority transitory and ephemeral, on the often-criticized assumption that Africans belonged to their homeland in the rural areas. In this vein, what Jørgen Eskimose Andersen, Paul Jenkins, and Morten Nielsen have written about Mozambique also applies to Angola: "Despite some attempt at population control, the Portuguese colonial state had a relatively laissez-faire attitude to urban in-migration of indigenous Mozambicans, who constituted a much-needed labor force, albeit without rights of urban citizenship."[9] As such, they were left on their own to build their houses outside the formal urban perimeter, until they were removed and the land their houses had occupied was used for the expansion of the formal urban grid.

Central here is the way in which the colonial state dealt with difference, particularly racial difference, and how this mindset was reflected in housing policies. For the colonial state, there were two major categories of people: on the one hand, the civilized, formed by the settler population and a few Africans, and, on the other, the large majority of Africans, who were thrown into the category of the uncivilized, or more specifically the Natives.[10] These anthropological precepts were codified in law, in the early 1920s, in the infamous Estatuto do Indígena (Native Statute), which, at the more practical level, turned the Native population, those who were not deemed civilized, into the target for conscription as forced labor for public works. With the growth of the Black population in urban or peri-urban areas, the design of cities had to accommodate such distinctions. The expansion of the urban grid of Luanda from the early 1940s onward was an expression of such a social arrangement, which was the dubbed the *fronteira do asfalto*. The instantiations of colonial paranoia Ole reveals are also present in the work of many other artists whose crafts were conterminous with the unfolding of these processes. The Angolan writer Luandino Vieira is perhaps the one who most forcefully has attempted to make sense of these social and racial divisions and their impact on the fabric of the city. In his collection of short stories, *A cidade e a infância* (City and childhood), written in the late 1950s, he cogently describes the *fronteira do asfalto*:

> Virou os olhos para o seu mundo. Do outro lado da rua asfaltada não havia passeio. Nem árvores de flores violeta. A terra era vermelha. Piteiras. Casas de pau-a-pique à sombra de mulembas. As ruas de areia eram sinuosas. Uma ténue nuvem de poeira que o vento levantava, cobria tudo. A casa dele ficava ao fundo. Via-se do sítio donde estava. Amarela. Duas portas, três janelas. Um cercado de aduelas e arcos de barril.

> (He turned his eyes to his world. On the other side of the asphalt road there was no sidewalk. Let alone trees with violet flowers. The sand was red. Agaves. Reed houses in the shadow of *mulemba* [ficus] trees. The sandy streets were sinuous. A thin cloud of sand raised by the wind covered everything. His own house was located toward the end. He could see it from the place where he was standing. Yellow. Two doors, three windows. A fence made of jambs and barrel arcs.)[11]

In this passage it is clear what this frontier line represented for Vieira. On the one hand, the planned city, with its amenities and infrastructure. On the other, the slum, with its precarious architecture and all the social ills associated with it. This is not particularly different from other colonial situations.[12] However, what made the existence of such a frontier more pungent, as one can infer from the quotation, was that these different worlds were in many segments of the city not separated by railway lines, or green parks, as in many cities in apartheid South Africa, or by the many other devices (stone fortresses, security rings) that compound what Wendy Pullan has called "frontier urbanism."[13] In most cases, the role of separation was performed by a simple road, behind which, more often than not, there was not any deliberate planning intention. Therefore, the *fronteira do asfalto* was enacted through very particular repertoires for enforcing difference. On the one hand, circulation was allowed across the road, particularly during daytime. On the other, the *musseque*, which was on the other side of the road, was not considered a place as such but rather a temporary problem, something to be dealt with through public or private investments that would eventually allow for the removal of its inhabitants and the expansion of the formal city. This book is, then, about the ways in which these lines of division in the city came about, contracted, and expanded through history. I will demonstrate this process by extrapolating the view of Ole and others on the formation and enactment of borders within the city, to discuss the ways in which the social—largely understood as Luandans, or Luanda's residents—has been enclosed, cut off, encircled, or removed from the various urban units that I use to make sense of the skin effects, or agents of separation: the fort, the street, the apartment, the *bairro* (neighborhood), and, in the national reconstruction lexicon (after the period 2000-2010), *urbanização* (urbanization), *centralidade* (centrality), and the Reserva (land reserve). I will come back to these units later in this introduction.

As has become abundantly evident, I have drawn from Ole's conceptual work several insights discussed above. However, I should point out that my use of the concept of skin is also strategic. Here, skin is not simply that which divides or protects and envelops something; I am also using it in the bodily sense of the word itself: skin as a thin layer that, more than encapsulating something, arbitrates the relationship between interior and exterior. It allows fluids to leave the body, but it does not constitute a particularly strong protection against exterior invasions. More important, skin self-regenerates and can recede or expand. The notion of skin I am elaborating here takes its cue from Roberto Esposito's concept of *immunitas*—so deeply imbued in Western political thought, and, consequently, in Western rationales for colonial expansion—as the operation through which the "other from which immunity would have secured us, still constitutes merely the 'other,' that is the foreign and the exterior. It is thus 'excluded' from the privilege that only the 'exempted' one enjoys, namely, the immune."[14] Colonial city making in this sense has always been about the protection of a class of humans, the privileged, from the aggression of the outer world.[15] The replacement of these regimes by the postcolonial order does not necessarily abolish the category of the immune altogether. It rather creates new systems of segmentation, new modes of separation. In the following chapters, I will be amplifying such a view in two ways. First, I will engage the notion of skin as a narrative device to make sense of how the city of Luanda has been formed and transformed throughout its history, and particularly from 1975 onward. Second, I will focus not so much on very specific processes relating to the city—on its construction or regimes of governance—but on its edges and limits, particularly on the ways in which these urban elements came into being and how they have been transformed, reconstituted, and negotiated in the course of history.

Part of this book, particularly chapter 2, engages with the dualities, and their derivatives, of colonial urbanization, which several scholars of urban Africa have examined.[16] David Morton, in a book on Mozambique, traces this dual description back to Frantz Fanon's urban typology, in which the colonial city is divided into, on the one hand, the "white folks' sector" and, on the other, the shantytown.[17] In his attempt to move away from such a duality, Morton criticizes the "historians of the built environment" in Africa for limiting themselves, particularly "when they address only how cities were split unequally between colonizer and colonized and, relatively, the role of European administrators and professional architects and planners in doing the dividing."[18] As such, he proposes an alternative history based not only on the formation of the *cidade de cimento*, the cement city, but also on the *subúrbios*, the peri-urban areas in the city of Maputo.

I am inclined to agree with Morton that such a framework, which sets aside the unplanned from the planned, the formal from the informal, obfuscates more than it illuminates the myriad ways in which such divisions are hard to maintain. In the case of Luanda during colonial times, for instance, there were sections of the city that resembled the *musseques*, and there were whites living in the *musseques*, which countered a stark ascription of race to place. Sandra Roque has written an illuminating article on the legacies of such colonial partitions—based on her research in Benguela but with application to most cities in Angola—on how, still today, many of Luanda's inhabitants cling to the colonial-era designations *cidade* (city) and *bairro* (neighborhood) to make sense of their relation to the city.[19] Having this in mind, I am less concerned with identifying the particular categories of people that belong to specific places, or even how these places came into being, but rather with the notion of borders, or how these divisions between the city center and *musseques* emerged, how they were negotiated, and how they have expanded, receded, or melted away. Ultimately, this book is concerned with the social dimension of geopolitical formations and how behind the recalibration of frontiers lie the inclusion and more frequently the exclusion of certain classes of human groups. Putting it differently and, perhaps more emphatically, the chapters that follow are an attempt at writing a description of a city through the notion of the margin itself rather than through what such a margin separates.

For what interests me most in this book, and what in fact drives the narrative, is the notion of borders, in their more sociological constructs, such as race and class, and the corresponding topographical descriptions that anchor such differences. As such, I will not be approaching Luanda as a static reality whose borders and limits can be easily and unproblematically pinpointed and determined. Rather, the thrust of the argument throughout the book lies on the malleability and, somehow, the undecidability of these borders. For instance, chapter 2 deals for the most part with the modernist intervention, or how colonial architects and urban planners have attempted to separate the city center from the surrounding *musseques* by what then was called the *fronteira do asfalto*. Chapter 3 discusses the collapse, with the country's independence in 1975, of the norms that sustained the Portuguese colonial order and its effect on the city and how, with the flight of hundreds of thousands of Portuguese settlers, the city center was progressively occupied by those Luandans who during Portuguese rule could not afford, and were not allowed, to live in the so-called consolidated urban core. Here, the notion of the border, or the city's skin, no longer pertains to the separation between the city, as the consolidated urban, and the expanding and sprawling *musseques*, but instead relates to how occupants of the apartment concocted ways to keep the city's anomy at bay. Here, the kind of separation that is examined is between the apartment, as the sphere of an illusory and fleeting intimacy on the one hand, and the city as the realm of the public on the other—not a colonial and bourgeois public, but a characteristically African public. I am particularly interested in how the culture of those who come to occupy a space exerts a transformational effect on it.

At the heart of this book and key to understanding the various regimes of separation that Luanda has been through, and the systems that have arbitrated such separations, is the notion of the *bairro*. I will be purposefully using the word in Portuguese to convey a concept that is not easily translated into the English word *neighborhood*. Luanda was subdivided into Junta de Freguesias (Civil Parishes), by the time continental Portugal, and by extension the empire, adopted such a subdivision of municipalities in 1916. However, while the old *bairros* in the city center went on to be designated as Juntas de Freguesias, the new ones, built in the periphery—and to where the Portuguese sent the Africans removed from the city center—were simply called *bairros*, such as *bairro indígena*, and then *bairro popular* and *bairro operário* (which were on this account integrated into Civil Parishes). There is also enough evidence to conclude that the difference between these types of settlements was not only in their names but also in the ways in which they were administered, along the lines that Mahmood Mamdani has argued in his famous *Citizen and Subject*.[20] Whereas Mamdani seems to push aside the pertinence of how the distinction between the categories of citizen and subject might have played out in African urban settings during colonialism, it is quite evident that in Luanda the Juntas were governed by elected bodies, while the *bairros* were controlled by local authorities appointed by the colonial state. Interestingly enough, by the time the country became independent, Juntas de Freguesias were erased from the postcolonial governing order, and the *bairro* became the single unit of urban subdivision. Reforms of 2016 turned the *bairro* into a "nonadministrative unit," and the city came to be subdivided into urban districts. Losing its political claim, the concept of *bairro* was reduced to the meaning by which it is for the most part understood in Luanda: it pertains to belonging. As such, the *bairro* is still the topographical description that squatters use when land they have built on is seized and its location needs to be named. But for governmental authorities, new areas of expansion, such as the ones I discuss in chapters 5 and 6, are hardly conceived as *bairros* but rather as *urbanizações* or *centralidades* (urban growth areas), thereby perhaps reflecting the scale on which urban transformation is unfolding.[21]

Of Singularity, and a Singular City

Proponents of Southern urban theory have made a name for themselves by insisting that the major tenets of mainstream urban theory do not hold much significance for understanding cities in the Global South. They have rightly argued that classical urban theory was shaped in order to explain and account for urban processes in the cities of the North, particularly Chicago, around which much of the urban conceptual armature came into being.[22] Cities in the Global South, the argumentation goes, have come about mostly through uneven relations between North and South and, accordingly, perform a very subaltern role in the global economy, mostly as producers of primary commodities and as reservoirs of unskilled labor. As such, their trajectories do not conform to the evolutionary schemes proposed by the Chicago urban scholars, who viewed cities as, among other things, spaces for the performance of citizenship. But Southern urbanists do not merely interrogate the shortcomings of urban theory on historical grounds. They have forcefully made the case that some of the principles for understanding cities sketched by classical urban theory still pervade the tool kits deployed to grasp the indeterminacies of cities in the South. Chief among these is the concept of cityness, or the proper form of a city.[23] The sometimes rigid and inflexible definition of what should count as a city has for the most part been used as the yardstick through which countless geographic locations in the South are reduced to a non- or quasi-city status.

In a more recent attempt at theorizing the city otherwise, the charge against the work of Christian Schmid and Neil Brenner is a case in point for several reasons. Schmid and Brenner have proposed the notion of planetary urbanization, gleaned from the work of the French philosopher Henri Lefebvre, to grapple with urban processes that are no longer city-centric, or driven by the city, and imply the eclipse of a range of dichotomies, particularly the one between the urban and the rural. More specifically, planetary urbanization theorists have relentlessly attempted to put forward the understanding that an emphasis on the single city framework is no longer theoretically pertinent, for, to simplify the argument, city demarcations can no longer be taken for granted. For them, "conceptualizations of the urban as a bounded spatial unit must thus be superseded by approaches that investigate how urban configurations are churned and remade across the uneven landscapes of worldwide capitalist development."[24]

Responding to the, most of the time, vituperative criticism of postcolonial urban theorists, Schmid and Brenner contend that "in politico-epistemological terms, we share much common ground with many of our critics who work in feminist, queer and postcolonial traditions of critical theory."[25] For they also "insist upon the social constitution of political mediation of all knowledge formation," "reject the positivist/technoscientific contention that knowledge can be constructed from some disembodied Archimedean point exterior to social relations, power hierarchies, spatial politics, and political struggle," and, more important, "connect all essentializing, transhistorical knowledge-claims to formations of power, domination, exclusion, and normalization."[26] Convincingly, they have made the case for the similarities between both schools of thought. Both Southern urbanism and planetary urbanization theories take major cues from the invectives of the so-called LA school against classical urban theory. For LA theorists of the 1980s also vigorously claimed that the theoretical elaborations and methodological approaches proposed by classical urban theory failed to capture the richness and formal complexities of conurbations such as Los Angeles.[27] As such, there is a more immediate commonality between both theories, which consists of the inclination that stems from the attempt to carve out alternative spaces for theory making within classical urban theory. Both schools tend to approach the margins of global theory as, according to Gilles Deleuze and Félix Guattari, "abstract machines of overcoding."[28] They were obviously referring to power, and particularly the State apparatus, but there are nonetheless inferences to be made about the ways in which theory is produced and the truths it reveals or conceals. In this way, any urban phenomenon can be explicable through the theoretical frameworks they propose. Crudely put, for theorists of the planetary urbanization persuasion, the "city is dead," and any fact that emerges out of the ashes of the city can be explained through the selected precepts that they have been refining throughout the years.[29] Southern urbanists have taken as a principle the notion that only specific urban phenomena produced in the South may count as theory, and they have done so mostly by stressing the comparative method. For instance, scholars such as Garth Myers have maintained that the "Global South approaches give us tools to see the making of globalised cityscapes differently, from the margins and shadows that run parallel to, connect with or contest Northern understandings of urbanism and urbanisation."[30]

However, none of these theories has been able to present a solid and robust body of work that provides an alternative to the impetus of the Chicago School. Mostly because one sees in many of these attempts at theorizing the city otherwise, particularly those that engage with the comparative framework, an insistence on elaborating episodic engagements and making problematic generalizations with cities of different scales and with divergent histories. On this critique, I will have more to say in the coda.

The chapters assembled in this book mainly rebut some of the major premises of both theoretical positions. I will do so partially by taking issue with the notion that the trends and contours of modern urbanization supersede the pertinence for an engagement with the city-centric paradigm. Key to my reformulation for "seeing like a city" is David Wachsmuth's injunction that "the city is an *ideological representation* of urbanization process rather than a *moment* in them."[31] In my own terms, the city is that which allows the urban to unfold by obviating the conditions for the urban to emerge, as discussed in chapter 6. More specifically, throughout this book I will be showing the extent to which the urban in Luanda is not a modern process. There was already an urban process underway by the time the Portuguese were busy expanding the consolidated core, or the cement city (chapter 2), as there is an urban process taking place in modern Luanda that has taken the form of an etiolation of the (mostly colonial) city-periphery dialectics. To put it in slightly different terms, the task I will be undertaking in the chapters that follow pertains to an examination of Luanda's urban expansion and more specifically to how such an urban process has taken place through the articulation, or dearticulation of boundaries from the so-called *fronteira do asfalto* to its various historical derivatives and reconfigurations. Particularly relevant to my argument is that even though these boundaries—and what they enclose: the *bairro*, the *centralidade*, or the *urbanização*—are endowed with their own scalar properties, they have as a common denominator the faculty to articulate within them dichotomies such as inside and outside, which, on their own terms, arbitrate over regimes of inclusion and exclusion of various social categories. In brief, by examining urban expansion through the lenses of what it encloses and what it does not, I hope to come to terms with an ethnographic description of the myriad repertoires for inhabiting Luanda. I will do so without losing sight of how these repertoires speak to urban theory in general.

On a metatheoretical level, the following chapters have been written as a corrective, or at least as an alternative, to another problematic aspect of social theory in general and urban theory more specifically: metaphysics. My thinking regarding this question is influenced by Jacques Derrida and the philosopher Kojin Karatani, who in many ways have denounced and attempted to dislodge the metaphysics that looms large in social and urban theory. In his famous reading of Claude Lévi-Strauss's theory of myth, "Structure, Sign and Play in the Social Sciences," Derrida not only reveals the metaphysical residue that lurk behind Strauss's structuralism but also conveys the difficulty at moving beyond them. For even when this gesture is attempted, more often than not, as in the case of Strauss, what happens is the reinforcement of outdated categories such as the distinction between nature and culture. Part of the problem, for Derrida, is that "we have no language—no syntax and no lexicon— which is alien to this history; we cannot utter a single destructive proposition which has not already slipped into the form, the logic, and the implicit postulations of precisely what it seeks to contest."[32] In the same vein, building on Derrida's critique, Karatani deconstructs the metaphysics implicit in the work of the architect and planner Christopher Alexander, particularly the unconvincing distinction between natural and artificial cities.[33] Whereas natural cities are those that have "emerged over the course of many years," artificial cities are those "deliberately created by designers and planners," lacking, consequently, the "ingredients of natural cities."[34] For Karatani, then, Alexander's methodology is profoundly marked by what he calls "the Platonic will to architecture," which "rather than resorting to the illusion of nature as exterior to the man-made, it reveals the exterior as a negative figure at the heart of the man-made."[35] Putting it differently, for the sake of my argument, the concern of Karatani lies with the tendency in social theory to conceive of the man-made as a representation of a perfect and superior order, or what Max Weber called the "ideal-type."[36]

Throughout this book, I will be implicitly proposing a way out of these residues of metaphysics imbued in social sciences in two ways. First, in regard to cityness: the intention behind the following chapters is not positing the somehow incompleteness or disorder of Luanda against the backdrop of what things should look like. For the question I am mainly concerned with is not what the city is, or to what extent the concept of city is universal and applicable to other locations, but whether such a notion—the city—may not particularly coincide with any given physical location and is merely an ideal type, a thinking model, or an exemplary center. As such, my insistence on referring to Luanda as a city, in its various historical incarnations and iterations, is not to come to terms with or to propose any other usable definition of a city. My intention is more basic, for what I want to foreground, as mentioned before, is the ideological underpinnings of the notion of city itself. Such a stance precedes from a basic anthropological teaching, the one according to which anthropologists need to take seriously the concepts deployed by those they attempt to understand: the so-called Natives. To put it crudely: if Luandans have referred and refer to Luanda as a city, I will refrain from deconstructing it as a city.

A second rebuttal of metaphysics concerns the question of land and land rights: particularly how land has recently been articulated in relation to citizenship in significant segments of urban scholarship. Under the rubric of the rights to the city, the vague and abstract right that for Lefebvre should be claimed by Parisians—the right to centrality—has been appropriated and used by an increasing number of urban scholars as a rallying cry to address land distribution in many parts of the world. For Edésio Fernandes, for instance, this concept should be "understood from a combined philosophical and political perspective providing substance to the formulation of both [a] general discourse of rights and social justice and a more specific rights-based approach to urban development."[37] His contention that countries such as Brazil have "already formally incorporated the 'right to the city' into their national legal system" has become the natural corollary, or the horizon, of much of this theory.[38] On Luanda specifically, the right to the city has also been evoked, directly or obliquely, by scholars such as Sílvia Viegas and Claudia Gastrow, so as to make the connection between land occupation and claims on citizenship. Analyzing autoconstruction in contravention of the law, for instance, Gastrow states emphatically that "by insisting on the value of *casa de bloco*, they were shaping the ground through which claims to rights could be made."[39] I partially sympathize with Gastrow's argument that there might be a sort of claim for political incorporation in how Luandans build their houses on land under the control of the state and, in doing so, carve out their place in the city. However, to equate such a gesture to a claim on citizenship renders the notion of citizenship itself unproblematized. Moreover, such a formulation speaks more directly to the currency, or excessive use of this concept in urban scholarship, than any particularly specific examination of how it has been locally apprehended and mobilized.

To bypass the universalizing, programmatic, and metaphysical categorization of citizenship, I will historicize the land question, so as to bring forth the notion that citizenship (in the crudest sense of the relationship between the city's structures of power and the status of those who live in the city, the citizens) dovetails with the shifting regimes of the state-society apparatus. These regimes are conjectural, purely assemblages, having their own historical significance before being superseded by other regimes, not particularly in any teleological way. Putting it differently, land-based claims on citizenship only make sense in the context of specific state-society relations at particular historical moments. Chapter 1 will show that land was not an issue at a time when the whole economy gravitated toward movable commodities: slaves. Chapter 2 discusses the expansion of the modernist urban grid that came hand in hand with the migration of settlers and Angolans from the countryside to Luanda, people who were allowed by colonial urban authorities to squat on public land. The tacit calculation was that the wages of the African labor force could be kept low if the costs of reproduction of the same labor force were also low. Chapters 3 and 4 cover a moment in Luanda's history when the notion of the right to the city becomes applicable, because, after the flight of the settler population, the socialist government nationalized built property to distribute it to the citizenry. Chapters 5 and 6 demonstrate how the city became increasingly fragmented through the alienation of state property—as if pieces of the city were being sliced up and distributed to the population—a process that further intensified with the emergence of gated residential communities. These two chapters also reveal how this process needs to be understood as part of a shift to authoritarianism, promoted by former Angolan president José Eduardo dos Santos, with ripple effects on urban expansion and land rights. I use the term *bifurcation of the urban* to make sense of the conditions through which Luanda has been transformed as the consequence of the direct intervention of central power, which has manifested itself through the split between citizenship and land-based claims. Citizens may be given houses by the state in the new *centralidades* and *urbanizações*, but for the most part they do not own the land on which their houses are built. Social housing in this sense dilutes property and turns the beneficiaries of these schemes into the target for the government's operations.

Chief among the resources I will be deploying to destabilize the universalist penchant of citizenship, and therefore its metaphysical claims, is the figure of the squatter. I will elaborate further on this notion in the coda, but for now, it suffices to say that squatting is that which renders the act of living in Luanda contingent. Squatting is a universal phenomenon, as Mike Davis has so painstakingly shown.[40] But squatting in Luanda is also contingent because it brings together a myriad of practices (of building houses), repertoires (what kind of house in which part of the city, using what kind of materials), and regulatory apparatuses (under which terms of the legislation, regulation, or constitution). On this, I could not agree more with Roque when she concedes that building a house does not translate into tenure, since the house is susceptible to being destroyed by the state and invites us to think of squatting in more nuanced ways. For, she writes, land occupation "provokes a particular relationship with the law and to what is legitimized by the law as being 'urbanized': people desire to be included in the urban and in what is legitimized by the law; but they are in reality excluded as they cannot afford to do so."[41] In sum, it is not because of its sheer materiality that the structure erected by the squatter is precarious; it is precarious because of its relation to the law.

Hence, the notion of squatting that pervades this book is one in which squatters are not simply the subjects who refuse to comply with sacrosanct ideologies that sustain private property, nor are they those who occupy land in defiance of state principles, rules, and regulations regarding land use; rather, they are those who stand on the margin, or the skin, for they always arbitrate and negotiate the boundaries, not only physical boundaries but legal ones as well: the ones who can simultaneously exist inside the government and outside the law, as Sylvia Croese has so aptly and succinctly put it.[42] More important, it is because of their sheer presence and existence and the challenges they pose to the state-enforced order that the boundaries and frontiers within the city come to be drawn and redrawn. I will be showing this not only ethnographically but also historically.

In sum, this book is written from the perspective of someone who, instead of walking within the city, decides rather to take a stroll along its edges and limits. My point, in doing so, is not to contrast this perspective with a top-down description from the point of view of the government and the urban authorities; nor will I take the corrective position of writing from the bottom up, focusing on the perspectives of the urban poor and their legitimate struggles. I am interested, rather, in taking a more "sideways" approach, one that enacts a sort of "lateral thinking" as defined by Stefano Boeri in his concept of the "Eclectic Atlas."[43] For, as Boeri adduces, it is this sort of lateral gaze on the city that "may help us not only to see how individual tremors change the territory, but also to understand the strangely evolving assonance that binds these tremors together."[44] Accordingly, I will not be providing detailed anecdotes or full descriptions of particular individuals, the ways in which they eke out a living, or even transcriptions of interviews, as anthropologists are expected to do. Instead, this book is an attempt at coming to terms with the formation, transformation, and fragmentation of Luanda from the standpoint of its border, or the skin. As if the city's skin could speak.

What follows in the various chapters of this book is, therefore, an attempt at producing urban theory without relinquishing the insight one can draw on by engaging with the singular city paradigm. Instead of asking what the city is, I intend to ask: On what ground, and through whose action and desire, is the idea of the city produced? I will do so by finding my way through the tenets of modern urban theory, by bringing a basic lesson in social theory to the fore: the same causes can generate different and sometimes contradictory effects. Luanda's historical trajectory from the highly concentrated urban core into a sprawling polycentric urban metropolitan area (and not necessarily decentralized, as I will show in chapter 6) fits into the teleology of urban theory. However, to fully understand the ways in which this process has historically unfolded, one needs to pay close attention to and engage with conceptual tools such as singularity and contingency.

An Ethnography of Tracing Associations

It has been more than ten years now since I started thinking about this project and, in a way, unconsciously writing this book. Back then the focus of my research focused on the dollarization of the Angolan economy that forced most citizens to carry, and use interchangeably, on an everyday basis, both American dollars and the national currency, the kwanza. However, the beginning of my anthropological investigations in Luanda, which took place in 2008, coincided with two events whose full magnitude I would only later begin to understand. The first was the oil boom, which provided the government with unprecedented means to buy dollars elsewhere to subsidize the kwanza. This drastically diminished the mundane operations in dollars I had found worth investigating. For during the time of my doctoral research in Luanda, there was not much to observe in terms of the repertoires Luandans were using to navigate the double exchange system. It was during the reflections that always come with the prospect of failure that I was taken to Roque Santeiro market by a Brazilian photographer, André Vieira, and met Makassamba, who became my main informant for the research I would start doing later on. In the next six months or so, I became a regular of Roque Santeiro and documented my experience.

The second and more important for the argument in this book was that during these years the Angolan government embarked on a comprehensive overhaul of urban Luanda. The oil boom, and more specifically the oil-backed loans from China, created the conditions for deliberations over the building of housing and infrastructure through contracts with a myriad of construction and consultancy companies whose work aimed at tackling the dysfunctionality of Luanda. Only later on, back in New York, in the early 2010s, did I realize that during the time I was busy trying to understand Luanda's economic anthropology, a book on Luanda's urbanization was practically writing itself in my head, a book that cobbled together my research interests, sporadic participation in political commentary for Angolan newspapers, my flirtation with architecture (first as a student at Columbia University and more recently as an anthropologist in a department of architecture), and, most important, the experience of being born and raised in Luanda.

In chapter 4, I will discuss the emergence of Roque Santeiro and the role it played in Luanda's urban transformation more thoroughly. Here it suffices to say that Roque Santeiro was a gigantic informal marketplace that came about around 1985 when informal traders and operators chased from other informal selling points in the city congregated in a waste dump and opened their businesses. By spending a great part of my time in the market—meeting sellers, interviewing public officers, riding with taxi drivers through the city, and becoming familiar with places that I would not have any interest in visiting or have access to were I not doing research—I was forced to ponder the importance of two interrelated questions. The first one pertained to the craft of anthropology, when anthropologists are locals or natives. The second one pertained to notions of networks, particularly when anthropologists themselves are not exterior to the networks (kinship, for instance) they are trying to describe, and they are able to engage and mobilize them to advance their research. Finally, and more important, it also seemed to me that my interrogations of monetary circulation would become irrelevant if I failed to take into account the physical places I was trying to grapple with in their own terms.

Roque Santeiro and the zone where Roque Santeiro stood was not simply a place I was approaching as an anthropologist for the first time. As mentioned above, I was born and raised in Luanda. Part II of the book, or chapters 3 and 4, even if not written from an autobiographic point of view, are infused with the emotional and psychological demeanor of someone who was a participant in the events he describes. I moved to Baixa (downtown Luanda, close to the Provincial Government of Luanda), in the late 1970s, when my parents squatted in an apartment. There I spent a great part of my childhood and adolescence, and I still stay there when I visit Luanda. From these years, I remember the almost deserted city, the times when the children of the neighborhood could play soccer on the frequently carless roads. The site of Epic Sana, now one of the most expensive hotels in town, was a wasteland, for us, the kids of the Baixa, a mere shortcut to the slopes of São José de Cluny School—where we used to go for birdwatching.

However, my involvement with Roque Santeiro is of a different nature, which cuts through the very argument of this book. The colonial *fronteira do asfalto* was not abolished with independence; it was simply nationalized, as discussed in chapters 3 and 4. In the early days of independence, people like my parents, who managed to secure apartments in the city center, had an easier way into upward social mobility in contrast to several of my relatives. Living in the Baixa meant that we had access to better equipped and better staffed hospitals and schools, compared with other parts of the city. Being from this section of Luanda where in the late 1970s and early 1980s one could conduct an entire life within a radius of less than one mile (for all the facilities one needed to attend such as school, church, and the sports clubs were in close reach), I saw, not without bewilderment, that the city was growing at its margins, in the area of Roque Santeiro, a place that during my childhood was beyond what was then considered the limits of the city, or the frontier between the urban and the rural. In those years, my father was a worker at a glass factory, Vidrul, and my brother and I would accompany him to the factory on Saturday and Sunday mornings. A fifteen-minute drive to the north of the city was enough to experience the change of the landscape. There were the buildings and the cement city, which was then replaced by the shacks and cobbled roads of Sambizanga. A little farther on, the city was left behind, and the rural area of Cacuaco started to dominate the landscape, with agricultural fields, animal husbandry farms, and salt pans interposed sometimes by factories, the port infrastructure, and warehouses. These sections of Luanda were at that time only very scantly populated.

The structure that upholds this narrative on Luanda, from the center to the periphery, from Baixa to Kilamba, is then more than a storytelling device. It is also personal, for this structure is in all earnestness shaped by my own experiences in and with Luanda that preceded the moment I decided to pen a book about it. Accordingly, this book follows this very personal trajectory from the known to the unknown, from the familiar to the less familiar. Despite the form, it is still an ethnography, but one of the kinds that is aptly described by Walter Benjamin. Writing on photography and quoting Johann Wolfgang von Goethe, Benjamin writes: "There is a delicate empiricism which so intimately involves itself with the object that it becomes true theory."[45] This is also a question the anthropologist Paul Rabinow has taken on in his more recent writings, particularly around the works of the painters Marcel Duchamp and Paul Klee and the historian and literary critic Hayden White. Rabinow suggests that there is a relationship between the shape of the problem and the form, or style, of ethnography that addresses this particular problem.[46] Accordingly, the shape of my research for this book, and the form of this book itself, stem from the *problématique* of the topic. It is not a coincidence then that I have started this introduction with a discussion of the artistic, abstract, and current work of Ole, whose original photographs of Luanda's shacks in colonial times constitute a kind of dialectical image, in the sense that Benjamin has defined this term.[47] Being not only a form of "presenting history in which the principle of construction is montage," it is also a "heuristic principle whose structure sets up systems of co-ordinates for plotting out the relation of the present to the past."[48] The geographical trajectory the following chapters revisit, from Baixa to Zango and Kilamba, is a historic-ethnographic description of Luanda's urban transformation: one that captures the shacks, the dwelling of the squatter, as a dialectical image; one that allows for an engagement with the present by finding alternative coordinations that are specific and contingent. As such, I could not help but write a book on city form, or city formation, that brings to the center the craft of research and the style of writing itself. I will come to this question in the coda.

On following this route, my intention diverges considerably from that school of anthropology, native anthropology, which posits the question of identity at the heart of ethnographic insight.[49] Conversely, I am using my Caluanda (those who are from Luanda) experience, not as a badge of identification with those I write about but rather as a methodological device. It was my experience in the city, the places I know or don't know, that allowed me to grasp urban transformation in a particular way. This book represents an amplification of such an insight, which I am tempted to call an ethnography of tracing associations. I obviously follow Bruno Latour, who, in *Reassembling the Social*, demolishes the supposed disciplinary coherence in the social sciences that prevents social scientists from working in a truly interdisciplinary domain. For him, "[the] social does not designate a thing among other things, like a black sheep among other white sheep, but a type of connection between things that are not themselves social."[50] Sociology for him, and by extension anthropology for me, is a form of academic inquiry concerned with the tracing of associations.

By taking seriously Latour's injunction, what lies behind the ethnographic premises of this book is not an attempt at describing Luanda through the lenses of Actor-Network Theory (ANT). I concur with Latour, and with many other contributors to this theory, that objects as much as humans may be imbued with agency. And central in my argument in this book is the suggestion that enclosures and other forms of spatial delimitations are agentive in many ways. They involve various forms of expertise, they are shaped by the production of legislation, and, more important, they constrain, inhibit, or enhance human action. Moreover, ANT's antimetaphysical approach, its attention to the singular and the contingent, pervades my engagement with urban theory. Central to the descriptions and discussions that follow in these chapters is a genuine attempt at understanding networks and their interconnections. For instance, the gist of chapter 5 is an attempt at understanding the interconnection between Cidade Alta, the precinct of the presidential palace, and the emergence of the southern expansion of the urban grid. However, the way I organized these assemblages diverges considerably from the premises of ANT. Instead of simply explaining the formation and interconnections among these networks, synchronically, I also take pains at tracing their diachronic dimension. Elinga, the house of the theater company targeted for demolition, which is the starting point for discussing Luanda's foundation, in chapter 1, does not only epitomize the disjuncture between cultural heritage and urban speculation. Elinga, being a relic in which slavery and other forms of extraction were themselves the raison d'être for the formation of Luanda, opens up ways in which one can devise networks at work. This shows the ways in which history, or the history of the city, becomes itself a network through which action is undertaken in the name of cultural preservation.

To bring the interplay of all these networks together, and, in this way, to convey the uniqueness of Luanda's urban process, my own methods have for the most part deviated from what is taught in anthropological schools. Most of this book is not the result of a well-prepared and articulated research project, but it has behind it a curiosity instigated by the question of how to follow associations to understand the recalibrations of the borders that constitute the idea of the city itself. Chapters 1 and 2 are based on archival work, for they deal with the history of the city. Chapters 3 and 4 are the most ethnographic because they are for the most part based on my own experiences and fieldwork notes. Behind the structure of chapters 5 and 6, even if they also provide some ethnographic details, is a collage of disparate bits of information. These chapters, which form part III of the book, convey much of the transformation that took place after the removal of Roque Santeiro, which has deserved a fair deal of attention from numerous urban scholars.[51] But my approach diverges significantly from many explanations of Luanda's urban expansion. The idea of urban expansion as a manifestation of the late capitalist and neoliberal forces that have contributed to flatten the world is not far-fetched. But such an interpretation should be considered in conjunction with the local agency behind transformation. By saying this, I do not aim to retrieve the old debate over the primacy of structure versus agency. My goal here is more modest. If reality is formed by the disjointed elements that Latour and many others have called assemblages, then those assemblages have their own historicities. This book is then an attempt at a contextualization of these assemblages.

There are numerous ways in which the singularity of cities has been approached in urban theory. Some of the precedents I am working with, and whose discussions are in a way distilled in this book, range from urban modernism in James Holston's the *Modernist City* and crime and segregation in Teresa Caldeira's *The City of Walls* to various regimes of informality, as in Filip de Boeck's *Kinshasa* and especially the collective project edited by Sarah Nuttall and Achille Mbembe on the worldliness of the African city of Johannesburg. What I have tried to do here, contrary to the propositions advanced in most of these books, is to write not simply on a specific aspect of Luanda—say, on the city's informal economy—but on a topic or a set of issues that could be taken as defining urban principles of the city itself. I focus on the question of the *fronteira do asfalto*, or how to approach the urban process through separation rather than agglomeration. I have taken this cue from Ole and other Angolan artists who have mused on this question, but in doing so I am also revisiting a trope more central to architecture than to urban planning, a trope whose very condition, according to Pier Vittorio Aureli, is to separate and be separated.[52] Or, to put it differently, architecture is always about this dialectic between interior and exterior, inside and outside. The major concern in this book with the units of living (the apartment and the single-family detached house) and with the units of urban organization (the *bairro* and the Reserva) stems directly from this postulate. Ultimately, the concern that is carried throughout this book pertains to the skins of the city, even if those skins may take on different names throughout the chapters.

To sum up, at the center of this book is an attempt to go beyond the dualities that have been used to deal with African colonial and postcolonial cities in most of the literature by evoking a kind of dialectical thinking. I see dialectics, along the lines proposed by Georg Wilhelm Friedrich Hegel, as a useful methodological tool, one that helps us to get critical purchase beyond the false dichotomies in which most of the urban studies scholarship is caught up. More than coming to terms with the calibration of what is formal and informal, or what is the center and the periphery, what moves me throughout the book is a desire to understand the ways in which these categories came about, how they provide ascriptions and regulations for society and space, how people understand these categories, how they negotiate and navigate them, and ultimately, how these categories recede or are transformed by mostly those in power but not rarely by the powerless too.

The Structure of the Book

In one way or another all the chapters in this book attempt to make the case for how social or physical boundaries came about in the city and how they were pushed farther or receded as the city went through the growth and expansion of the urban grid. The structure of the chapters, and how they relate to each other, can easily be described as a series of maps, for each chapter presents a given stage in the geographic development of the city. To flesh out this argument, the book is divided into three parts, titled "Formation," "Stasis," and "Fragmentation."

Part I, "Formation," is subdivided into two chapters. Chapter 1 is titled "Unbuilding History to Build the Present," and it has two aims. First, it provides a historical overview of the city, which is the oldest settlement founded by Europeans below the equator in Africa. It describes the early urbanization and demographics of the settlement and discusses in detail the role of the slave trade in Luanda's formation. Trade in slaves, and other economic ventures associated with it, not only made the implementation of state-led projects possible by providing significant financial resources levied as taxes but also brought about an enduring social taxonomy in the city. For most of Luanda's history, the population was divided into the enslaved and enslavers, and the city space was deeply influenced by the social and racial dichotomies that arose from this division: they created a distinction between those who could claim land, and build their houses accordingly, and those who languished in the *quintais* (backyards), which were the antecedents of the informal settlements that would later be called *musseques*.

Chapter 1 begins with a description of modern-day battles to preserve an old building, occupied by the theater company Elinga Teatro, to foreground and set the stage for the rest of the book, since several dynamics have historical resonances. It notes the irony that the Elinga Teatro was at the center of a social mobilization, not because it had also become a shelter for dozens of squatters (and since its occupation is against the law, it is now a squatting site itself), but simply on historical grounds. The second aim of this chapter is thus to introduce the notion that squatting is not only a modern-day tool used by the disenfranchised to claim a place to live but also an expression of the historical conditions under which Luanda has always been inhabited.

Chapter 2, "Ordering Urban Expansion," narrates the process through which Luanda passed from a derelict settlement by the end of the nineteenth century to a fully-fledged African city by the end of the 1960s. At the heart of this process was how the Portuguese approached modern colonization. The proclamation of the republic in Portugal in 1910, and later on, the formation of Estado Novo, led by António Salazar, were behind a fresh approach to the colonial question. A natural resource-endowed colony such as Angola was, according to colonial thinkers and policymakers, expected to contribute to the development of Portugal through intense extraction. For this to take place, the colony itself had to be developed. During this time, then, major infrastructure projects such as ports, an airport, and dams were implemented, alongside the construction of hundreds of thousands of kilometers of roads and railways. Of utmost importance was the arrival of a considerable number of Portuguese settlers in Angola, particularly in Luanda.

The expansion of the modern grid of Luanda, through the work of modernist architects, came about in response to profound changes in the city's demographic makeup. Not only settlers were moving to Luanda but so too were many Angolans who for many reasons were leaving their land in the countryside to find better opportunities in the city and, as such, joined the population that languished in the *musseques*. The Estatuto do Indígena played an important role in the social and physical differentiation that separated the settlers from the Native population because it contributed to the enforcement of segregation. Whereas whites lived in the booming city center, the Natives were deprived of land-ownership rights and were forcibly removed and relocated to the *bairros indígenas*, later renamed the *bairros populares* (people's neighborhoods), for whose construction the city struggled to secure funds.

Modernist intervention, then, marked the most successful attempt at creating borders and boundaries between different social and racial groups by using the built environment. Whereas by the 1960s the lower echelons of the settler population lived shoulder to shoulder with Africans in the *musseques*, the city center was for the most part occupied by white settlers. These years corresponded to the thickening of the city's skin, to the times when the so-called *fronteira do asfalto* attained its highest level of effectiveness. Most of the postcolonial process of city making, I will be arguing, is contingent on the terms on which the city of Luanda was transformed in the last decades of Portuguese presence.

Part II of the book, "Stasis," also has two chapters; it covers mainly the first decades of postcolonial Luanda, when the city's authorities and central government were struggling to find their feet in terms of governing the city. By stasis, I mean those times in the city's existence during which, in terms of both physical expansion and demographic composition of the population, very few developments of note were taking place—even if the city was bustling with new ways of using and relating to it. Chapter 3, titled "A Place to Dwell in

Times of Change," focuses on the most dramatic period in the city's history. It narrates the end of the Portuguese empire through the coup that ousted the inheritor of Salazar's Estado Novo, Marcelo Caetano. Colonial power quickly disintegrated after that, and the national liberation movement that controlled Luanda, the MPLA (Movimento Popular de Libertação de Angola [People's Movement for the Liberation of Angola]), did not show any inclination to protect the lives and property of settlers. As such, the Portuguese government was forced to organize Operation Air Bridge to evacuate the more than 300,000 settlers who were living in Luanda (out of half a million living in the whole country).

This chapter is concerned, then, with this political change and the power vacuum that ensued, as the city of Luanda lost the population for whom most of the urban facilities had been built. The central government started to distribute the vacant houses to the general population, but several houses left by the Portuguese were simply squatted in. The chapter brings to the fore the role played by squatting in the production of the postcolonial urban.

Chapter 4, "A City Decentered," discusses the physical collapse of the city, on the one hand, and, on the other, the rules and norms that had allowed the colonial administration to keep the formal city functioning and which no longer worked under the independent government. Of central importance in the creation of an informal economy in Luanda was the creation of Roque Santeiro, the informal marketplace at the margin of the formal city. Roque Santeiro was the quintessence of the frontier economy, the place people turn to when the formal economy no longer works. However, more than extolling the virtues of the informal economy, I will be concerned here with the ways in which Roque Santeiro contributed to the decentering of Luanda in the late 1980s and early 1990s, since a great deal of the economic life of the city that passed through the market and the system of public transportation now had Roque Santeiro as its epicenter, allowing Luanda's residents, for the first time, to commute from one point on the periphery to another without transitioning through the city center.

Part III, "Fragmentation," deals with the ways in which the Angolan government attempted to regain control over the city. The government was then trying to respond to, on the one hand, the urban collapse that affected the city center and, on the other, the alternative strategies for urban survival that were being developed by the social outcasts, such as the traders, customers, and neighbors of Roque Santeiro. Chapter 5, "Reversing (Urban) Composition," is concerned with the progressive fragmentation of the urban through the demise of holistic approaches to urban design. This chapter discusses the implementation of major policies for reorganizing the city—namely, the privatization of the housing stock and the introduction of legal mechanisms such as surface rights, which opened the way for land ownership and consequently urban fragmentation.

Of particular importance to the processes discussed in this chapter is the place of the presidential palace in relation to the city. In the late 1990s, the presidential palace was moved from Futungo de Belas to the city center, Cidade Alta, vacating a significant tract of land that was then used for the expansion of the urban grid to the south, Luanda Sul, which allowed for the construction of various gated communities. From then on, Luanda could no longer be defined through the tension between *cidade* and *musseque*, or center and periphery. Luanda Sul not only provided an alternative way of living but also created the conditions for the expansion that followed, particularly after the end of the civil war, in 2002.

Chapter 6, "The Urban Yet to Come," engages with the unfinished business of Luanda's urban expansion. It examines the growing role the president of the republic played in the city's transformation, roughly from the country's shift into a neoliberal market economy and the promulgation of the Angolan Constitution in 2010. The chapter discusses the construction of several government-led developments to accommodate either war veterans and civil servants or residents of demolished informal settlements. The big picture here is that these processes of accommodation have become possible only under the new legal dispensation pertaining to land, which allows the government to clear informal settlements, sometimes without compensation, and move residents to newly built social projects such as Zango.

Central in these developments is the place that the former president of the republic, dos Santos, claimed in the process of urban transformation. It was not enough to form agencies under his own control to overhaul Luanda's urbanism, which entered in direct competition with local bodies such as the Provincial Government of Luanda. In the end, the key for Luanda's transformation was not an urban solution but a political one. It came through the approval of the constitution, in 2010, which on the one hand furthered presidentialism and on the other proclaimed the right of the state to create land reserves, within which citizens could not make any claim on land.

The concluding chapter of the book, the coda, focuses on the contributions of this book to the literature on cities, particularly on Southern urbanism. It takes as its starting point a stroll through Paris whose purpose is not particularly to compare this city with Luanda but rather to emphasize the extent to which one can produce insights on the urban in more general terms. It does so in two major ways. First, it acknowledges that the singular framework does not occlude the possibility of deriving critical understandings from other cities, apprehended in their own singularities too. Second, it suggests that a possible comparison between Luanda and Paris should consider a methodological approach rather than a simple epistemological and ontological one. By asking why, contrary to Luanda, Paris is for the most part a walkable city, the coda engages with the figure of the squatter to propose a more attuned method for grasping the contingencies of the African urban condition.

Part I. Formation

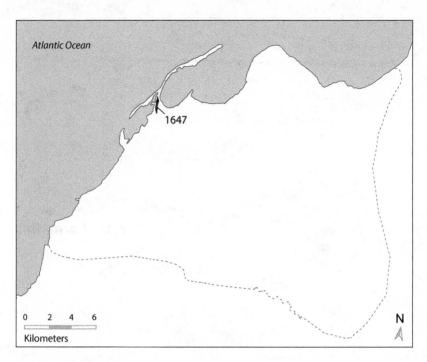

Map 1.1. Luanda circa 1647.

I. Un-building History to Build the Present

Os angolanos, tão orgulhosos de viverem numa das capitais mais antigas da África negra, em breve deixarão de ter de que se vangloriar. Nada de antigo restará na cidade.

Angolans, so proud of living in one of the oldest cities in Black Africa, will not have anything to be proud of. Nothing of the old will be left in the city.—José Mena Abrantes, quoted by Christophe Châtelot in "Morte de um teatro em Luanda," 2012

• • •

In a city that has almost freed itself from the weight of history, one may find it hard to comprehend, in present-day Luanda, the commotion caused by the attempted destruction of the *sobrado* (townhouse) in downtown that has for a couple of decades housed Elinga Teatro.[1] The building had been classified as a national monument in 1981. However, in 2012, the same building was *declassified* to open the way for its demolition. Several concerned citizens launched a campaign for its preservation, and Elinga Teatro was spared from destruction.

In reality, however, what saved the building from being torn down were not the various bouts of mobilization by those interested in saving it but the economic crashes of 2008 and 2014 that deprived public, and above all private, interests of the appetite to raze old buildings in order to erect postmodernist skyscrapers in their place. Despite this, it should be added, the success achieved in preventing Elinga from destruction is merely a half victory, since no document has been issued on the need for its preservation. Moreover, since plans for the razing of Elinga were still pending, as of December 2020, the theater company that uses its premises has been left with a dilapidated building and deprived of any means to raise funds for its renovation. In the end, Elinga may face the fate of most historical buildings in downtown Luanda: abandonment, followed by rapid deterioration to the extent that one day its demolition not only becomes necessary but is viewed as a favor to the building itself and to the city.

Although the destruction of Elinga has captured the public imagination, this *sobrado* is just one of several buildings in the entire block between Rua Major Kahangulo and the Praça Bressane Leite targeted for demolition. As of early 2020, some of the businesses in this quarter, such as a supermarket, had

Figure I.I. Artist intervention along the façade of Elinga Teatro in 2014. Source: Jika Kissassunda, @JikaKiss.

already relocated elsewhere, but others, a restaurant and a car rental agency, still remain there. At least three of the *sobrados* in this square are emblazoned with plaques that confer on them the distinction of national monuments. And while the final decision on the future of these structures is still pending, a couple of them, the most derelict, have become home to dozens of squatters. Some of these new occupants are simply youths whose main source of income is washing cars, but others are more seasoned, such as an artist who does his paintings on the walls and who has collected Angolan newspapers from the time of the country's independence. This occupation encapsulates an irony that is at the heart of Luanda's processes of historical transformation, for it is precisely these buildings in the city center that came into being through conjunctural social relations, on the basis of specific understandings of ownership and belonging throughout the history of the city, that are prey to squatting. Putting it differently, through occupation of these old mansions, squatters are living remainders of the city's cruel past, the one produced by slavery and the Atlantic slave trade. Elinga Teatro may stage the most compelling plays or the most abstract dance shows, attracting the most brilliant and sophisticated minds in the city alongside members of the government and the diplomatic body accredited in Angola, but for the duration of these performances the members of the audience on the second floor share the building with the squatters who inhabit the first floor. The virtual impossibility of telling apart groups of people who perceive themselves as different (in terms of either race or class) is central to understanding Luanda historically. As I will demonstrate, this feature not only reproduces perennial social relations in the city; it also speaks to the spatial organization in Luanda, or the impossibility of erecting borders, or limits, to separate social groups. As such, this *sobradó*, in particular, not only enacts the prototype of Casa Luandense (a hybrid of the Portuguese and the local), which I will address later in this chapter, but also reproduces the sorts of social relations that animated these structures in the past: the cohabitation of enslavers and the enslaved. It is as if the mere existence of the theater company in this building was enough to reproduce such perennial relations. This is of course a metaphor that speaks and refers to a past that the city would like to get rid of, that of slavery. But such a metaphor can also be amplified to comprehend modern-day forms of inhabiting. For when it comes to tearing down buildings in the city center, or even informal settlements, it is as if these places were endowed with an aura, a force, or what anthropologists would call mana, around which social forces coalesce, forcing the government to ponder the opportunity to raze the buildings.[2] Putting it differently, it is as if the mere presence of these structures, or the social forces that inhabit them, brings the government into the calculation between the economic and other benefits of having these structures out of the city's way versus the uproar and mobilization it may elicit among concerned citizens or among those whose livelihoods are pulverized.

At stake here is a dialectic between destruction and preservation that is not specific to Luanda. Cities change, it goes without saying. But, as Ackbar Abbas has noted, "cities change at different rates, in response to different sets of circumstances, in different historically specific sites, acquiring in the end different urban physiognomies."[3] Building on this insight, my aim in this chapter is not to provide a historiography of urban change in Luanda but rather to introduce from the outset the question of Luanda's foundation. By foundation I am only very cursorily mentioning the chronological foundation of Luanda, which occurred in 1576. For taking this date in all its seriousness would amount to disallowing the precolonial occupation of that part of the Angolan territory that was then, after numerous iterations, called Luanda. Foundation here means mostly the setup, or the laying down, of several concepts, that will be expanded in the following chapters. By tracing Elinga's history against the history of the city itself, I intend to provide an account of the ways in which Luanda has freed itself from the weight of history or—to put it in different terms—from its original skin. This is an important step toward urban renewal in the city center, a process that has historically disregarded the city's past. Charges that modern-day Luandans attach little importance to matters of conservation are uncannily similar to the ones articulated by, for instance, the Portuguese architect Fernando Batalha in the 1950s. Batalha's attempt at theorizing about Casa Luandense as an architectural prototype of the past will be taken as the production of a signifier that will be allowed to play freely in the chapters that come. But, here, in this chapter, it will also be used as a metaphor to shed light on the many dichotomies, such as inside/outside and formal/informal, that Luanda is made of and the tensions they bring about. Squatting is then a case in point, for squatters have been, historically, allowed to inhabit the city; politically, if not sociologically (as those who can claim belonging), they are not a part of it. As such, they navigate the inside/outside dichotomy, or the skin of the city itself.

Enduring Entanglements

For most Luandans in positions of power, or those who are members of the elite, what renders the city's historical formation intractable and difficult to address is the role of slavery, and particularly the role played by the slave trade in this process. It has already been established, contrary to the mainstream of Africanist historiography, that Luanda was the main port of departure for the millions of Africans taken from the continent during the three hundred years of the Atlantic slave trade, since the Portuguese controlled a great deal of that trade.[4] Even though other parts of the territory claimed by the Portuguese, such as Mbanza Congo or Benguela, were also important points of departure, the old Porto de Luanda (Port of Luanda)—located about 2000 meters (6561 feet) from Elinga Teatro, the Portas da Cidade (Gates to the City), and the Portas do Mar (Gates to the Sea)—was the nerve center linking labor and expenditure, the Americas and Europe, in an economic triangle of death.[5] Oral tradition tells us that Luanda's geography played a role here, for as most of the area where the city was located was swampy, the early settlement became propitious for the breeding of slaves. It was a natural prison.[6]

Admittedly, the slave trade might not have been on the minds of the Portuguese who arrived in this part of the African continent for the first time. Even though they were already active along Africa's west coast—with the "discoveries" of Cape Verde and Guinea-Bissau in the mid-fifteenth century—they sailed farther south, with a fleet led by Diogo Cão, in 1492, and established their presence in what became Angola after making first contact with the powerful Kingdom of Congo. In the following years, the Portuguese tried to expand their influence southward, under the pretense of spreading the gospel—religion always played a fundamental role in (Portuguese) imperial forays—but they were also busy searching for precious metals, especially silver. The navigator Paulo Dias de Novais, who had been dispatched to the coast of Angola by the Portuguese king Dom Sebastian in 1560, was the first to visit the Kingdom of Ndongo, south of the Kingdom of Congo, another important contender in the dispute for the possession of Luanda. Novais was captured and, upon his release in 1566, returned to Portugal, where he petitioned the king for the title of *conquistador* (conqueror) or *donatário* (land grantee), analogous to the titles given to Portuguese explorers in Brazil.[7] He returned to Angola in 1575 as a *conquistador*, settler, and the first governor of what would later be called the "Kingdom of Sebaste,"[8] a name given in homage to the Portuguese king Dom Sebastião, who died in an attempted invasion of Alcacer-Quibir, in present-day Morocco, in 1578.

On this trip, Novais arrived on the Luandan coast with a fleet of seven ships and about 700 men, among them soldiers and traders, masons, shoemakers, a doctor, and a barber. They settled on Ilha de Luanda (Luanda Island).[9] Only in 1576 did Novais venture onto the mainland and settle on the top of a hill that was baptized São Miguel (Saint Michael); the whole surrounding area was called Cidade de São Paulo da Assumpção de Loanda (Saint Paul's Assumption at Loanda), Loanda being an abbreviation of the Kimbundu term *axilu-anda* (those of the net), a clear allusion to the main occupation of its original inhabitants: fishing.[10] Soon the Portuguese saw their expectation of finding precious metals dashed, but they found the territory full of another commodity in high demand: slaves. For the next 250 years or so, they would not only invest an overwhelming part of their energies in capturing and breeding slaves but also use slavery as the main driver for the economy of the incipient settlement. During this era in which the trade in slaves became the main social and economic activity of Luanda's *moradores* (residents), it also, understandingly, became the basis for the operation of the incipient colonial state itself. The administration acquired its main financial resources through taxation levied on slaves and on other trade items, such as weapons and alcohol, which were imported as means of payment for the slaves. The Angolan colonial government also profited from the slave trade in that many of its public works were built by the enslaved, sometimes working alongside, or under the command of, *degredados* (convicts) from Portugal, who made up an important number of the *moradores*.[11]

The establishment of Luanda's municipality in 1605 has been credited to Novais, as a response to the demands of the town's *moradores* that the newly founded settlement should have the same city status conferred on it as had been granted to Porto, whose inhabitants had fought to keep their town's autonomy vis-à-vis Lisbon.[12] Under this arrangement, *moradores* would be able to manage "os seus próprios assuntos da administração da cidade que não implicassem com a coesão nacional" (their own affairs concerning the administration of the city as long as they did not interfere with the national cohesion).[13] However, at various moments in the city's history, the Senado da Câmara (Chamber Senate), the legislative body of the municipality, was so strong that it took on executive power to govern its own affairs without any interference from the kingdom.[14]

Since slavery was the raison d'être for the existence of the settlement, it does not require a stretch of the imagination to conceive of the extent to which it lay behind the settlement's earliest layout. This urbanization allowed for the expansion of the original settlement beyond the perimeter of the Fortaleza de São Miguel (Fortress of Saint Michael), the earliest building in the city. The series of buildings that were erected subsequently, with the intention of rendering any attempt at attack from the sea difficult, occupied the top of the same slope, opposite the entrance of the bay. Since these early constructions were primarily military fortifications and religious structures, the tone of the early development of the settlement was set. In the following decades and centuries, the royal state, alongside the church, tended to occupy the upper side, Cidade Alta, whereas the merchants preferred to build their houses and tend to their commercial activities in the lower section, Cidade Baixa, near the sea. More important, this layout spoke to a conception of power and commerce whose remnants are still part of the city's typology.[15] Cidade Baixa was strategically located close to the sea, allowing merchants to have direct access to the port, either to ship slaves or to receive their imported goods. As part of this political economy, then, the *sobrado* came to be the main housing style in Cidade Baixa, which allowed owners of these houses to live and store their goods in the same physical location. It is important to note that whereas today nobody refers to downtown Luanda as Cidade Baixa—even though the simplified version of this designation, Baixa, still stands, particularly for pre-independence residents— the site of the presidential palace, alongside the Paço Apóstolico (Archbishop's House), is still called Cidade Alta. This site is then the foundation of power in the city, such that even the postcolonial state has been able to avoid emulating it. Old Luanda, then, consciously or unconsciously reproduced, or tried to reproduce, the medieval dyad of political and religious order. Present-day Luanda is now left to refer to the colonial foundation, Cidade Alta, as the repository of perennial authority. I will come back to this point later in the book.

Even though, during the early days of Luanda, the *moradores* exercised an almost unrestrained control over the settlement's affairs, this situation did not exist without a reaction by a colonial government eager to mark its presence. The Angolan colonial government was behind the construction of several early buildings, mostly in Cidade Alta, including the residence of the governor during the tenure of Governor Manuel Pereira Forjaz (1607–11), which was built by transforming a jail and butchery into the Câmara de Luanda (Municipal Chamber of Luanda).[16] The governor's quarters did not undergo any particular change in their "modest form" until the administration of Governor Lourenço de Almada (1705–9).[17] The expansion of the governor's lodge, in the eighteenth century, signaled also the settlement's growth in line with expanding interests on the part of the military, which had the task of protecting Portuguese trade routes and interests, and of the Catholic Church, which besides working to spread the gospel and caring for the *moradores*' souls, also served as a fiduciary entity.[18] It was not surprising, then, that the military and religious establishments came to determine the original layout of the city in formation.

Fear that Luanda could be forcibly taken by another enslaving nation—the justification for the presence of the military apparatus—should not be interpreted simply as colonial paranoia: Angola's abundance of slaves made it the object of substantial interest and greed on the part of other imperial powers. The French launched an unsuccessful attempt to occupy the city in 1600. The Dutch succeeded in their attempt in 1641 and were able to hold on to the town until 1648. The Dutch occupation was subsumed in the history of the European wars: with Portugal's loss of independence to Spain in 1580, it became an enemy of Holland. The Dutch, in turn, having conquered the northwestern part of Brazil in 1630, required a secure supply of slaves to run Brazil's sugar economy.[19] When the Dutch fleet under Captain Peter Houtbeen arrived at Luanda's bay, it faced almost no resistance, as most Portuguese citizens had abandoned the city together with their slaves. Led by Governor Pedro de Menezes, they found refuge in a little settlement called Massangano, allegedly founded by navigator Paulo Dias de Novais in 1582, to the southeast of Luanda.[20]

The withdrawal from the settlement allowed the residents to mount a resistance against the Dutch over the next few years in an effort to regain control of the city. They failed at least twice. In the first attempt, a troop of soldiers who were disembarking on their arrival from Brazil were attacked and annihilated by warring natives. In the second attempt, Portuguese reinforcements tried to join up with the local resistance but, going astray in the jungle, were surrounded by the Dutch and lost their combative spirit. In the month of August 1648, a messenger brought the news to Massangano that General Salvador Correia de Sá e Benevides, admiral of the southern seas and mayor of the city of São Sebastião do Rio de Janeiro in Brazil, had arrived—commanding a fleet of twelve ships equipped with 1200 men—recaptured the city, and expelled the Dutch.[21]

The recapture of Luanda after seven years of Dutch control was a watershed moment in the expansion of the colonial state into the city's affairs. Correspondence from Luanda's residents to the king in Lisbon tended to condemn the Dutch and accuse them of raping women, killing several men, and destroying buildings and archives in the city. In these documents, the Dutch are portrayed as having burned down the Portuguese buildings that predated their occupation, which, according to various Portuguese historians, explains the lack of any architectural pre–Dutch occupation landmarks.[22] Arguably, these accusations were fodder for the argument, put forth by Luanda's residents, in favor of a larger degree of autonomy from the central government. Charles Boxer has suggested that the *moradores* could put their demands forward more easily after the proof of cunning and courage they had given during the occupation. As such, the Portuguese crown, represented by the governor, was more willing to accede to these demands. It was during this time that Luanda began to be transformed from a mere military and religious camp into a settlement resembling an inchoate city. Since the availability of manpower was never a concern, most of the transformation was driven by public works. In any event, the reoccupation of the city marks the beginning of a new era in which steady investments were made in improving life in Luanda's settlement.

In the following years, the city underwent several other improvements that laid the groundwork for a stronger presence by the colonial state. Francisco Inocêncio de Sousa Coutinho (governor of Luanda from 1764 to 1772), described as one of the "mais lúcidos, mais entusiastas e mais dinâmicos a quem coube a missão de dirigir esta Província" (most lucid spirits, most enthusiastic and most dynamic among the many who governed this Province) has a particular role in the ways in which these transformations have been written about.[23] He has been credited with overseeing the construction of the *terreiro público* (public warehouse), with a tank holding 250 pipes through which water circulated and cooled the stored goods. This was a critical improvement for Luanda, since the settlement did not offer many opportunities for agricultural production because of its dry climate. Cashing in on these insufficiencies, previous owners of storehouses had sold their products at exorbitant prices for profit. To prevent speculation, the state urgently needed a public storehouse in which *moradores* could safely and hygienically store their own provisions. However, this measure was also meant to give the state unprecedented control over the commercialization of products by undermining the role that intermediary brokers could play.[24]

Other important constructions that are credited to Governor Sousa Coutinho are the settlement of Novo Redondo as a stopover for the trade between Benguela and Luanda—the two main commercial centers at the time—a hospital in Luanda, an iron factory in the village of Oeiras, the fortress of São Francisco do Penedo in Golungo, and other defensive buildings, as well as the court next to the navy's arsenal, from which slaves were dispatched, and the Casa das Contas (Customs House) to house the tax authority and the criminal court. Last but not least, Sousa Coutinho has also been credited with initiating oil prospecting in Dande and Sulphur in Golungo, starting a public education system in Luanda "com a criação de muitas escolas primárias e de uma aula de estudos superiores de geometria e fortificação" (with the establishment of a number of primary schools and another school for the study of geometry and military matters),[25] and paying particular attention to the formal expansion and early urbanizing work of the settlement by ordering the opening up of various arteries and the widening of the streets between the Igreja de Nossa Senhora da Nazaré (Church of Our Lady of Nazareth) and the fortress at Penedo to allow for circulation between those two sections of the city.

On account of these improvements, Sousa Coutinho has been hailed as the trailblazer of the modern colonization of Angola. Anticipating José Maria Norton de Matos (1867–1955), the governor-general of Angola in the first half of the twentieth century, Sousa Coutinho was perhaps the first Portuguese political authority to view white colonization as crucial for the development of the colony. During his tenure, he not only encouraged soldiers to settle in Angola, which was not a particularly difficult task, but also worked relentlessly to bring married couples to Luanda from various parts of the Portuguese kingdom, such as Madeira, the Azores, and even Brazil. However, despite these efforts, two hundred years into the settlement's foundation, by the 1790s, most settlers still lived in the confines of the *Fortaleza*. For most of these earlier *moradores*, beyond the fort was the wilderness. The development of the early settlement gained momentum with the arrival of the first contingent of white females, "15 donzelas" (15 maidens), from Casa Pia de Lisboa, sent by the queen, Dona Leonor, in 1657, to "casarem com pessoas beneméritas" (marry decent people)—where for the most part *moradores*, and in particular the troops, were otherwise left to engage in unions with "prostitutas condenadas ou mulheres acusadas de bruxaria, enviadas à força de Lisboa para Luanda" (condemned prostitutes or women accused of witchcraft, sent by force from Lisbon to Luanda).[26] By the time of the census taken in 1781, the white population in Luanda comprised more than 400 souls.[27] This number is impressive, taking into account the life expectancy in Luanda. Epidemics were rife, and Luanda was known pejoratively as the white man's grave.[28]

With this effort to turn Luanda into something that was not only a fortification but also a place worth living in, the growth of the population was inevitable. To accommodate these newcomers, the city needed some basic infrastructure. It could live without a sewerage system as long as a great number of its inhabitants were servants, if not slaves, whose most important daily chore was taking human waste to the beach—with the result that for many years travelers would complain of the pestilent air in the city, which was the cause of the many epidemics that ravaged Luanda. Garbage could be seen at any time on the streets and was devoured by the crows, which, as a report ironically put it, were considered "funcionários municipais" (municipal clerks).[29] However, the city could not go without water.

Water provision was considered the real battle for the city. Lying in an area with a dry climate and insufficient agricultural production to feed its entire population, Luanda was since its early days afflicted by "many instances of famine."[30] What made life possible in the city was the availability of money, or other means of exchange, since most of the *moradores* made so much through the slave trade that it did not bother them to have to purchase everything they needed, including water. In the early days of the settlement, people in Luanda drank the "diminuto e insalubre líquido dos seus poços e cacimbas" (scarce and unhealthy liquid of its wells), while the better-off pumped water through pipes from the Bengo River, about 40 kilometers (25 miles) from downtown Luanda.[31] During their occupation, the Dutch had attempted to bring clean water into the city, starting, in 1645, to engineer works "grandiosa para o tempo" (ambitious for the time) in order to build a tunnel through which water could be piped in from the Kwanza River.[32] But when they left, the project was abandoned. Successive governors who took over from the Dutch were more modest in their plans and were content to use water from the *cacimbas* (wells). A century later, from 1753 to 1758, the Portuguese were still trying to find ways of pumping water into the city. No construction ever took place, however, as it was considered too costly and laborious to build the necessary infrastructure. Thus, Luanda would remain without access to water for many years to come. Yet the population did not stop growing. In 1800, Luanda had about 6,500 people, of whom 443 were Europeans (map 1.2). In 1887, the population had mushroomed to 14,500 people, of whom about 2,000 were Europeans. The city authorities reached such a state of despair that, in 1886, the Câmara weighed the possibility of building a rainwater retention system in Kinaxixe Lagoon, located to the north of the old city center and known for its stagnant water. The plan was to expand the lagoon so that the city would be able to store sufficient rainwater to last for a year. But, once again, this project was never implemented. Luanda's residents had to wait about one hundred years after its reoccupation by Salvador Correia for the Compagnie Generale des Conduites d'Éaux de Liège to figure out how to construct a hydro-engineered system to pump water to the city center from 50 kilometers (31 miles) away. The water pipes were finally dedicated on March 2, 1889.[33]

Since the slave trade was the motor of Luanda's early development, the abolition of this infamous commerce had a devastating impact on the city, particularly when it came to its population, which was for the most part transitory. Even though, during the three hundred years since its foundation, the limits of the city were for the most part unaltered—even if some *moradores* had economic ventures beyond such limits, in places such as Kinaxixe or Maianga— the population of Luanda did not stop growing despite the various outbreaks of pandemic diseases that periodically ravaged the territory and the trade in slaves that was coming to an end.

In March 1807, it was declared illegal for British subjects to hold slaves after May 1, 1808. This led British subjects in the New World to put pressure on nationals of other colonial powers to heed the same law so that they would not be placed in an economically disadvantageous position. This was not an easy task for the British to accomplish. When Brazil became an independent country, in 1822, by seceding from Portugal, Great Britain made the recognition of its independence

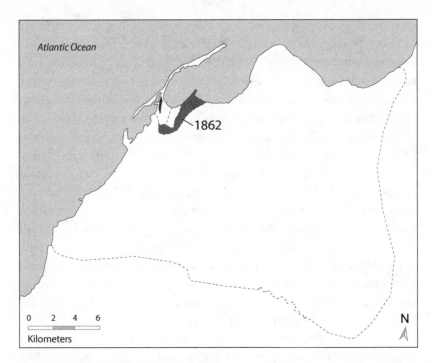

Map. I.2. Luanda circa 1862.

contingent upon the abolition of the slave trade in this South American territory. The terms of recognition and abolition would only be signed in November 1826. The Portuguese resisted this, for according to a historian of Luanda, José de Almeida Santos, "a estrutura económica portuguesa, como de resto a de outros povos coloniais, não estava preparada para uma abolição brusca do desumano tráfico" (the Portuguese economic structure, as of other colonial powers, was not ready for a sudden abolition of this inhuman trade).[34] He voices the sentiment of numerous slave traders for whom "havia a necessidade de uma mutação gradual, aliás reconhecida no tratado do Rio de Janeiro de 1810" (a gradual transition was required, as recognized by the Rio de Janeiro Treaty of 1810).[35] But, more important, he also acknowledges, implicitly, that the British's prohibition did not in fact end the transport of slaves to the New World, particularly to Brazil: "E essa mutação foi-se processando gradativamente, apesar das impaciências e das prepotências dos britânicos" (This transition did indeed take place gradually, despite the impatience and arrogance of the British).[36] From the signing of the Anglo-Brazilian abolition treaty to the moment when abolition became a local law in Brazil, about 150,000 enslaved people were transported from Africa, mainly from below the equator.[37] One of the unintended consequences of this risky phase of the slave trade was that Africans, or Africa-based enslavers, had more control over the business, which, in the case of Angola and particularly Luanda, was epitomized by the increase of unions between Portuguese soldiers and local women, something that had already been reported by the first historian of the city, António de Oliveira Cardonega, in the late seventeenth century.[38]

Such a mix was then the ferment for the emergence of the so-called Creole society, whose most prominent members competed with the Portuguese and traders of other nationalities operating in Luanda. They were the offspring of interracial unions with Europeans; they called themselves Angolenses, harbored nationalistic feelings, and made strides into the social, political, military, and business life of the colony. Many of them, such as Ana Joaquina dos Santos Silva, made a fortune during the slave trade and left architectural marks on the city. Others had agricultural business ventures and organized the supply of foodstuffs.[39] Since colonial law prohibited white settlers from negotiating directly with the local populations in the hinterland, Creoles were critical intermediaries between colonizers and the colonized, and were also instrumental for Portugal in the so-called scramble for Africa. To prove that it was managing to control its African territories effectively under the obligations assumed at the Berlin Conference of 1884–85, Portugal lured in Creole individuals to fight on its side and expand its sovereignty throughout Angola. In return, these individuals were granted land in Luanda in the form of a *sesmarias* (land grant) allocation that the Portuguese king distributed to subjects who had provided crucial services in the consolidation of the Portuguese empire.[40] As a result of these allocations, Africans were in transit in the city, waiting for ships to take them to the New World, and also landlords, deriving a great deal of their income from renting out residences and commercial establishments, a situation that remained in place until the early twentieth century.

To return to the discussion earlier in this chapter, Luanda's historical architectural heritage is the legacy of this convoluted and traumatic past. These are the enduring entanglements that still linger in the city's imaginary. Even though it has not been possible to account for the owner of the *sobrado* that houses Elinga Teatro, it is not far-fetched to surmise that its original owner, or the owner of the building in its various incarnations, could have been one of the members of the Creole community. The active involvement of *filhos da terra* (Native children) constitutes the original sin of the city and has had powerful implications for debates about the conservation of these *sobrados*. It is not simply that Luanda was built and expanded by means of the exploitation of the bodies of millions of people. It is not even that Luandans themselves took part in, and made fortunes out of, the suffering of the enslaved. The crux of the matter is that Luanda was formed through the separation of enslavers and the enslaved and, consequently, through the distinction between those who belonged and those who did not belong, even if the line between these groups was thin and not particularly well policed. And the fact that today several supposed descendants of enslavers of the past may use the history of the city as the basis for their claim to it as a place of belonging renders it unnecessary for those who cannot claim this belonging to protect and strive to preserve its main historical landmarks. Furthermore, it is also conceivable that the loathing for this era derives from the fact that a great many nationalists, who would later join the nationalist movement to claim independence from Portugal, or even members of the first generation of leaders, were descendants of these enslaving families of the past.[41] For many of them, then, the city's history is tainted by slavery.

Casa Luandense

In the early 1900s, Luanda was visibly a poor city, as was any other colonial African city back then. But it was endowed with sumptuous houses from the previous era of the slave trade, the *sobrados*. They consisted, typically, of two floors built on a site of considerable size. The second floor was normally reserved for residence, and the first floor was used for business activities. The basement could be used either to store slaves or to pursue economic activities, such as the sale of alcohol. By the late 1800s, a number of these basements had been converted into taverns.[42] They were built through the application of elaborate construction techniques. The first floor and the walls were made of wood, and the walls were covered with *taipa* (rammed earth) that had to be thick enough to support the upper floor, which was, properly speaking, the *sobrado*. Some buildings in the city had an additional, smaller floor that the locals called *sobradinho*. The tiles for the *sobrado* were imported from Lisbon, whereas the wood used in these structures came from Brazil in the very ships that had transported enslaved people from Luanda to the New World.[43] A local addition to this type of housing, the hybrid element, according to Batalha, was the Indigenous coating on the walls, which was produced by locals and created by mixing mortar and a lime that came from the burning of sea shells. In 2010, at the height of a wave of demolitions, the city could still boast eighteen of these *sobrados*, whereas by 2018 only twelve of them remained.[44]

The neglect to which Luanda had been left prevailed until the 1920s, for reasons that I will discuss in the next chapter. Here, it is enough to point out that the turn to the twentieth century came with a fresh interest for the colonies, particularly those well-endowed with natural resources such as Angola. Timidly in the beginning, the Portuguese started to invest in infrastructure to allow the production of commodities in high demand internationally, such as cotton and coffee.[45] Demand for these products became even higher in the 1940s, when an unprecedented speculative financial frenzy accompanied urban renewal. For new buildings, tracts of vacant land were used. But countless architectural remnants from the past were also destroyed for the same purpose. It is interesting to note that it was precisely during the city's modernization, in the early 1940s, and the rapid urbanization that was taking place, epitomized by the rising up of new buildings where the old ones stood, that reflections on the history of the city and its architectural past were being articulated by a number of colonial public servants, journalists, and writers. Overall, these authors seem to be torn between, on the one hand, extolling the Portuguese presence or civilizing mission in Angola—and glorifying the history of such a presence, encapsulated in four centuries of material culture—and, on the other, celebrating modernization as the beacon of the Portuguese presence in Africa. This precisely required the demolition of the old.

So, by the 1940s, entire blocks of old buildings were being torn down, and even churches were being destroyed to make space for the squares and other open and public spaces that could still be found in the late 1970s. At the same time, voices arguing for the preservation of historical artifacts were also starting to make themselves heard. The champion of this movement was certainly the architect Fernando Batalha, who for many years worked in various government departments concerned with the city's conservation, such as the Comissão Provincial dos Monumentos Nacionais de Angola (Provincial Commission for National Monuments of Angola). In the various contributions to the issues of preservation penned by him, he complained of the alarmingly impossible task of protecting monuments: whenever a building was considered a monument, its owners would leave it to rot until nothing else could be done but tear it down. It is not that hard to assume, then, that Batalha must have felt relieved and vindicated when the Companhia de Diamantes de Angola (Angolan Diamond Company, CDA) purchased a *sobrado* in the city center and, instead of tearing it down to build something else, decided to turn it into offices.

The discussion of such an act of preservation was presented in a slim book, published in 1966, *Uma casa setecentista de Luanda* (An eighteenth-century house in Luanda), in which Batalha tries also to put forward the concept of Casa Luandense that characterizes the city's architecture, defining it as the architectural, or vernacular, hybrid between Portuguese technique and local materials. Elaborating on this, he describes Casa Luandense as a mixture of Portuguese civilization and

African culture that resulted in a vernacular architecture consisting of "casas térreas e grande número de casas de sobrado, bem proporcionadas para as ruas desse tempo" (one-story houses and a large number of manors, well-proportioned for the streets of the times) and forming "um conjunto urbanístico coerente e com unidade de estilo e criavam um ambiente cativante e harmórico que, pela sua arquitectura, constituíam uma feliz e rara fusão do corpo físico africano com o espírito europeu—e, mais diferenciadamente, português" (a coherent urban set, with unity of style, creating a captivating and harmonic ambience that, by its architecture, constituted a rare fusion of the physical African-style body with an European spirit—and, more pronouncedly, a Portuguese one).[46]

It is obvious that the main point of reference for Batalha is Lusotropicalism, the theory concocted by the Brazilian sociologist Gilberto Freyre that was increasingly being appropriated by the Estado Novo to justify the "sociedades multirraciais" (multiracial societies) that the Portuguese were supposedly building in their settler colonies, particularly in Angola and Mozambique.[47] Paying particular attention to material culture, Freyre famously discusses, in *Casa-grande e sanzala: Formação da família brasileira sob o regime da economia patriarchal* (*The Masters and the Slaves: A Study in the Development of Brazilian Civilization*), the extent to which this complex connection between the mansion, for enslavers, and the shantytown, for the enslaved, has been formative of Brazilian culture.[48] Freyre tested his theory on the built environment that was the outcome of Portuguese colonialism. In his view, the propensity of the Portuguese to mix with the Native women was extended into a general predisposition to sustain hybridity, which could also be seen in the cultivation of a particular form of architecture that fused Portuguese-style houses with elements of Amerindian dwellings. Freyre thus suggested that the Casa-Grande e Sanzala complex, a mansion and shantytown, was not only a particular form of dwelling created in the tropics but also an apparatus that illustrated the microcosm of Brazilian society and was thus an explanation for the formation of the Brazilian people itself. For Batalha, such an example had purchase in Luanda, and he staunchly defended the preservation of the colonial structures built by the Portuguese, mostly churches. Or, at least, Batalha might have thought that creating an architectural prototype of a particular form of relations would contribute historical character to Luanda and, thus, help preserve such remnants of the past. However, he also realized that even if the measures he was advocating were put in place, it would already be too late, since a number of iconic buildings that constituted "um padrão real da nossa acção civilizadora . . . um modelo da nossa arquitectura e da nossa integração no meio local" (a real mark of the Portuguese civilizing action . . . a mode of our architecture and our integration in the local environment) were already gone.[49] What happened, in fact, was precisely the opposite of what Batalha was advocating: old structures were being systematically destroyed as their owners resisted all pressure to conserve them or respect their classification as heritage buildings.[50] He would attempt to do so, theoretically, by proposing a disembodiment of these buildings, so to speak, by tearing apart form and function.

The *sobrado* he discusses in the book was derelict and abandoned when it was purchased by the CDA, restored, and dedicated on December 28, 1961, as the headquarters of the company.[51] Situated at the crossroads of Rua Direita and Rua da Nobreza (Friedrich Engels and Cerveira Pereira Streets today), this building was just one of many in that part of the city sharing the same characteristics: "tipicamente local, cujo modelo predominava expressivamente na Cidade, tinha como composição especificadora uma frontaria simétrica, geralmente de cinco vão em cada andar, com a porta ao centro e duas janelas de casa lado, muito frequentemente enquadradas por pilastras" (typically local, in a style that was predominant in the city and is characterized by a symmetric façade with five beams on each floor, a door in the center and two windows on each side, frequently framed by pillars).[52] The interior of this house did not differ from other old manors in Luanda in which "no piso inferior situava-se o establecimento e o armazém de mercadorias, e o andar superior destinava-se à habitação do proprietário" (in the basement were the emporium and the storeroom, and on the upper floor was the owner's residence).[53] Aesthetically, Batalha saw the archetypal Casa Luandense as one of two or three remaining buildings that best demonstrated this vernacular(ized) style.

The building was renovated using "materiais e processos modernos" (modern materials and processes); the renovation included the restoration of the façades "para dar destaque à harmonia da sua composição e das suas proporções" (to preserve the harmony of its composition and proportions).[54] In the interior of the building, its "espontânea singeleza primitiva" (spontaneous primitive simplicity) was retained, and in only a few cases were elements of the structure reinforced with modern materials.[55] In terms of reconstruction, Batalha also notes that several features were added—namely, two large interior arcs as supports for the upper floor, a clay tile floor, split roofs for each section, and a roof and a floor consisting of round beams and large old wooden beams, and so on. The house was used for a couple of years as the offices of the CDA and was then turned into the Casa-Museu Ernesto Vilhena (Ernesto Vilhena Museum),[56] which was intended to be turned into a museum of African art, as a branch of the Museu do Dundo (Dundo Museum) that the company had set up in the diamond-rich Lunda province. Furthermore, the CDA considered buying the whole block where this *sobrado* was situated, to turn it into a cultural center that would accommodate ten rooms for permanent exhibitions; space for temporary exhibitions; an auditorium; storage space for archeological collections; a laboratory; a restoration workshop; offices for cartography, iconography, and photography; as well as a public library, work and study offices for researchers, and offices for services and administration.[57] However, the owners of the surrounding buildings refused to sell their properties to the company, which was thus left with the original plan of the Casa-Museu. By the time Angola became independent, in 1975, the Casa-Museu Ernesto Vilhena had been taken over by the state, which turned it into the Museu Nacional de Antropologia (National Museum of Anthropology), whose repository came from the Museu do Dundo.[58]

What Batalha leaves out of the shifting of Lusotropicalismo to the formulation of the Casa Luandense are the more sociological aspects of Freyre's elaboration on the formation of Brazilian society. One then has to push such an analogy even further so as to make sense of the Luandan society confined in the Casa Luandense. As such, Casa Luandense is not just an architectural hybrid but a social phenomenon, too, for it allowed cohabitation of enslavers and the enslaved under the same roof. From this initial arrangement, then, the Luanda emerging therefrom was sociologically an expansion of the Casa Luandense complex. For instance, toward the end of the slave trade, the number of enslaved people coming to Luanda was so high that their enslavers could not fit all of them into the storage areas of their *sobrados*. So, they built *quintais* (backyards) throughout the city, where enslaved people lived in transit to the New World.[59] A number of these *quintais* subsequently became full-blown *bairros*, such as Coqueiros, Ingombotas, or Maianga, and were partially or entirely razed later on when the colonial authorities became increasingly more concerned with hygiene and sanitation. Here, one can also use this metaphor and extrapolate it to explain the social evolution of the colonial society. Casa Luandense, or the original epitome of the skin of the city, was then expanding, without necessarily altering the structural differences between the haves and the haves-not. I will evoke such a concept in further chapters, for it also evokes a certain, so to speak, sociology of inhabitation, or a hybrid between architectural form and the particular sociopolitical regime in place.

Building History

One may certainly argue here that the CDA, later Museu de Antropologia, was saved from destruction by the function it was called to perform in times of urban renewal and not for the particular history that it embodied, reversing the principle so cherished by architectural modernists that form follows function. At play here was that an old form had been given a new function, that of culture. To put it differently, it was as if the building were given a new soul. The CDA's *sobrado* was no longer an old building that does not speak back to a city in transformation but a renovated building embodying the history of the city. Money is not the only factor to take into account in this transfiguration. What is important to highlight here is the discursive component in this campaign, or how the case was made to preserve a building on historical and cultural grounds. This was, however, a case that more problematically could be made during colonialism. Even though the Portuguese colonial intelligentsia disavowed the country's involvement in the slave trade, they also uncritically extolled the benefits of their colonization. Africa was, and still is, for many historians, architectural historians, and Portuguese architects who took part in this process, as Ana Vaz Milheiro has put it, "um território disponível para a experimentação construtiva" (a territory available for constructive experimentation).[60] This experimentation took place at the expense of the destruction of old Luanda. Emulating such a mindset, postcolonial authorities have never been able to convince themselves of the importance of preserving history in the form of material culture. This explains part of the neglect that followed independence, and the activism to counter it.

Even though the first Angolan president, Agostinho Neto, was a published poet and a man of culture, and even though one of his first public acts as president of independent Angola was the proclamation of the União de Escritores Angolanos (Union of Angolan Writers), on December 10, 1975, it was only after his death that the politics of recognition started to encompass historical buildings.[61] Under the law of nationalization (to be discussed in detail in later chapters), the state had become the owner and, in some cases, the landlord of these buildings, but it did not take steps to promote their conservation or renovation, except for those buildings to which particular functions were ascribed—such as the headquarters of the CDA. It was only in 1981, six years into independence, that forty-two of these buildings became protected under a law that regulated historical monuments.[62] Such was the case of the famous palace of Dona Ana Joaquina. The palace was named after its owner, Dona Ana Joaquina dos Santos Silva, an Angolan slave trader who was one of the richest and most prominent residents in the city in the late eighteenth and early nineteenth century. Certified as a national monument after independence, by the 1980s, this *sobrado* was in an advanced stage of dereliction and had become an eyesore in the city. Dozens, possibly hundreds, of squatters had moved into it. The talk of the town was that these newcomers to the city, mostly refugees and homeless kids—people who were for the most part being displaced because of the civil war—were responsible for the levels of criminality in that part of the town. The fact is that the area around this old mansion had become the downtown red-light district: early in the evening one would see dozens of teenage girls with heavy makeup stopping cars to offer their services. When the city authorities decided to act, there was too little to save. The building was demolished without any resistance or reaction from Luanda's residents. That was perhaps because the state promised, and fulfilled its promise, to reconstruct the building in a more radical way than it had done with the Museu Nacional building. In this reconstruction, the beams of wood, which are the most distinctive feature of *sobrados*, were replaced with beams of steel and concrete.[63] What is today the palace of Dona Ana Joaquina is in fact a modernized version of it, a replica, with little resemblance to the original.

A similar tactic was used to bring down another building of a different, but no less important, epoch. The building in this case was the emblematic Quinaxixe Marketplace (hereafter spelled Kinaxixe, according to the current custom), designed by one of Luanda's leading architects and urbanists, Vasco Vieira da Costa, an "absolutely extraordinary [example] of the epoch of modernism," according to the Angolan architect Ângela Mingas.[64] The marketplace was deactivated in the late 1980s, and the decision to tear it down came thereafter. However, this time, the government did not intend to renovate it or build a replica in place of the old one. The Ordem dos Arquitectos de Angola (Order of Angolan Architects), the official regulator of the profession, was against the destruction of this modernist building, which was being considered by the United Nations Educational, Scientific and Cultural Organization (UNESCO) for classification as a world heritage site for humanity.[65] When the government announced that the Kinaxixe Marketplace would be razed so as to make way for a six-story shopping mall with two gigantic towers, one at either end, various groups of concerned citizens filed a complaint in the provincial court. For about ten years, the ruined building subsisted under a covering of corrugated iron. In the end, however, the intention of the economic group behind the planned construction of the shopping mall prevailed, and the iconic Kinaxixe Marketplace came down. For Mingas, the destruction of Kinaxixe was a wake-up call for Luandans, and "not because of the demolition itself, but because with these demolitions people were losing urban references in the city."[66]

Mingas also believes that from then on, Luanda's residents became more receptive to the notion that the city's architectural heritage should be pre-

Figure I.2. Palácio Dona Ana Maria Joaquina, prior to reconstruction in 1992. Source: John Liebenberg.

served. She was herself the director of the Centro de Estudos e Investigação Científica de Arquitectura (Center for the Study and Scientific Research of Architecture; CEICA), linked to Lusíada University, which conducted the most exhaustive report on colonial architecture in Luanda to date.[67] Later on, the center teamed up with the Associação Kalú, an association of friends and residents for the conservation of historic Luanda, and developed a campaign, according to Mingas, aimed to foster an awareness of the importance of "social space" among Luanda's residents.[68] For Mingas, it was the absence of such an awareness among Luandans that prevented them from conceiving of these relics as historic buildings and not mere blots on the landscape. Arguments for the preservation of these buildings, Mingas and many other people believed, should not be based on historical reasons alone but also on the fact that they have become a sort of mnemonic for people to remember the history of their city and, consequently, to orient themselves in the city.

These two demolitions contributed to the fostering of a consciousness of, and resistance to, the destruction of old buildings, particularly because of the intentions that lay behind these actions. The acclaimed Angolan writer Pepetela, for instance, maintains that the Angolan elite suffer from a "horror ao vazio" (horror of emptiness), which accounts for the inclination to replace parks and squares with skyscrapers.[69] For them, Pepetela would certainly add, old buildings amount to emptiness. So by the time the government announced the plan to demolish Elinga Teatro, a group of people had already organized themselves and were ready to push back. Times had changed: the demolition of Elinga was part of the most ambitious overhaul of the city since the construction frenzy of the 1950s and 1960s. If these *sobrados* had for the most part been abandoned since independence, 2002 was a turning point for a drastic transformation of the city. On the one hand, the civil war ended that year, with the killing of the rebel leader Jonas Malheiros Savimbi. As a result, financial resources that had been siphoned off to sustain the war effort started very slowly to be diverted into other channels of expenditure. On the other hand, the years that followed, particularly from 2008 onward, coincided with an unprecedented increase in oil prices in international markets and oil production in Angola. Consequently, oil production, as Ricardo Cardoso so succinctly put it, became the "reconfiguring element of the urban form."[70] Construction and demolition activities in Angola could be tracked by reading the average annual Organization of Petroleum Exporting Countries (OPEC) crude oil prices. Prices started to rise in 2003, with the average annual price reaching US$28.10 per barrel, and continued rising until 2008, when the price reached US$94.10. In the two following years, prices plummeted but then began to rise again in 2011, until by 2015 the annual average was above US$96. To have an idea of the impact of the price rises on Angola's economy, in 2003, Angolan's gross domestic product reached US$124.20 billion, most of it derived from oil exports.[71]

Urban transformation and infrastructure revamping took place in two major ways. The central government used a great deal of these new resources to fix and modernize most of the infrastructure destroyed by the war and to provide the country with many other new infrastructural resources such as airports, ports, dams, and so on. But most of the urban investment in the city was driven by private interests even if, as we will see shortly, the central government was explicitly or implicitly behind most of them.

Elinga Teatro received its eviction order on April 1, 2014, as the last move in a standoff that had pitted the government against artists and many other concerned citizens interested in the preservation of the building.[72] The rationale for the demolition of Elinga was, primarily, that the building was old and did not comply with the legally required safety measures. Nowhere in the rationale was there any mention of the fact that the building belonged to the state, which, thus, would have been the entity responsible for its lack of maintenance. Those who were fighting for the preservation of the building based their argument on its historical value, attested to by its classification as a national monument after independence and confirmed in 1995.[73] However, only three years after this confirmation, the then minister of culture, the historian Rosa Cruz e Silva, signed the executive decree number 134/12 of April 30, 2012, to declassify the building as a national monument.[74] She justified her decision with the argument in that "as razões de natureza histórica que determinaram a classificação do referido edifício já não subsistem" (the reason of historical nature that determined the classification no longer prevailed).[75] The laconic document did not specify, however, which historical value she was referring to and why the building had lost it. One cannot fail to recognize here the irony of history in relation to the same kind of processes that Batalha was writing about fifty years earlier.

The larger picture here was that downtown Luanda, in the vicinity of Elinga Teatro, was at the heart of the city's overhaul, the epicenter of public-private investments, alongside the new satellite city of Kilamba, a new urban development that I will discuss in chapter 6. A bit of background is required here. When the Portuguese moved the port from Portas do Mar to the entrance of the Bay of Luanda in 1942, a move whose implications will be discussed in the next chapter, they turned the now-vacant area into a recreational space, originally called (appropriately) Avenida Paulo Dias de Novais, also known as Avenida Marginal. Residents could walk or run along a wide sidewalk stretching from the entrance of the bay, past the new port, to the fort, or even farther up to Ilha de Luanda. The bay as such was transformed into a fishing area and a site where nautical sports also took place. The uses of the Marginal, rebaptized Avenida 4 de Fevereiro after independence, did not change much in the years that followed, even though dereliction could not be prevented. At the height of the period of urban land speculation, post-2002, a private group, Luanda Waterfront Corporation, led by the Portuguese citizen José Récio and his Angolan partner António Mosquito, approached the government and proposed the refurbishment of the Marginal through a set of interventions. The first

Figure I.3. Marginal de Luanda, viewed from Cidade Alta, 2016. Source: Rui Magalhães, @rui_magalhaes.

would involve the cleaning up of the bay, since during the Portuguese era, the city's sewage had flowed into it. The second phase would include the renewal of the bay, which would consist of the enlargement of Avenida 4 de Fevereiro, through land reclamation, and an accompanying sidewalk to allow for the construction of sports and leisure facilities. Through this, the city would win about 100 meters (about 300 feet) from the sea. In exchange, the group would be allowed to build two artificial islands, to be developed with residential and office space, so as to increase the city's urban stock.[76] However, soon after the first phase of the project was concluded, the group filed for bankruptcy, forcing the government to buy back the project through public debt to the value of US$379,000,000.[77]

Since that area of the city had become the fulcrum of urban speculation, several other commercial groups started to buy property for development in the expectation that prices would go up. Elinga Teatro was located 200 meters (658 feet) from Mutamba, the core of Baixa, and 150 meters (492 feet) from the Marginal; more specifically, it was situated in one of the most physically uneven and morphologically diverse parts of town, only two blocks up from the Bay of Luanda—today referred to as the Nova Marginal de Luanda (New Marginal de Luanda)[78]—and halfway between the Fortaleza de São Miguel and the Igreja de Nossa Senhora da Nazaré (Church of Our Lady of Nazareth), on what a couple of centuries ago constituted the main artery of the city. The area in which the building stood was, thus, one of the most coveted locations in the whole country in terms of urban redevelopment and, concomitantly, urban speculation. In the government's vision, through the aforementioned development plans, this part of the city would boast a Dubai-like waterfront.[79] The developers of Empreendimento Elipark acquired the right to raze the whole block and to erect in its place a building of about 4,600 square meters (15,091 square feet), comprising a cultural center, commercial spaces, and a large parking area fourteen floors above ground, alongside apartments and offices. The promoters of the project provided a guarantee that the theater company would be allocated a space in the new urban complex, consisting of a single large room, that would have better amenities than those available in the old building.

Even if Elinga was not the only classified building on that block, it had made a name for itself on account of the theater, or put differently, the function that it housed. As I have said earlier, the Elinga Teatro *sobrado* was built in the nineteenth century, and its original owner is still unknown. Over time, the building has been used for many different purposes. Originally possibly the residence of a well-to-do family, by the 1950s it served as a school. After independence, as urban structures were nationalized, the building was allocated to the Universidade Agostinho Neto (Agostinho Neto University), which used it primarily as a social center, providing offices for, among others, the Brigada Jovem da Literatura (Young Literature Brigade). Later on, it housed the theater company of the university's medical school, and even later Elinga Teatro, the name by which the building is currently known.

Over the ensuing years, the history of the Elinga theater company became inseparable from the history of the building itself. Elinga Teatro became one of the most acclaimed theater companies in the whole country, in a context where there were no professional companies nor even formal training courses available for actors.[80] It became part of a wider network of theaters in Portuguese-speaking African countries, and its troupes performed in many other African countries, while it frequently invited companies from elsewhere to perform in Luanda. In this manner, the building came to constitute the cornerstone of Luanda's cultural life. By the time of the eviction notice, the building housed not only the theater but also the studios of the artist António Ole—with whose work I began the introduction to this book—and of the fashion designer Mwamby Wassaky. It also served as the home to Kussanguluka, a traditional dance company. Finally, it operated as an art gallery, where international artists exhibited their work and where local artists first became known to a wider Angolan public.[81]

The selling point of Elinga was that it mixed the old with the new, not only in terms of architecture but also in social terms. In a city that, in recent years, had been losing its young people to the outskirts of town, as this was the only place where affordable housing was available, the Elinga Teatro became the meeting point for artists, tourists, nongovernmental organization (NGO) activists, and expatriates who worked for oil and other international companies and organizations. A bar, and parties with resident or invited DJs, kept the establishment financially afloat. The theater was one of those vibrant places that blended things that were otherwise conceived of as different and separate. It was a place of music and art that often showed creative work that was at the cutting edge of Luanda's cultural production. The area around the Elinga Teatro became a magnet for homeless children who helped visitors park their cars in a desperate attempt to make some money.

By the time members of the Associação Kalú and other groups launched a campaign to save the building, they could count on a well-known and well-connected group of people whose interests gravitated toward Elinga and who could advocate against its destruction—unlike the situation with other buildings that were destroyed, or scheduled for destruction, which did not evoke the same type of outcry. The director of the Elinga Teatro, José Mena Abrantes, was himself a speechwriter for the president of the republic and warned publicly that the demolition would mean that Angolans, "tão orgulhosos de viverem numa das capitais mais antiga da África negra, em breve deixarão de ter de que vangloriar. Nada de antigo restará na cidade" (so proud of living in one of the oldest cities in Black Africa, will not have anything to be proud of. Nothing of the old will be left in the city).[82] This was a feeling widely shared among the people who put their weight behind the campaign. At the same time, the Elinga Teatro itself increased the number of its productions, to emphasize its importance as the city's cultural heartbeat. Moreover, it also became a common point of reference among people whose politics could not be more divergent. A handful of members of the so-called Movimento Revolucionário de Angola (Revolutionary Movement of Angola), a group of youth who staged a number of protests to oust the long-serving president José Eduardo dos Santos), also converged in Elinga; they included Luaty Beirão and Nito Alves, who took part in various awareness campaigns around the preservation of Elinga. In the end, then, the case for the Elinga Teatro was easy to articulate from the point of view of civil society. It set the interests of the people, and history, against the greed of individuals whose only concern was to make money, even if in order to do so historical buildings had to be razed. To date there has been no decision yet about the future of Elinga; the show still goes on.

The controversies surrounding the Elinga Teatro show not only the extent to which Luanda is still entangled in its past but also the ways in which history is never settled; it is always dynamic or dialectical. It reveals how history has been used, or appropriated, to justify contending agendas that put emphasis either on the preservation of relics or on the modernization of the city that inevitably implies the destruction of the buildings from previous eras. On the one hand, the argument about the historicity of these buildings may be deemed fraught with inaccuracies and melt in the air, as Marx would say. Unlike the Dona Ana Joaquina Palace, Elinga Teatro is more like a ghost in the city, for almost nothing is known of who the original owners were and how it was occupied. On the other hand, the push for the clearing of old buildings from the city center can also be depicted as insensitive, to say the least. But these two seemingly contrasting views meet in the overdetermination of the function. Those who supported the destruction of Elinga Teatro have based their position on the argument that the city center would be better served with more office space, parking lots, and a shopping mall. Similarly, behind the survival of the Elinga Teatro is the successful disjunction of form, or the rationale that presided over its construction and function. Putting it differently, the Elinga Teatro has survived not because of its history, and not even because of its status as a national monument, but because of its function, or the life it came to host as the home of a theater company—not very different from the reasons for the survival of the CDA building, later on transformed into the Museum of Anthropology. In the end, *sobrados* such as the Elinga Teatro, which are the very few remnants of a time the country does not want to be reminded of, are the last shackles to be thrown off before the city frees itself completely from history. As such, destroying landmarks in the city does not simply involve getting rid of them physically; there is also something more profound at work here, which I have tried to encapsulate in the term "un-building history." It is as if there is a belief that, once the enduring entanglements are discursively put to rest, by insisting for instance that it is better to forget than to remember Luanda's traumatic past, we can remove everything else far more easily.

Furthermore, the fate of Elinga Teatro speaks to something deeper about Luanda that is also at the core of this book. I have tried to articulate this idea by borrowing, without of course its ideological frame, the concept of Casa Luandense as proposed by the architect Fernando Batalha. For Casa Luandense does not only bring the mix of people from different social standings (in terms of race and class) to the fore, it also allows us to see the relationship between these houses and the rest of the city, or between architecture and urban form. As such, these sumptuous houses were like fortresses, or enclosures for the well-to-do, in a city that was overwhelmingly inhabited by the destitute, many of them enslaved. The fact that these buildings have been, after independence, taken over by squatters accounts for more than a simple historical irony. I would like to construe it as the condition for inhabitation in Luanda itself. Or to put it differently, the building that Elinga Teatro occupies is also a theater itself for a sociology of inhabitation in present-day Luanda. It shows, primarily, the extent to which life in Luanda has always been about separation and enclosure—about those who are within or beyond the limits of that which is considered interior or exterior. The ways in which these modes of separation come about are always relational, or dialectical, for these lines of separation—the house, the *bairro*, or the city itself—may recede or expand. As such, the squatters in present-day Luanda are not, in any way, different from the enslaved people who inhabited the first floors of these buildings. This is not so in relation to labor patterns, obviously, but in relation to an understanding of slavery as conceptualized by early philosophers such as Plato, for whom slaves were those who did not have a public presence and were subsumed in the domus, or domestic sphere.

In saying this, my aim is to counter the assertion that, through appropriation, the urban poor or the squatters lay claim to the city, as a burgeoning literature has been arguing under the rubric of the right to the city, and as I have discussed in the introduction. My intention lies elsewhere. I would like to argue that in present-day Luanda no one can claim the right to the city because of the ways in which belonging, ownership, and appropriation are mediated by legal redefinition of the relationship between the state and the land. Or, to put it differently, the state here is not a metaphysical category but one that forces us to engage with the contingent ways in which it relates to the citizenry. I will come back to this point in further chapters. Here, it suffices to say that the Angolan postcolonial state has conceived of itself as the sole owner, or originator, of the land. As such tenancy is always unstable, and the law can always change so as to render sections of the city in contra-vention. For law is the foundation itself that renders senseless any reference to metaphysics, or the notion that a concept such as right to the city may have any purchase so as to understand law making in Angola. The outcome is the always-latent production of the condition of squatting, after the fact. In the chapters that follow, I will seek to magnify this vision.

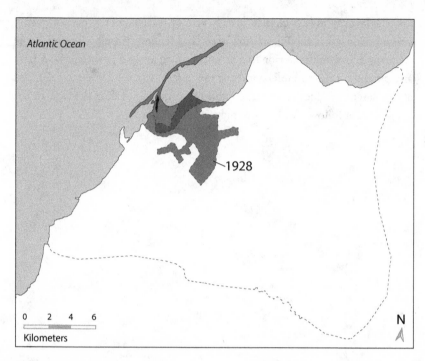

Map 2.1. Luanda circa 1928.

2. Ordering Urban Expansion

Luanda é um porto que trabalha para toda a colónia

Luanda is a port that works for the entire colony.
—Vasco Vieira da Costa, "Cidade Satélite no. 3," 1948

. . .

By the time the competition over available land was becoming fiercer in down-town Luanda, for the reasons I discussed earlier, Portuguese urban authorities were considering the expansion of the city's borders. The hilltop of Kinaxixe was deemed an apt and natural section of the town for such a scheme. Adjacent to downtown Luanda, it consisted for the most part of unused land until the late 1930s. The area was occupied by a few public buildings, some private estates, and mushrooming settlements, in which poor whites lived to-gether with members of Luanda's traditional families. The urban expansion that colonial authorities had in mind was enabled by a number of interlinked factors—namely, the appreciation of prices for commodities such as coffee and cotton in the international market, which provided colonial governments across the continent the confidence to embrace developmentalist policies. In the context of Portuguese colonialism, particularly for the case of Portugal's most precious colony, Angola, such a mindset was bolstered by two interlaced beliefs: first, that colonial development could be channeled into addressing the high indices of poverty in continental Portugal by encouraging migration to the colonies, and second, that massive investment could be used to provide transportation infrastructure, such as roads, bridges, the railway, and particularly on the industrial-port complex. The modern Luanda that starts to emerge in 1945, over the ashes of the lingering effects of the slave trade, is a by-product of the application of these principles.

The construction of the Port of Luanda played such a pivotal role for the further expansion of the urban grid that Vasco Vieira da Costa, one of the city's chief architects, equated the whole city with the port itself. Luanda, for him, was a "porto que trabalha para toda colónia" (port that works for entire colony).[1] By this, Vieira da Costa was making the case for viewing the port as an instrument for economic growth in that it made possible the increased shipment of commodities out of the country and vice-versa. But the port was also a potential anchor for urban growth. The construction of Porto de Luanda was not imagined by modernist architects, but modernist architecture provided a lexicon for envisaging and planning Luanda's expansion in a more holistic manner. Taking advantage of a clear-cut, almost cohesive historical center—albeit with historically diverse housing types—most urban designers in Luanda at that time considered natural the radiocentric expansion of the city. Such a scheme was the blueprint followed until the mid-1970s when the colonial order came to a halt.

At a more sociological level, what comes to the fore by reading the city's plans from the 1940s onward, and the discourses attached to them, is the intention at purifying the city center by removing those groups whose lifestyles contravened the image of a modern city in the tropics that Portuguese modernizers wished to emulate. This desideratum was attained through, on the one hand, conceiving of what was then called the consolidated urban core, or the concrete city, which was progressively achieved by removing informal and precarious housing and settling the occupants on the outskirts of the formal city, beyond the frontier—that is, when the occupants or owners of such precarious housing had not already decided by themselves to relocate beyond the border of the formal city on account of the fact that urban modernization was making their lives untenable financially.[2] On the other hand, however, there were not, for the most part, major buffers separating the *cidade* from the *musseques*. In some sections of the city, there were obviously major pieces of infrastructure, such as the port, cutting through two *bairros* whose inhabitants held opposite economic standings in the colonial city. But generally, separating most of these *bairros* was a simple road. It was as if the Portuguese were willing to sustain the tension between *cidade* and *musseque* through these thin lines that the Angolan writer Luandino Vieira has called the *fronteira do asfalto*.

It will be my contention in this chapter that inscribing race, and to lesser extent class, as the main descriptor for the ascription of residents to their respective and secluding *bairros* is part of the reason Luanda kept its status as the colony's capital. In the early 1900s, Huambo came close to dislodging Luanda from this position, because it offered the opportunity to envision city building from a clean slate. However, the higher agricultural production in the northern provinces made Luanda the more logical and economically wise point for export, through the construction of the Port of Luanda alongside other auxiliary pieces of infrastructure such as the railway and the road infrastructure network. What one reads in the various planning initiatives since the early 1940s is how the various social groups were meant to be clustered in the interstices of infrastructure (without abolishing for the most part the thin lines that constituted the *fronteira do asfalto*). Modernist Luanda worked at superimposing an urban order made of clear-cut streets, wider avenues, public spaces, a long promenade by the bay, and towering buildings, onto the architecturally hybrid, messy, and racially mixed city Luanda.

The city's modernization through the idiom provided by modernist architecture is then the most elaborated attempt at enforcing the skin of the city on the urban, which was accomplished, on the one hand, by making starker the difference between city and *musseque* and, on the other, by successfully demarcating the differences among the various *bairros* in the city. With this, a whole system was recast, particularly through recalibrations of whom the right to the city belonged, which, ultimately turned most Natives into potential squatters.

The Colony, the City, and the Port

The Atlantic slave trade was certainly the main reason Luanda became the principal settlement for the Portuguese in Angola. Luanda's poor arable land was compensated for by optimal conditions for breeding slaves. The coast was endowed with a sizable hill, on top of which a fort with heavy artillery was installed. Overtaking such a settlement, as the Dutch did in 1641, would never be any easy task. Furthermore, the bay itself constituted a natural harbor, which made it possible for the Portuguese to become the largest purveyors of slaves in the modern world, without having to invest in permanent port infrastructure.

However, with the end of the Atlantic slave trade, in 1836, the position Luanda occupied in relation to the rest of the country, most of which was still to be brought under colonial authority, was being severely challenged.[3] The commodities that still arrived on its shores (besides enslaved people who were illicitly abducted and transported to Brazil)—such as rubber, wax, manganese, and agricultural produce—were not enough to keep the economy afloat and prevent the most affluent members of the population from leaving the city with the fortunes they had amassed. Those who stayed, and those who came after, were then turning their attention to other economic opportunities. Luanda's hinterland was endowed with arable land, where there were better conditions for the mass-production of agricultural goods. Accordingly, traders in Luanda were cogitating on and plotting ways to transport produce more quickly, efficiently, and in greater quantities to Luanda. Feeding Luanda's population was what they had in mind, but they were also aware of profits to be made on exports.

Aware of the potential of an emergent technology, the railroad, a few traders, Silvano Pereira, Arsénio Pompílio de Carpo, A. Y. R. Shut, and Eduardo Possolo, set off on a venture to bring it to Luanda. In 1848, they distributed a pamphlet on a project to "para o melhoramento do comércio, agricultura e industria" (improve commerce, agriculture, and industry) through transport, with the aim of finding potential investors to finance their plan to build a railway linking Luanda and Calumbo, northeast of Luanda.[4] They promised all those who joined the proposed society a profit of 10 percent at the end of the first year of operation of the railway. British investors were the main target of the campaign, for their interest in expanding railway technology throughout the world, their acumen in investing overseas, and particularly their effort to suppress slavery, which, given the weight it occupied in the Angolan economy, was, for the promoters, the main cause of the colony's decline. As such, they expected the British to be sensitive to and support their search for alternative economic ventures beyond the slave trade.

Such a consortium, when formed, would be expected to realize two goals: first, they were interested in transporting produce to Luanda; second, they also aimed at acquiring the rights to the extraction of timber and all the minerals found in the course of the construction of the railway. From the colonial state they expected to receive tax exemptions for all the materials they imported, as well as support in the recruitment of *degredados* to perform mostly skilled labor and assistance in facilitating the recruitment of the Native labor force.[5]

This undertaking failed, but it inspired many other groups to ask the colonial government to financially support them in the construction of the railway. A tender advertised in 1896 by the Portuguese state was won by the Companhia Real dos Caminhos de Ferro Através de África (Royal Company for Railways across Africa), which formed a subsidiary firm, the Sociedade Constructora do Caminho de Ferro the Ambaca (Society for the Construction of the Ambaca Railway). This group delivered the 364 kilometers (226.17 miles) of rail linking Luanda to the hinterland at Ambaca, a project officially inaugurated on September 7, 1899.[6] A few years later, the colonial government carried out a plan to merge all the rail routes that existed and were being privately exploited, linking Luanda to several other localities under the designation Caminhos de Ferro de Luanda (Luanda Railway; CFL). The line that started in Ambaca, with stops in dozens of localities, traversed Luanda and had its final railhead at a station near Cidade Alta.[7] Despite the intentions of their promoters, this service was primarily designed to transport passengers. In just its first year of operation, 462,071 individuals were transported.[8] In the next few years, with the improvement of the infrastructure and the use of more powerful locomotives, transportation of commodities increased. This movement of people and goods would have a profound impact on the modernization of Luanda.

While privately owned businesses were busy attempting to revitalize the city's moribund economy, the colonial state was trying to find alternatives for raising revenues. The prohibition of slavery had left Portugal devoid of concrete ideas for how to turn the colonies into profitable ventures. At the famous Berlin Conference that took place in 1884–85, England imposed on Portugal what has been referred to in the literature as an ultimatum, in which the Portuguese were bound to either effectively occupy the territories they claimed to possess or transfer them to any other colonial power better equipped to administer them. In the debates that raged in the Portuguese press, well-established members of the intelligentsia argued that Portugal would be better off without the colonies and should simply sell them.[9] Clarity about Portugal's colonial mission only started to emerge by the early 1900s, particularly after the republican revolution in 1910 that put an end to the ineffectual Portuguese monarchy. Fresher ideas flowed into the public debate, particularly on the applicability of colonial polices being experimented with across the continent by the British and the French. From these discussions emerged the mindset that African colonies could better serve the empire if they enjoyed a certain degree of autonomy. The largest colonies, Angola and Mozambique, were thus granted a semiautonomous status.[10]

To help manifest the potential of the Portuguese-dominated territories in Africa, General Norton de Matos was dispatched to Angola with powers that no other colonial leader in that territory had previously held and that none would hold again in the years to come. First, as governor-general of Angola between 1912 and 1915, and then in a second mandate as high commissioner from 1921 to 1923, Norton de Matos encapsulated his ambitions for Angola's modernization under the banner "desenvolver Angola, promover o negro e reforçar a soberania Portuguesa" (develop Angola, promote the Negro, and strengthen Portuguese sovereignty).[11] He has been hailed as a trailblazer for setting the foundations for the country's modern state by promulgating countless colonial policies, founding new settlements, such as Huambo—as I will show later in this chapter—and opening up commerce with the Natives through the construction of infrastructure such as bridges, roads, and the expansion of the railway. More important, Norton de Matos decisively acted to put an end to slavery.[12] With the oath he took as a Freemason before his first stint in Angola, Norton de Matos pledged to fight slavery not because he particularly abhorred the abduction of human beings but because he was inclined to believe that slavery could be replaced by another no less compulsory but inevitably more efficient system of work.[13] He then took decisive steps toward the institutionalization of the infamous *indigenato* (from *indígena*: Natives), which consisted mainly of the colonial state's creation through law of a category of human beings who could be deprived of the rights to be members of civil society.[14]

Part of the rationale for Native people to be outside civil society was cultural, in that they were deemed not to possess civilizational attributes and thus should be governed by their traditional authorities, according to their own cultural structures.[15] A number of Africanist scholars have shown the extent to which the *indigenato* legislation was also used as a tool to prevent Africans from leaving the countryside and migrating to major cities.[16] This was also the case for Angola, and yet the *indigenato* also had a powerful impact on the ways in which Luanda came to be planned from the early twentieth century onward.

Given Norton de Matos's views on the place of the Black population in the whole architecture of the empire, it may not require a stretch of the imagination to conjure up the extent to which Luanda may have appeared an oddity to him. In the previous chapter, I mentioned that the slave trade, particularly in its dying phase, allowed for the emergence of a Black elite who called themselves Angolenses and who enjoyed considerable economic, political, and cultural standing, especially after the abolition of the slave trade. By the time Norton de Matos arrived in Luanda, descendants of this privileged group owned property in various sections of the city, particularly in Ingombotas. Having spent time in Asia, particularly in India, Matos was aware of the British distrust of in-between categories, such as these civilized subjects, and geared his administration toward the separation, as much as possible, of whites and Blacks. He emulated the model of the New World, in particular North America, as a way to impose Western "hegemonia em todo o continente" (hegemony on the whole continent).[17] For such an order to come into being, the Portuguese would have to "fixar nas terras de África que nos pertencem, a nossa raça, com a maior intensidade, para que as suas qualidades de perseverança, de resistência ao desânimo e de coragem indomável [. . .] lhes deem um cunho bem português" (settle our race on that part of the African soil that belongs to us with greatest intensity, so that the [Portuguese] qualities of endurance, resistance, as well as untamable courage [. . .] give it [Angola] a Portuguese imprint).[18]

Suffused with ideologies of social Darwinism and eugenics, Norton de Matos conceded that he was not against the uplifting of Black people, as he so candidly expounded, but that he favored the view that races should develop in different directions. He was thus reiterating the conclusions of a number of his contemporaries, particularly Lord Lugard, the governor of Nigeria, for whom colonization had two objectives: to benefit the colonial power and to uplift the Native, the latter through the preservation of African institutions.[19] Norton de Matos argued that a crucial way to implement Portuguese hegemony was to separate the races as much as possible by actively preventing any form of miscegenation. Alarmed by the potential consequences of the migration of single men as the main cause of interracial relationships, he posited the need to transplant not only Portuguese men to Angola but also entire families.[20] Norton de Matos was also inclined to believe that if one wanted to improve colonization, urbanization, "uma das mais nítidas características da civilização" (the most distinctive characteristic of civilization) had to emerge on African soil.[21] Formal and European-style cities and settlements would attract more whites and would thus endow these places with "uma imagem portuguesa" (a Portuguese image) through the construction of houses resembling those in traditional Portuguese villages.[22]

Luanda was not a viable candidate for Matos's scheme, owing to the widespread presence of what he considered miscegenation and other forms of promiscuity, such as interracial marriages. In the previous chapter, I left implicit the fact that old Luanda was characterized by a promiscuous cohabitation between enslavers and the enslaved, for shacks, or *cubatas*, could be found everywhere in the city. Repulsed by this state of things, Matos turned to the countryside. His vision, which he wrote about prolifically, was to build Angolan

Figure 2.1. Settlers on board the ship *João Belo* departing Portugal for Angola in 1936.
Source: Arquivo Nacional da Torre do Tombo.

pastoral villages for industrious Portuguese who would work the land in a self-sufficient manner, dispensing with all Black manpower. The Colonato da Cela (Cela Settlement), for instance, which was only built later on, showcases how the Portuguese tried to concretize this vision.[23] But Norton de Matos's dream pointed toward a far-reaching goal—namely, the very production of a new colonial center where the criteria of race, hygienic purity, and economic organization could be integrated from the outset.

Norton de Matos also has been credited for contributing to the groundwork for the establishment of Huambo, a city the Portuguese attempted to build as a replacement for Luanda as Angola's capital city. And the creation of Huambo provides important clues to what would later on feature in Luanda's transformation from the 1940s onward. For this transformation was only made possible through the implementation of several principles that had been experimented with and tested in the construction of Huambo. This settlement stemmed directly from the railway and emerged from the concession the Portuguese had given to Robert Williams, one of Cecil John Rhodes's close friends, to the right to build a railway line that crossed the entire Angolan territory from east to west, from the coastal town of Benguela, about 500 kilometers (340 miles) to the south of Luanda, to Zambia. Williams became the director of the company called Companhia do Caminho de Ferro de Benguela (Benguela Railway Company; CCFB).[24] In the early 1900s, the railhead was in Cuma, where a small settlement had been set up 317 kilometers (196.97 miles) from the coast. In extending this line, the Portuguese were first of all eyeing the copper mines of Catanga and, secondarily, the construction of a new city, Huambo.

As Huambo's existence was due to the expansion of the railway to the hinterland, the CCFB requested an area of 404.68 hectares (1,000 acres) on which to build infrastructure and services for the railway, such as headquarters for the company, workshops, storage, housing for personnel, and a sanatorium. It occupied a considerable area of the city's initial plan, with its repair shops and other workshops and facilities for the operation of the railway. From there, the city grew, designed in the shape of a polygon, with the sides being formed by the road grid, the railway, buildings, and water lines. Huambo was designed to be linked by five arterial routes, springing from a circle with nine roads that constituted the civic center, with a roundabout around which public buildings, commercial concerns such as banks, and recreational facilities such as cinemas would be erected. Long avenues, wide boulevards, public spaces, and green areas were also part of the city's design. The garden city principle that was transplanted to Huambo was the zoning, through which residential areas were separated from industrial ones, with the civic center at a considerable distance from the train station and other railway facilities. In the residential areas, the larger houses were to face the main roads, whereas the smaller ones for the natives, alongside the sewerage lines, would be at the back. Even though the designation "garden city" never appeared in the justification and rationale for Huambo, produced by its putative father, Carlos Roma Machado, its town plan was nonetheless called "English," because of its "specific guidelines for the development of this town."[25] The garden city model had proved to be very effective at eliminating slums and unemployment in other cities in Africa through its use as an effective mechanism to preside over organized "migratory movements of populations for the purpose of settling land, either in overseas territories or within the metropole."[26] So it was obvious that the model of the garden city could be deemed adequate to the foundation of Huambo.[27]

Although Huambo was conceptualized during the governorship of José Augusto Alves Roçadas (1909–10), the final project for the settlement was only later on approved by Norton de Matos, who was also given the honor of inaugurating it on September 12, 1912. It would certainly be the capital of Angola had it not been for the recalibrations of the global economy I mentioned earlier in this chapter. However the reversal of fortune that prevented Huambo from becoming Angola's capital city came with the steady progress in the construction of the Port of Luanda. This project had become a priority for the colonial government, since investments had been made in the north of the country and the production of cotton and coffee was starting to yield returns. Economically, it made more sense to have these commodities shipped out from Luanda. However, even though Luanda had been one of the most important exit points for slaves on the African continent, the city did not have a proper port in the modern sense of the word. Wharves may have been used, but for the most part slaves and goods were rowed on smaller boats to the large vessels anchored farther out in the deep natural bay of Luanda.[28] This makeshift port was situated in the Pedro Alexandrino Square, at the center of what is now the Marginal de Luanda, and was also known as Portas do Mar.[29] Only after the abolition of slavery did the construction of a new port become a pressing issue for the Portuguese. The need to provide the city with a port was driven less by the pressure to modernize the city than by drastic changes in methods of transportation and technology, as well as in the organization of worldwide logistics systems that required particular conditions for ships to anchor.[30] Without such an infrastructure, Luanda would be on the margins of worldwide maritime navigation. Even though construction of the new port began in 1888, there was no significant progress for decades. Not even the overenthusiastic Norton de Matos managed to accelerate the completion of this vital infrastructure during the time of his governorship. In fact, only in 1942, fifty-four years after the end of slavery, was Porto de Luanda finally inaugurated.

For Luanda, the construction of the port constitutes a sort of Haussmann moment. Baron Georges-Eugène Haussmann's conviction that public works could pull France out of an economic crisis by creating jobs and increasing public and private consumption has been enacted many other times and in many other contexts in the world since then.[31] In the case of Angola, while the colonial government was not particularly geared toward tackling any economic crisis, it was clear to many colonial officials that the construction of such an infrastructure would have important ripple effects that would reverberate through the entire economy.

The intimation that the construction of a permanent port of such magnitude could usher in urban expansion and renewal of the whole city was already present in the writings of one of its main engineers, Afonso Mello Cid Perestrelo.[32] In the various articles, reports, and at least one book he authored, it is clear that the proposal to construct Porto de Luanda was more than a way to provide the city with this vital facility; the thinking behind it was also that such a construction could, and should, be geared toward promoting the city's growth. The city, then, was perceived as an extension and consolidation of the port, or, more specifically, the structures that would allow bigger ships to berth, together with all the other associated buildings and infrastructure. The plan proposed the construction of the Praça do Porto (Port Square)—which in the terminology of the colonial city's design was known as Praça do Império (Imperial Square)—as a nodal point in the network of axes to satellite cities outside the city's center and the point of convergence of the transport system. In the end, though, this square did not represent the empire (in terms of making room for the construction of representative elements of the empire), for the economic interest once more prevailed. Whereas the main building in the square is still the customs building, following the Estado Novo architectural model adopted by the state for the colonized territories, the square is filled with many other buildings of modernist inspiration. These buildings, commissioned by various companies operating in Angola, represent a growing private-sector interest at the time in the fabric of the city.[33]

Since the area originally was a beach, intensive land reclamation work needed to be done for the construction of the port and its adjoining avenue, the Avenida Marginal. It was this reclaimed land, reinforced with concrete, that provided the ground for the construction of the first generation, so to speak, of Luanda skyscrapers, which came to adorn a significant extent of the bay from Igreja de Nossa Senhora da Nazaré (Church of Our Lady of Nazareth) to Praça Pedro Alexandrino (Pedro Alexandrino Square). This set of buildings, which extends along the Marginal de Luanda, creating its distinctive skyline, replaced the old *sobrado* mansions and other commercial establishments that were being purchased and torn down at a rate that alarmed the conservationists. In the next few decades the consolidation of the coast continued, with further land reclamation, particularly through the construction of a bridge that linked Luanda's mainland to Ilha de Luanda. With these interventions, Ilha de Luanda was being transformed into the main recreational zone of the city, with manicured beaches, nautical clubs, and restaurants, interspersed with fishermen's villages along the coastline.[34]

The role the port would play in ushering in Luanda's urban expansion is clear in the first city plan—the Plano de Urbanização de Luanda (Plan for the Urbanization of Luanda)—submitted to the city's authorities in 1944.[35] This plan likely was drawn up by the same team that had also submitted to the authorities, in 1943, the Plano de Urbanização da Parte Marginal de Luanda (Plan for the Urbanization of Marginal Luanda). These included the Portuguese David Moreira da Silva, trained at the prestigious Institut d'Urbanisme de l'Université de Paris (Urbanism Institute of Paris University; IUUP), and Étienne de Gröer, a Russian-born French citizen, resident in Portugal, who had taught at the IUUP. They were coming of age professionally in Portugal when Duarte Pacheco, Salazar's minister of public works, made it mandatory for every city in Portugal to have a master plan.[36] As a team, they worked on a couple of master plans for cities in Portugal, such as Coimbra. Moreira da Silva tried for many years to expand Duarte Pacheco's requirement into the colonies, traveling to Angola many times to convince municipal authorities in Angola to buy into this creed. He eventually managed to sell his proposals to Luanda and Gabela, a little town in the province of Kwanza Sul.

Like many other professionals who came from the IUUP, Moreira da Silva and de Gröer's professional practice was situated between the garden city model and French urbanism.[37] Unsurprisingly, the garden city model was what they proposed for the expansion of Luanda. Persuaded by Howard Ebenezer's recipes for improving urban life, they highlighted the need to impose the zoning principle on Luanda in their plan so that activities such as housing, commerce, industry, and recreation would be allocated to different sectors of the city. Marginal de Luanda is, to a great extent, a good example of the emulation of such an urban philosophy, in that it was built to accommodate discrete activities—namely housing, banking, and other commercial activities—from Porto de Luanda to Igreja dos Remédios (Church of our Lady of Remedies), and then mostly recreational activities and housing from the church to the end of Ilha de Luanda.

Despite the fact that this master plan was unexecuted, it nonetheless presents a trove of information regarding the role the port was expected to play in the expansion of the city and how the growth of Luanda was perceived and anticipated.[38] In Moreira da Silva's and de Gröer's view, central to the future of Luanda was the imperative to prevent the expansion of the urban center through, among other measures, the construction of five satellite cities, each removed about 6 kilometers (3.72 miles) from the center. Conceived essentially to absorb Luanda's natural population growth, they would connect to the main center through seven axes, with the other two providing direct linkages to Funda and Foz do Kwanza. Those five centers would be vast enough to accommodate a population of 400,000, in which, as Maria do Carmo Pires writes, "os quarteirões destinados à população indígena, localizados nas zonas nascente e sul, são provisórios e serão transformados em quarteirões normais *à medida da civilização dos negros*" (the quarters for the Native population, located in the eastern and southern zones, are provisional and will be transformed into normal quarters *at the pace of the civilization of the negroes*).[39] Aiming as much as possible to isolate historic Luanda from the rest of the province, the plan envisioned the establishment of green belts that were expected to perform several tasks, including providing fresh and clean air to each city's inhabitants but also restricting the physical expansion of the cities' limits. In the end, only two of the five satellite cities proposed in the Moreira da Silva and de Gröer plan were built, namely Cacuaco and Viana. However, the intention to, as much as possible, insulate the white population from the Black population was never abandoned, and it would crop up in every planning initiative until the end of the colonial order.

Gröer and Moreira's city plan might have been too ambitious for the time, particularly because the city could not claim enough land to execute it. However, beyond land ownership, there was also the disjunction at the core of the planning process between the technicalities of the plan that were intended to conform to garden city principles on the one hand and, on the other, the reality of land values in Luanda at the time. De Gröer writes, in his *Introduction to Urbanism*, that he was against vertical construction for several reasons—namely, that tall buildings rely on the proper functioning of elevators, that they become dangerous in case of fire, that the cost of construction would be onerous, and that the buildings would not provide privacy for their occupants.[40] In fact, Moreira da Silva and de Gröer were putting forward a new concept of a city that would be less dense and be served by a more efficient system of transport—which was not a priority for those with vested interests in Luanda. More important, they also "edificação espaçada de casas"[41] (spaced building of houses) in relatively small volumes, which contrasted with the notion, more and more prevailing, that high-rise construction was more profitable, since it allowed for the highest concentration of both people and economic value per square meter.

In hindsight, these early planning interventions in Luanda can be read as an attempt to impose the garden city model on a city that, up to that point, had grown quite spontaneously. The founding of Huambo may have provided lessons for Luanda since, among other things, modern Luanda was the product of infrastructural encroachment into the hinterland, through the expansion of the railway and its linkage to the port. The fundamental difference between the planning and development of the two cities, however, is that whereas in Huambo planners and builders had a clean slate as their starting point, in so far as land disputes were almost nonexistent as a direct consequence of the pacification wars, in Luanda that was not the case. In Luanda, most of the land had been privately owned for centuries, and planning had to take this reality into consideration. Whereas the city had to be engaged in negotiations and confiscation of land so that infrastructure and public facilities could be built, the expansion of such infrastructure and facilities ended up giving even more power to landowners, in the sense that they were then able to benefit from serviced land, or the land that held the infrastructural network set up by the state. As such, the state's intervention for ordering urban growth made possible for these landowners to accrue even more land in the city.

Reading Moreira da Silva's and de Gröer's plan retrospectively yields important insights into how the city evolved from the late 1940s onward. The plan is still a fundamental repository of insights into how the formal urban center would expand, and it would be consulted by future generations of planners, as I will shortly show. However, the city would expand in precisely the opposite direction from the garden city principles, particularly because that expansion was driven by speculation. Or, to put it in slightly different terms, this speculation-driven expansion exerted dramatic effects on the city's form itself. The pace of such transformation became even more pronounced with the entrance on the scene of a newer generation of architects and urban planners. They were moving to Luanda equipped with the determination to turn Luanda into a modernist city.

The Modernist Skin

When, in the early 1940s, a student of architecture at the Escola Superior de Belas Artes do Porto (Porto School of Fine Arts), Vasco Vieira da Costa—born in Aveiro, Portugal, and raised in Luanda—was looking for a topic for his design project, the final requirement for his bachelor's degree in architecture, he turned to Moreira da Silva's and de Gröer's city plan and used it as a canvas to design Satellite City No. 3—one of the satellite cities they had proposed for Luanda. In the end, then, he could trace an association between the city's previous planning intervention and the future he anticipated for it. In this project, Vieira da Costa went further than just reproducing the content of the initial city plan. He added a modernist sensibility developed through the influence of the masters of the movement, such as Le Corbusier, particularly their attempts to take into consideration climatic (specifically aeolian) and geographic conditions, such as slopes and inclinations, in their projects. In this plan, he specifically tried to reconcile several things: the still-accepted precepts of the garden city movement as they had been proposed by Machado and, more particularly, by Moreira da Silva and de Gröer; the more aesthetic aspirations proposed by tropical modernist architecture; and the political demands of the Portuguese presence in Africa.

By the time Vieira da Costa was musing over the expansion of European culture on African soil, certainly echoing Norton de Matos, Portugal's position toward the settlement of Portuguese in Africa had changed. During the time of the slave trade, the Portuguese used Angola mainly as a place to deposit *degredados*. After slavery, Portugal did not encourage migration to the colony because of the suspicion that massive migration could increase white poverty, which could have a negative impact on the supposedly Portuguese mission in Africa.[42] Things changed drastically from the 1940s onward. Cashing in on the favorable prices of primary commodities in international markets, the colonial government, like elsewhere in Africa, started pushing a more developmentalist agenda by investing surpluses in many areas of socioeconomic life, such as infrastructure, health, and education. In countries like Kenya, Nigeria, and Ghana, millions of African farmers were entering the economy not just as producers but also as consumers.[43] However, in Angola that was not the case, as the Portuguese attempted to benefit from these global changes in a different way. Rather than taking Africans out of poverty by giving them the means to become members of the middle class, the Portuguese used this opportunity to take, first and foremost, Portugal itself out of poverty by sending hundreds of thousands of poor Portuguese to the colonies, particularly Angola. The initial plan followed the dream of Norton de Matos: that these Portuguese would embrace agriculture and form the white rural communities like those in South Africa, Namibia, or Rhodesia. Some of them did.[44] However, most Portuguese found economic opportunities in urban settings such as Luanda.

The more the city grew, the more people it attracted. Demographics, particularly white migration to the colony, are key to an understanding of this urban expansion. In 1940, Luanda's population included about 9,404 whites, but within ten years this number had increased by 123 percent, reaching 21,081 in 1950. In 1960, the white population of the city had risen to 55,667, an increase of about 164 percent; and finally, in 1970, the decade of independence, whites in Luanda constituted a staggering 123,226, an increase of 127 percent from the previous decade.[45] This evolving demographic makeup not only placed housing policy at the core of the colonial endeavor but also put the racial question at the heart of the urban project. Whereas poor whites and Blacks whose economic status was rising could mix and live together in the *musseques*, central Luanda, or the consolidated core as it came to be known, was becoming an exclusive zone for white residence. Modernist Luanda is, then, the moment in the history of the city when the idea of the separation between races achieved its highest concretization by providing the technical and internationally recognized vocabulary for the enforcement of the *fronteira do asfalto*.

The principles of modernist architecture started to circulate in Portugal in the early 1940s. During these years, the *Revista de arquitectura* (Architectural review) published several articles on modernism, including Le Corbusier's

Athens Charter.[46] In 1948, Estado Novo sponsored the first Congresso de Arquitectos Modernistas (Congress of Modernist Architects), where architects had the opportunity to share ideas about modernism. The movement then split into two organizations: the Iniciativas Culturais Arte e Técnica (Cultural, Artistic and Technical Initiatives), with Keil do Amaral, Francisco Castro Rodrigues, and João Simões, among others, as members; and the Organização dos Arquitectos Modernos (Organization of Modern Architects). It was the former that developed its activities in Africa.[47]

The first attempt to produce modernist architecture took place on Portuguese soil itself. Members of both architectural associations developed several modernist projects, including the Bairro das Estacas, a neighborhood in Lisbon located between Avenida Brazil and Avenida Estados Unidos da América, and the Bairro Rumelde, a suburb in Porto.[48] However, modernist architecture never gained traction in Portugal for many reasons, particularly because it failed to dislodge the building style derogatorily called Português Suave (Soft Portuguese) that the Estado Novo regime favored.[49] In addition, it came to Portugal already stigmatized, since much of the application of modernist architecture was taking place in Brazil, and to a lesser extent in Europe, and the style was therefore scorned by mainstream European architects and urbanists.[50]

Eager to find well-paid job opportunities in a growing and demanding environment, and anxious to leave their own mark, architects of modernist persuasion turned to African cities such as Luanda.[51] In Luanda, not only could they experiment with a form of architecture that was experimentalist at its very core, but they also faced lower levels of regulation. Besides, these professionals could count on the complacency of regulators, such as Vieira da Costa, who professed themselves in favor of the same kinds of influences.

The Portuguese architectural historian José Manuel Fernandes conceives of them as a single group, which he called the African generation, because of the undeniable imprint they left on Luanda's cityscape.[52] Part of the reason for the apparent uniformity of architectural style in Luanda at this time was the fact that they had been trained in the same places, under the same instructors, and were exposed to the same kinds of references. Vieira da Costa was probably one of the first architects of this generation to arrive in Luanda after his graduation, in 1946, and a stint as an intern at one of Le Corbusier's ateliers, where he had been given the opportunity to develop his dogma on modernist architecture. In 1949, he moved back to Luanda, where he was given a job as a technician at the Câmara Municipal de Luanda (Municipal Chamber of Luanda). During most of the time that da Costa held an official position in the Câmara, being responsible in this capacity for the approval of construction projects, he also, like many other architects of his time, kept a private atelier in what is now Avenida Rainha Ginga. Through his practice, he not only constructed several buildings in the city but also groomed several other architects who would themselves propose urban interventions. In his regulatory position, he proposed a new plan, in 1957, for the growth of Luanda called the Plano Regulador (Regulatory Plan), which built on some of the proposals presented by Moreira da Silva and de Gröer, adapting them to the new situation the city was experiencing. In this plan, geared like the previous one toward the need to control the city's growth, da Costa proposed the enforcement of zoning, in which downtown Luanda, including the Marginal de Luanda, would be devoted to commercial and administrative activities, on account of the infrastructure and facilities installed there (the port, the railway, storage sites, banks, commercial establishments, and so on), whereas Cidade Alta would accommodate government and residential activities with the construction of new neighborhoods. An industrial park was also proposed, particularly to respond to the increasing demand for construction materials.[53]

Vieira da Costa can be credited, then, as one of the urbanists of his time who most forcefully pushed for the expansion of the city beyond the *barrocas* (escarpments), if we consider that the construction of the new port and then the Marginal de Luanda had turned these cliffs into prime land. The geographic pattern of Luanda, in which cliffs and slopes rise abruptly hundreds of meters into the mainland, had long been a concern for engineers. In a study conducted in the early 1950s, it was noted that these escarpments posed two serious problems for the city—namely, that they were constantly moving toward already-consolidated sections of the urban area and that, during the rainy season, water flows produced erosion.[54] Additional recommendations detailed in the study included consolidation of these encampments, which could be done through the creation of greenbelts, the remnants of which can still be found in Miramar. The study also encouraged construction of roads such as the one that links Porto de Luanda to Praça Lusíadas (Lusíadas Square) and, at, a later stage, the construction of concrete terraces and plateaus.[55] Only through these series of engineering interventions could the Praça Lusíadas, which in the early 1950s became the first showcase of modernist architecture in the city, be prepared to receive construction in concrete. Vieira da Costa commissioned his friend Manolo Poitier to prepare the design for the square, from which four arteries depart to other points of the city—namely, the one that descends to Porto de Luanda, a second one that connects to downtown Luanda, a third one that extends to the north of the city, and the fourth, the famous Avenida Brito Godinho, which not only linked Kinaxixe to another important center of modernist architecture, Maianga Square, but was at the time also known as the asphalt frontier. Below the avenue, in the direction of Cidade Alta, this frontier separated the consolidated urban core from the *musseques* and the zone above, to be overthrown by modernist architecture.

In front of the square, Vieira da Costa himself designed what has been referred to as the masterpiece of modernist architecture in Luanda, the Kinaxixe Marketplace. Opened to the public in 1952, Fernando Mourão has called the marketplace "um manifesto da arquitectura moderna" (a manifesto of modernist architecture).[56] The influence of Le Corbusier was discernible in the voluminous building, which resembled a box and occupied a whole block of one hundred meters (328 feet) in length and sixty meters (197 feet) in width. It was supported by *pilotis* (pillars), in Le Corbusier's jargon, along the entire outer edge of the galleries. The exterior arcades were punctuated by built-in stores, at a considerable distance from the edge, which gave the impression that the building was suspended. The market itself was made up of open-air galleries, enclosed by concrete slabs of ten meters (thirty-three feet) in height "que recorrem a componentes construtivos de sombreamento e ventilação" (that use architectural elements to provide shade and ventilation),[57] creating the almost poetic impression that the market was devoid of walls.

From there, the stage was set for the expansion of modernist architectural structures in the city, particularly residential buildings. In the next few decades, thousands of other modernist buildings were erected. The pace of this urban development became even more dramatic, ironically, after February 1961, when a group of nationalists attacked colonial prisons to free other nationalists, an action that launched the anticolonial struggle.[58] Following the colonial regime's cry "Para Angola em força" (To Angola, in force), military units, alongside settlers, moved to Luanda, an event that produced another wave of urban expansion. To explain this seemingly contradictory development, António Campino, one of the members of the African generation, has been quoted as confiding to a friend, the architect Fernão Simões de Carvalho, that he had been given the task of designing a monument to Luanda's urban transformation in modernist architectural style. He would propose erecting a machete in the middle of Kinaxixe Square in Luanda—for which he allegedly designed a model that adorned his office. According to him, the machete, which symbolized the uprisings in northern Angola, was also the symbol of the unprecedented construction frenzy in Luanda.[59] Campino was certainly being ironic, but this irony captures the entanglements between anticolonial struggle, colonial economic growth, and massive migration of continental Portuguese to Angola, particularly Luanda.

Figure 2.2. Portuguese troops marching along the Marginal de Luanda in 1961.
Source: Arquivo Histórico Ultramarino.

Key to an understanding of Luanda's process of urban transformation is the division of labor that I have been discussing, in which the state occupied itself with providing infrastructure, whereas the private sector reaped the benefits of the developed land given back to the city. This explains the shape of the urban form that, from this time on, came to characterize Luanda. Mass construction work, particularly of buildings, not only permitted the standardization and the optimal use of construction resources but also made it possible, from an economic point of view, for a greater number of dwelling units to be built on smaller plots of land, which contributed to the densification of the city. Involved in this process of providing housing to settlers and, to a lesser extent, the Native population, were not only numerous Portuguese companies that owned land in Luanda but also individuals who saw the construction of buildings as a good way to invest their money. The promulgation of the law on horizontal property, in 1956, opened the way for the formation of cooperatives that allowed even middle-class Portuguese settlers in Angola to invest in and buy their own apartments.[60] Private appetites such as these fueled the expansion of the city and the progressive encroachment of the urban consolidated core into the *musseques*. Modernist architecture was then the chief instrument for arbitrating the separation of bodies in the city.

Clustering the Social

In the previous chapter, I showed that inhabitation in Luanda during the slave trade was predicated on the Casa Luandense, a concept borrowed from Fernando Batalha. I reworked this concept to mean something else, as I sought to understand the social scaffolding that allowed enslavers and the enslaved to share the same premises. I did so because I am taking this concept as a zero, an empty signifier, an empty vessel, so as to allow for engaging with the various moments of Luanda's sociology of inhabitation. If in the previous moments in the history of the city inhabitation was anchored on *sobrados* for the few, as Batalha discussed, or shacks for the majority, the apartment building became, from the 1950s onward, the dominant way of living in the city. This was not because more people were living in apartment buildings than in the *musseques* that encircled these apartment buildings. It was simply that various *musseques* during this time were being cleared from the city center to create space for apartment buildings. At the core of such a demographic rearrangement was colonial social engineering.

The *indigenato* only became law in 1926, after the tenure of Norton de Matos in Angola, but he, nonetheless, can be credited as the governor who took the most decisive steps in institutionalizing it. Its central question was labor: how to channel the African manpower that otherwise, and not long ago, was being commercialized by using slaves as productive labor.[61] As such, the *indigenato* was the instrument used to create a category of humans deprived of civil rights, which came with two corollaries. First, the *indígenas* were subject to labor conscription, for it was only through labor that the *indígenas* could redeem themselves from their condition; and, second, the *indígenas* were to be governed according to their own cultural structures.[62] These regimes of "decentralized despotism," as Mahmood Mamdani has dubbed them, were easier to enforce in rural areas.[63] Cities, such as Luanda, with a long history of racial intermingling, were difficult grounds for the implementation of separatist policies. For there already existed in Luanda a local bourgeoisie who, in many cases, could not be differentiated by race, on account of miscegenation. However, from the early 1920s onward, the expansion of Luanda would go hand in hand with race and class separation. The greater the white population became, the higher the concern for clustering the various groups in their own residential zones.

By then, most of the informal settlements had been offshoots of the vast *quintais*, or backyards, on the premises of the residences of slavers, later taking the form of clusters of huts in neighborhoods such as Coqueiros, Maianga,

Ingombotas, and Bungo, inhabited by the enslaved and recently freed people. A novel preoccupation with hygiene prompted the colonial authorities to remove entire neighborhoods from the vicinity of the town center. Hygienic conditions were appalling, and epidemics of smallpox in 1856 and 1864 killed thousands of people, warranting the first demolitions of settlements and relocations of the African population. The demolition of 227 huts in the neighborhood of Coqueiros in the early twentieth century, for example, was justified by invoking the concern that winds would spread diseases from the informal settlements to the zones occupied by the most affluent population.[64] These concerns were at the heart of several proposals by urbanists for how to prevent whites from contracting tropical diseases.[65] In the case of Luanda, the most basic measure for creating such a separation was simply to move the natives from the center to the outskirts of the city, without compensation, and to legitimize this procedure with the argument that the land they occupied did not belong to them, on account of their political status as *indígenas*. There were also situations where members of the local bourgeoisie could not make the case that they were civilized and were simply reduced to the condition of *indigenato*. Even before the modernist intervention, entire neighborhoods were cleared on these grounds.

So even though the Estatuto do Indígena (Native Statute) was meant to address the political status of the rural population, it gave Norton de Matos an opportunity to address other pertinent urban issues.[66] Luanda was characterized at the time as a sort of mixture, in which a number of Blacks, including those who called themselves Angolenses, owned land and even buildings in the city. They were partly the beneficiaries of the assimilationist policies of the 1800s and formed part of the Creole society that had emerged in Angola as in many other places in Africa.[67] However, they became a problem for the colonial authorities when colonial policy shifted from assimilation to nativism.[68] In his attempt to turn Angolenses into natives, Norton de Matos implemented measures that eroded their rights, and particularly their positions, in the city. By confiscating urban land claimed by Africans, and by preventing them from owning land in the city, he and those colonial administrators who came after him were able to remove thousands of people and cluster them in the outskirts of the formal city, in what then problematically came to be called Bairros Indígenas.

Luandans today are known for their attachment to their *bairros* of origin, particularly those who were born before independence. This includes me, for instance. Even though I grew up in the Baixa (downtown Luanda), I tend to emphasize that I was born in Sambizanga. However, neither Baixa nor Sambizanga is a neighborhood in the proper sense of the word. They do not refer to limited and clearly demarcated geographic areas. In most cases, a *bairro* refers to a particular typology or to the main characteristics of inhabitants that occupy a given section of the city. Most of present-day Luanda, for instance, would associate Bairro Palanca with Angolans who have returned from Congo and with Congolese nationals—populations whose impact on the city will be discussed later. Bairro Popular, in contrast, is associated with social housing for single families built in the years of late colonialism. Incidentally, when the Angolan government announced, in July 2019, the project of erecting dozens of buildings in Cidade Alta to lodge the ministries of the central government, it called this project Bairro dos Ministérios. The origin of such a relationship between place and belonging is certainly colonial. A *bairro* was considered a critical juncture not only as a method to provide residents with a sense of belonging, particularly for newcomers migrating from Europe, but also as a device through which urbanists could devise ways in which the dialectical relationship between inside and outside could be approached. The main descriptors were city center and *musseques*. In this guise, the *bairro* was conceived as a tool that could allow for the creation of a sense of order and normality to set against the disorder of most of the city, as the *bairro* also allowed for the ascription of whole categories of people to the same geographic location.[69] More important, *bairros* would also allow for better control and surveillance of their residents, as they came into being alongside the early iterations of the pass laws that defined the zones of the city where Blacks could reside and circulate. Behind the formation of these urban conglomerates were then two objectives. On the one hand, they were meant to help the Portuguese purge the city of Blacks. On the other hand, the colonial state would also attempt to confine Blacks to their own *bairros* so that they did not have to visit the city center for any other reason but work.

The destructive fury with which the Portuguese tore down *musseques* in the city center was later, from the 1950 onward, deployed far beyond the city center and *musseques* such as Bananeiras, Burity, Cayete, Cabeça, Pedrosa, and Terra Nova. Other *musseques*—such as Catambor, Prenda, Cassequel, Calemba, Marçal, Rangel, and Caputo, Sambizanga, Mota, Lixeira, outside the urban perimeter—had been absorbed by other *bairros*, some of them partially constructed, such as Saiote or Caputo. By the 1960s, the cordon sanitaire had been pushed farther from the center, and settlements such as Bungo, Braga, Maculusso, and Viúva Leal had been destroyed and their populations moved farther beyond downtown Luanda, to newly formed *musseques*. Luanda's original population, composed mainly of descendants of the enslaved and enslavers, started to coalesce in the Bairros Indígenas, or the *bairros* that were later built to lodge workers, the so-called *bairros operários*.[70] Over time, these *bairros* were also constituting their own skin, for they were surrounded by shacks built by newcomers to the city, sometimes with the connivance of colonial administrators who turned a blind eye to these practices, convinced that the lower the cost of housing for unskilled laborers, the lower the salaries the laborers could expect to be paid.[71] From property owners, Blacks in the city by the late 1960s had become squatters.

Regarding the clustering of the social, Bairro Prenda is certainly a case in point. It was designed by the architect and urbanist Fernão Simões de Carvalho, born in Luanda in 1929. He studied architecture in Portugal, obtaining his bachelor's degree in 1955, before moving to Paris in mid-1955 to ply his craft by taking classes with Robert Auzelle at the Sorbonne and working, like Vieira da Costa before him, as an intern at one of Le Corbusier's ateliers.[72] Returning to Lisbon in the late 1950s, he found work at the Gabinete de Urbanização do Ultramar (Office for Overseas Urbanization) but resigned soon after under the pretext that the work he was involved in had more to do with design than architecture.[73] In Luanda, he founded a unit of the Gabinete de Urbanização Colonial (Office for Colonial Urbanization) at the Câmara Municipal de Luanda. As in the case of Vieira da Costa, Carvalho also worked for the public and the private sectors, for while he was involved in the preparation of a master plan for the city, he also worked as an architect on public and private buildings.[74]

Carvalho arrived on the urban scene in Luanda when the effects of the grandiloquent planning schemes of practitioners such as Vieira da Costa had started to become visible. The main consequences of these interventions were not only that racial segregation had found its way into the planning itself but also that land speculation had distorted or prevented the implementation of any city plan. He was educated in a school with a different sensibility compared with the one Le Corbusier's supporters were promoting, one which was coming to terms with the consequences of the strict zoning regulations that had been celebrated in the city's previous plans. In his understanding, the best way to tackle the disorderly growth of Luanda was to avoid approaching and planning it as a totality. He was convinced that the city should be broken down and divided up into manageable units, the so-called *unités d'habitation* (residential units). Part of the vision of Luanda's city making that he embraced is succinctly discussed in a short newspaper article suggestively called "Luanda do futuro" (Luanda of the future). In this short piece, he begins by declaring that Luanda would boast a population of about half a million people by 1980 and that the authorities should be prepared for this unavoidable outcome. In this future scenario, access to land would become a major problem, owing to the tendency of the city authorities to annex more and more land. The consequences, Carvalho predicted, citing Le Corbusier, would be "a apoplexia do centro e a paralisia nas extremidades" (collapse of the center and the paralysis of the extremities). To avoid this prospect, future master plans for the city should take the relationship between land use and population density more seriously, an issue that, according to Carvalho, had for the most part remained unexamined in previous city plans. In the future he was imagining for the city, Luanda's inhabitants would live in neighborhood units of 3,000 to 10,000 people, each provided with facilities such as primary schools, crèches, primary health care facilities, cinemas, churches, commercial infrastructure, and, particularly, sports facilities, all at "distâncias calculadas" (calculated distances) from where people lived. Each of these units would also provide access to open green spaces to help individuals retain their "equilíbrio psíquico" (psychic balance). More important, these proposed neighborhoods would be transected by thoroughfares.[75]

To showcase the city yet to come, Carvalho designed the Bairro Prenda as a prototype—as the first one of about a dozen that could be built—beyond the *fronteira do asfalto*, in the *musseque* of Prenda. The *bairro* he designed there would include self-built, single-family houses and semiduplex buildings for the white middle class. In the end, however, only six of the twenty-eight twelve-story apartment buildings he envisioned were actually built. None of the social amenities Carvalho had suggested were put in place, let alone the green spaces and sports facilities.

More important, Prenda was conceived not only as a solution to the housing issue but also as a way to address racial integration. From the mid-1950s onward, there was a debate on how to integrate Africans into the newly built residential areas. With Prenda, Carvalho proposed to build this Unité de Voisinage (Neighbourhood Unit) without removing the original population and by integrating Africans into it—but not on the same footing. Whereas whites could purchase their apartments and houses by applying to the various finance schemes available, Blacks were expected to build their own houses. To appease those who might not be interested in living in such proximity to Blacks, Carvalho also added that the purpose of this proximity was pedagogical, in so far as these *bairros* were conceived as schools where Africans would learn how to live in the city.[76]

Bairro Prenda was a failure in the sense that none of the facilities it anticipated were constructed, and it did not stir up a great deal of interest among the settler population. Part of the reason for failure was that Luanda was not industrialized enough for zoning to work. Factories could have been constructed in satellite cities such as Viana and Cacuaco, and workers could thus have lived in their vicinity without having to commute daily to the city center. However,

Luanda was for the most part a tertiary city, in which most of the economic activity was commercial. Ever since the era of slavery, most Africans had to provide labor to the white minority as a source of sustenance. And conversely, this meant that the whites who lived in predominantly white neighborhoods could not go without the labor provided by the Africans who lived in the *musseques*. This had an incredible influence on the layout of the city, which had to accommodate the long distances workers needed to cover to reach their places of work. Modernist planners such as Vieira da Costa had this in mind when they worked out how to separate the city's population according to class (and obviously race), without depriving the wealthy of access to cheap labor:

> Compete, pois, ao europeu criar no indígena necessidades de conforto e de uma vida mais elevada, impelindo-o assim ao trabalho que o levará a fixar-se, e que facilitará a mão-de-obra mais estável. A orientação das habitações e a localização dos bairros indígenas são os dois grandes elementos que devem reger a composição do plano de uma cidade colonial. . . . Assim, preferimos situar os bairros indígenas envolvendo o núcleo central, tenho todo o cuidado de localizá-los sempre a sotavento das zonas das habitações europeias, que mesmo assim serão sempre isoladas por um écrã de verdura, suficientemente largo para que o mosquito possa transpô-lo. Como parece ser indispensável, sob o ponto de vista higiénico e social, as populações indígenas formarão vários grupos dispersos, que como pequenos satélites abraçarão o núcleo europeu, ficando assim cada sector deste núcleo servido por um grupo indígena. Deste modo, encurtaremos a distância a percorrrer entre o local de trabalho e a residencia.

> (It is the work of the European to induce in the Native the need for comfort and a more elevated life, in this way compelling him to the work that will force him to settle down, and that will ease the availability of a more stable pool of labor. The spatial orientation of the housing and the location of Native neighborhoods are the two major elements that should dictate the composition of the colonial city. . . . In this way, we have preferred to situate the Native settlements around the central nucleus, trying carefully to locate them leeward of the European housing but separated by a green corridor, wide enough to prevent mosquitoes from crossing it. From a hygienic and social point of view it is imperative that the Native population form various dispersed groups that, as small satellite settlements, will encircle the European nucleus, in such a way that each nucleus will be served by an indigenous group. In this way, we shorten the distance from work to the residence).[77]

Vieira da Costa and others had the opportunity to realize such a vision in the ways they approached the planning of several neighborhoods in Luanda. Although the city was never fragmented according to the principle of the garden city, some of these solutions were nonetheless implemented. A case in point was the design of Alvalade and its relation to the surrounding neighborhoods whose inhabitants were supposed to provide domestic labor. Alvalade was partially encircled by a greenbelt, which protected it as an upper-end residential neighborhood from encroachment by the rest of the city—its class status was marked, for example, by the absence of sidewalks, signaling that the suburb was not intended for plebeian pedestrian traffic. But the greenbelt was crossed by pedestrian paths that gave workers access to their places of work in the suburbs. This design detail has eluded the most perceptive readers of Luanda's planning history, such as Mourão, who hails this solution as revolutionary since it allowed people to reach the center of the city by walking.[78]

The reshaping of Luanda according to modernist principles turned the city into material proof that the Estado Novo was civilizing Africa. Postcards produced for tourism and propaganda purposes could then depict the new buildings, manicured green spaces, and views of the Marginal de Luanda. But all of this posed new issues. White migration increased segregation and furthered social fragmentation. The problem went beyond Africans' being pitted against settlers: the settlers who considered themselves Angolans (some from families settled in Angola for generations) resented the newcomers and Portugal's administration of colonial matters.

In the 1960s, as a direct consequence of the anticolonial uprisings, the Portuguese initiated several reforms whose goal was to better integrate the colonies with the mother country. The abolition of the legal category of *indigenato* came with measures that rendered every native of Angola a Portuguese citizen. However, when it came to questions of housing and the right to inhabit the city, very few things had changed. At this moment, the squatter, the cognitive category I have been using, was not yet a citizen and was no longer the enslaved person who inhabited the city center but represented the indigenous Angolan, the Native. Although the question of the Native had been discussed for the most part in the context of rural Africa, the urban Native created a whole range of conceptual problems for the colonial legislator, as we will see.[79] Modernist Luanda operated through the expulsion of the indigenous from its core, as if the city had to immunize itself against the presence of the indigenous element.[80]

The frontier between the formal and the informal, or the city and the *musseque*, which had been porous and malleable for most of Luanda's history, became more rigid during these years. It was as if modernist architecture was forcing the city to thicken its skin, intensifying the separation between its two dichotomous poles. For the same railway network that allowed workers to arrive on time at their workplaces would also allow urbanists to plan the workers' residential areas farther and farther from the city center. This thinking was already intimated in a number of the city's plans and became more refined in the 1950s when, in his Plano Regulador, Vieira da Costa suggested the discontinuation of railway lines linking the peripheries to the center, at Cidade Alta Station, forcing those coming from outside the city to disembark at Estação do Bungo (Bungo Train Station) and continue their journey using other means of transportation, such as buses, or on foot.[81] Luanda, then, owed to these planning interventions the feature that predominated during the last decades of colonization and the early years of independence, and which the city has only recently been able to change: the formation of a radiocentric grid, in which the center, the consolidated urban core, was increasingly occupied by the well-to-do, and the *bairros*, surrounded by *musseques*, designed for the poor, were moved farther and farther from the center at the pace of the expansion of concrete buildings.

. . .

The decades in the history of Luanda covered in this chapter mark its most significant physical expansion. From a modest 320 hectares (741,316 acres) in 1926, Luanda burst forth into a city covering 6,714 hectares (16,591 acres) in 1975, when the country became independent. At the heart of these urban developments were a series of internal and external factors—namely, the appreciation of primary commodities in the global economy, the implementation of colonial development projects, and the sudden attractiveness of Luanda, which triggered migration from continental Portugal.

Colonial decision making structures in Lisbon certainly traced the broad strokes of the policies that permitted such developments to occur but not without the participation of Luanda's private interests. In a territory that was mostly controlled by private interests during the era of slavery—even the officials representing the colonial state conducted business privately—the weight of the colonial state only grew, particularly after the republican revolution in 1910. The private sector could certainly drive the colony's economy but would always fail to amass the resources to set up vital infrastructure for the circulation of commodities. By the time the colonial state was revitalized, particularly during the tenure of Norton de Matos, the lion's share of land was controlled by a handful of individuals and companies. For the expansion of infrastructure, the state was then forced to negotiate with these interests and, later on, create a legal mechanism for dispossession—with or without compensation. This is a feature of the colonial state that the postcolonial state would inherit and reinforce, as I will show later in this book.

The transformation of Luanda according to the Athens Charter principles was produced, then, by a conjuncture of circumstances, one political and the other technical. Politically, modernist Luanda emerged out of the conflict between, on the one hand, the interests of the empire, which wanted Luanda to be nothing more than a provider of unfinished raw materials and, on the other, the interests of an emergent white bourgeoisie, which was modeling its approach to the colonial endeavor on South Africa during apartheid. Such was a reading of the global situation when self-determination was gaining traction in Asia and Africa. On the technical level, one needs to evoke Le Corbusier, who was very aware of the unsavoriness of many of his proposals and knew that they needed to be backed by a strong regime.[82] For its dissemination in the colonized territories, modernist architecture relied on the Estado Novo, which had a strong grip on all forms of political expression and tightly restricted the space for dissent. Since most urban land and buildings were privately owned, the colonial state could not prevent, as shown in the previous chapter, older buildings in Luanda from being destroyed, even if they held heritage value. Luanda's inhabitants, in turn, consisted mostly of newcomers who had no attachment to its history and no interest in its preservation. Africa did not have a history, as it were. Even though the Portuguese authorities were reluctant to allow modernist buildings to be erected in Lisbon, they were also conscious of the benefits of doing so—namely, the creation of the modern image they wanted to give of Africa and the fact that such urban forms could dispel the negative images many Portuguese had of the continent and could therefore be used to attract metropolitan Portuguese to Angola, particularly Luanda.

Much of what has been discussed in this chapter entails the not always rosy relations between the colonial state and private interests. Whereas the construction of infrastructure was performed by the colonial state, under, for instance, the rubric of the various *planos de fomento* (development plans), the private sector certainly reaped the benefits of such improvements. For it was in the interstices of these improvements that they consolidated their own interests. Whereas urban planners and architects were instrumental for the expansion of the urban grid, or the *fronteira do asfalto*, they were also instrumental in the creation of the subdivisions that came about within the urban as a whole. Conjoining their oversight capacity with private practice, their involvement accounted for the construction of thousands of buildings under the modernist rubric. In this process, the social mix of Casa Luandense, and its corresponding urban makeup, was being replaced by outright segregation, in which the consolidating urban core was progressively expunging the poor.

The more perennial consequences of these urban and sociological arrangements were that toward the end of colonial rule, settlers controlled a staggering proportion of property in Luanda. Such control went beyond the city center, as most shacks in the *musseques* were owned by whites and rented to Africans. Those who could afford to rent houses in the *musseques* had the option to build their own shacks on informal land. Consequently, the expansion of the urban grid under the premises of modernist architecture was not only enforcing segregation by enclosing Luanda's residents in their own *bairros* but also creating a staggering class of squatters. This colonialism-induced squatting is what the postcolonial dispensation would address—in a revolutionary manner.

Part II.   Stasis

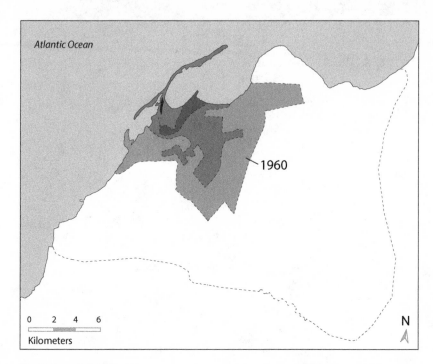

Map 3.1. Luanda in 1960.

3. A Place to Dwell in Times of Change

The city was dying the way an oasis dies when the well runs dry: it became empty, fell into inanition, passed into oblivion.—Ryszard Kapuscinski, *Another Day of Life*, 1987

• • •

In *Os transparentes* (most appropriately translated into English as *Transparent City*), the Luanda-born author, Ondjaki, describes the precarious and contingent life in postcolonial Luanda through the eyes of a dozen of occupants, probably squatters, in an apartment building in the *bairro* of Maianga. At the center of the novel's plot is Odonato and his journey into transparency.[1] For Odonato, becoming transparent is not akin to dying. Rather, it is a way to stop existing so that life becomes more bearable. Transparency, then, comes from this ability to be in a state of suspension between life and death. To provide such a metaphor with a critical purchase that helps us understand life in postindependence urban Luanda, I should say here that transparency, in the way I view it, is not tantamount to invisibility.[2] For whereas invisibility is the property of objects that resist reference or enumeration, as famously discussed by James C. Scott, transparency, conversely, posits the property of objects that can be vaguely seen and that allow the viewer to see through them.[3]

I am evoking Ondjaki's novel to make sense of the various repertoires for inhabiting most of the apartment buildings that emerged in postindependence Luanda. When the settlers for whom the city center was built fled the country in the wake of independence, their apartments were occupied by former inhabitants of the *musseques* and by the thousands of people fleeing from the civil war ravaging the provinces. Those new urban dwellers, then, became transparent. For it did not mean that the postcolonial state could not see them or how they were occupying these properties. But the state could not, or did not have resources to, make these inhabitants visible, or legible, for the purpose of extracting taxes and other property levies. In this sense, urban dwellers became transparent to the state. But there is also another kind of transparency Ondjaki's novel speaks to, which is the gist of this chapter. Most of the occupants of these apartment buildings had also become transparent to each other. For, in these years, the skin of the city had receded to such an extent that the limits of the city, the line of separation among the various groups that composed Luandans, was no longer at the level of the *bairro*, or even blocks of apartments. As we will see, the separation was at the level of the apartment itself.

The *fronteira* that the Portuguese attempted to erect between the city and the *musseques* was not a perfect one. Colonial rule had attempted to extend the cordon sanitaire of the city center as much as possible, and, in this process, pushed the undesirables, the colonized, beyond the borders of the formal city. Consequently, by the early 1970s, the asphalt frontier, or the separation between the planned and the unplanned city, had been considerably stretched out of the city center. Gone were the times, in the 1920s, when the city was still confined to its historical center, and gone also were the times when the limits of the city had been established on Avenida Brito Godinho. The setting up of infrastructure, transportation routes, and constructions in concrete had pushed the *musseques* farther away from the center, and those that survived the relocation turned into small islands of poverty in the midst of the urban core. However, as pockets of urban informality, the *musseques* had resisted and withstood destruction in various sections of the city. But this patchwork was at least a fabric the city's authorities could work with. But for the reasons that I will turn my attention to in this chapter, such an order could not be sustained after independence. The concrete city was still there, but the rules that arbitrated belonging, or the distribution of bodies in the city, had been severely smashed and compromised with independence.

Figure 3.1. A typical Luandan *musseque*, 1974. Source: Arquivo Nacional da Torre do Tombo.

Independence permitted the wretched of the earth, the colonized, to borrow Fanon's felicitous title, to dwell in the city center.[4] This process was of course an outcome of the redefinition of the social contract and the implicit promise of the national liberation movement that independence was a way to end the "exploitation of man by man."[5] The new nation that came into being would no longer make a distinction between colonizers and colonized, or between civilized and natives: every Angolan would be a citizen. Part of what was meant by *citizen* in those years was the right to live in proper housing, or at least in the houses left behind by the Portuguese. Hence, those Angolans who during the late colonial period had migrated from the countryside to the city and were squatting on private or public land were now, through occupation, turned into citizens. It was then through sovereignty that Angolans were righting the rights to the city. With the coming of independence, the Angolan authorities would not only create the conditions for massive squatting but also, within a few years, turn squatting into a protocol for inhabiting the city itself. In this process, the skin of the city, those systems of limits and limitations that the Portuguese had so consciously policed and surveilled, lost all purchase. Or, at least, from then on it was no longer a task for the state to police those urban boundaries.

Dismantling the Colonial (Urban) Legacy

On April 25, 1974, an event with unpredictable consequences took place in Lisbon. A group of officials from the Portuguese army marched to the city to oust the president of the council, Marcelo Caetano, in what became known as the Revolução dos Cravos (Carnation Revolution). The revolution that ended forty-one years of the corporatist far-right regime founded by Salazar in 1933 had started in the colonies, specifically in Angola and Guinea-Bissau. It was in Luanda, as discussed in the previous chapter, that a handful of nationalists attacked the colonial prisons on February 4, 1961, to free other nationalists being held there, and hundreds of ill-prepared guerrilla fighters entered the territory, coming from the Belgian Congo, to kill hundreds of Portuguese and thousands of Angolans in the coffee plantations of northern Angola.[6] But it was in Guinea-Bissau that the African nationalist Amílcar Cabral set up the most organized and theoretically sophisticated nationalist movement against the Portuguese, and where resentment against the war effort had bred and motivated the disgruntled Portuguese military to form the Movimento das Forças Armadas (Movement of the Armed Forces; MFA), the force behind the coup of April 1974.[7]

The effects of the Carnation Revolution were felt particularly acutely in Angola. This Portuguese territory had the highest settler population among the Portuguese colonies in Africa and was the most economically vital for the Portuguese economy.[8] Even if, according to the Angolan press, calm and quiet dominated Luanda on the morning of April 26, 1974, it was clear to many observers that the ideological scaffolding that supported the Estado Novo had been severely compromised. In the next few days and months, various voices emerged on the Portuguese political scene, putting forward divergent, if not irreconcilable, suggestions for how to deal with the colonial question. The most revolutionary and far-left voices were vying for total and immediate independence of the colonies, and in the middle of the spectrum, there were those arguing that Africans were not ready for sovereignty and that their territories should be placed under a regime of tutelage to prepare them for gradual independence. There were also those such as António de Spínola, the leader of the Junta de Salvação Nacional (Board for National Salvation), the governing body that replaced the Estado Novo, who saw in the revolution an opportunity to unearth an old project, which consisted of the formation of a community that included the Portuguese and the natives of its colonies.[9] However, it was too late for anything like this to be thought through and implemented, for during these times of uncertainty, the political situation deteriorated considerably, to the extent that the physical safety of the settlers could no longer be guaranteed.

Nineteen seventy-five was a kind of year zero for Angola on all accounts, particularly in regard to the question of urbanism and processes of urbanization. Independence brought with it the possibility of a new reconfiguration of space, and more important, one that could allow for justice in the ways in which bodies were ascribed to space. Putting it differently, independence provided the postcolonial order the possibility to right the rights to the city. However, the redress impulse predates independence itself. It was a consequence of the leftist leaning of the revolution in Lisbon and came to constitute, in times of transition (from April 1974 to November 1975), an ideological corrective to the fascism of the Estado Novo. Those people in positions of power, mostly whites, who had criticized colonial planning, now had the opportunity to produce alternatives that could undo the consequences of a problematic city making. Central to these recalibrations was the question of land, and by addressing this question, the reformers were hoping to at least deal with the real estate speculation, which could, subsequently, allow for the improvement of living conditions in the *musseques*.

However, things did not go this way. For the independence of Angola and other Portuguese colonies in Africa was subsumed into a broader political context that put an end to the Portuguese dictatorship led by Salazar's successor, Marcelo Caetano.[10] As a result, before the nationalists, Portuguese colonial authorities or settlers could start to imagine other forms of postcolonial society, the Portuguese empire began to crumble, and as this process unfolded, the settlers felt increasingly vulnerable in the colonies. Esposito's elaboration on "immunization" might be of help to grasp what was then going on. Luanda expanded under the conviction that settlers would be better off in a city center devoid of Blacks, who had been relegated to the outskirts. With independence, then, the settlers were the ones who were expelled from the community-information, precisely they for whom the modernist city had been built.

In Luanda, more specifically, the political uncertainties ushered in by the Carnation Revolution created a power vacuum. The colonial administration lost authority and respect in the eyes of the Luandan population. Political and social order could no longer be enforced. The settlers, and specifically the property owners, began to leave the country, or at least started to prepare for such a move by liquidating and repatriating their assets. By the end of 1974, more than 50,000 Portuguese settlers had left Angola.[11] In this social environment, in which popular views found more space for public expression, the most conservative elements of the settler population, still convinced that they could maintain their grip on the Black majority, organized militias not only to protect their lives and property but also to stage racist attacks against Black Angolans.

The British journalists Michael Wolfers and Jane Bergerol, residing in Luanda, describe how "after the April coup, angry white settlers rampaged through the shanty musseques, killing, as they had done in the 1960s [at the beginning of the struggle for independence]."[12] The residents of the *musseques*, in turn, set out to organize themselves into *comités populares* (people's committees), as a form of self-defense against both the settler militias and criminals and gangs that saw an opportunity in the ensuing disorder. Formed mostly by Blacks and mestizos, alongside some progressive whites, these committees emerged from what has been called *poder popular* (people's power), a concept later co-opted by the MPLA to organize Luanda's unruly population, particularly in the *musseques*.[13] They were the offspring of the popular political committees in Luanda that had been formed in the wake of the April revolution in Portugal, with reverberations throughout the colonial empire. But their origins traced back from the heart of the colonial endeavor.[14]

The emergence of these bodies can be traced back to the formation of the Bairros Indígenas, where the Portuguese had supported the creation of the Comissões dos Bairros Indígenas (Native Neighborhood Committees), as instruments for the enactment of indirect rule in the *musseques*. They may have evolved into Comissões dos Bairros Populares (People's Neighborhood Committees) when this designation replaced Bairros Indígenas. In those uncertain times, however, these bodies reached out and formed coalitions with many other interest groups. For at stake was how to bring order to the places where they lived in times of terror. As such, *poder popular*, expressed through the people's committees, became the de facto source of power in many of the city's neighborhoods, particularly in the *musseques*. Behind the emergence of these groups lay the notion, reinforced by the Carnation Revolution, that power should emanate from the will of the people. And since both the Portuguese soldiers and the youth in the *musseques* were reading the same literature, grounded in Marxism and its derivatives, this political conjuncture—of the coup against imperial power and a push for independence—became a major opportunity for reassessing colonialism and imagining the form of the postcolonial society to come. As the squalid *musseques* were an open and visible sore in the city, it was obvious that the energies created by these coalitions should be directed toward addressing the pressing issues the places posed.

These committees took over control of the city, and before governing bodies that could regulate social life were created, they were for the most part the ones that played this role. They were occupying the houses and apartments of the departed settlers, as well as the business premises of Portuguese shop owners in the *musseques*, "driving them out of the slums and setting up

Figure 3.2. Agostinho Neto (bottom left), first president of Angola, probably on his arrival in Luanda in 1974. Source: Arquivo Nacional da Torre do Tombo.

cooperative shops to replace the traders."[15] The committees organized protests against the Junta de Habitação de Angola (Angolan Housing Board), marching from the *musseques* to the city hall. The admiral António Alva Rosa Coutinho, the high commissioner during these times of transition, was forced to fire his highest officials and bow to the people's pressure to set up "an administrative committee to serve the interests of the majority."[16] But for many of those who were members of the people's committees, these measures were not enough. They were aiming at unraveling the effects of colonial planning in the places where they lived. To obtain some technical understanding of what needed to be done, they drew on the expertise of colonial expatriates working in Luanda at the time on other projects, such as Walter Shillinger, UNESCO's consultant on urbanism, and the Belgian architect Michel Toussaint. A key technician behind the project was the Angolan-born architect José Deodoro Troufa Real, who was the coordinator of Luanda's master plan of 1973.[17]

To address the people's demands, the collective formed by Shilling, Toussaint, and Troufa Real elaborated a multiphase plan that, according to Troufa Real, proposed a change of policy "concerning intervention in urban development."[18]

Supported by the Junta de Salvação Nacional (the de facto government that took over from Estado Novo and emanated from the Movimento das Forças Armadas), they produced a new housing policy with an "implementation strategy for Angola at five levels, classified as Actions."[19] The first action, seen as a "provisional emergency plan," was to be carried out in the *musseques*; its primary goal was to achieve an "immediate improvement of social services and infrastructure."[20] More specifically, at this level, the objectives to be achieved were an increase in the number of water points, the improvement of street lighting on main roads, and the setting up of a better infrastructure for sewage removal and refuse collection. The plan also envisaged the construction of primary schools, hospitals, and commercial cooperatives, and the development of an integrated public transport network.[21] According to Troufa Real, this action "involved the direct participation of the *Comités Populares de Bairro*, People's Neighbourhood Committees." In his review of the process, Troufa Real stated, with some fanfare, that in less than a year, "the programme had been almost concluded and results were beyond expectation."[22]

The second action proposed by the plan, also developmental in nature, involved the implementation of a primary sewerage network in the *musseques* and, critically, the drainage of the lagoons, particularly the one in Cazenga.[23] The third action was more ambitious and aimed at constructing houses through self-help cooperatives and small brigade schemes on plots of land identified and released by the Junta. Credit lines would be made available to wage earners for the purchase of construction materials to build their own houses, though these would be required to fulfill a set of minimum quality standards put forward by the Junta. The plan also envisioned the redistribution of land to decrease the population density in the *musseques* and facilitate rehousing.[24] These actions were only partially implemented.

As the site for a concrete intervention, the collective chose an expanding section of the city, mixing different housing types and selecting residents from among the settlers, who were eager to save money, as well as from among Angolans migrating from the rural countryside. Golfe was an apt choice, since the entire neighborhood was doomed to demolition under the provisions of Decreto-Lei (Decree) no. 576/70, which made land expropriation on behalf of the provincial government for the purpose of providing housing for low-income residents more expedient.[25] As such, following this intervention aimed at facilitating the "gradual recovery of *Musseques* in Golfe" while safeguarding the "character of the neighborhood as envisioned in the master plan,"[26] the land occupied by these informal settlements was "expropriated in the public and community interest."[27] This phase of the plan would create the conditions for the implementation of the fifth and last action—namely, "to control the flow of migrant workers from the rural areas to the city to counteract overcrowding and to avoid the emergence of new musseques in Luanda and other urban centers."[28]

In regard to the implementation of the fourth action proposed by the master plan, lower-class families from the *musseques* were selected and "encouraged to occupy their plot of land immediately and start the building work" so as to allow them to participate in the overall project from the outset, not only in constructing their homes but also by having access to a salary paid by the state.[29] As Troufa Real argued, this measure had important social implications at a time when unemployment was rising in the wake of the Portuguese leaving the country. At this point in his narration of the whole process, Troufa Real cites and criticizes John Turner—the British architect who became famous for championing housing for the poor in Latin America—and his propositions for housing the poor in Latin America, on the basis that it amounted to a "speculative practice in the supply of materials, land and labor [that] served other interests."[30] In Luanda, he countered, there was the opportunity to do something different, in that residents who were building their own houses were paid salaries, and the building materials were either supplied by the state or bought at "controlled prices by state organizations and by the People's Committees themselves." Furthermore, land was allotted for free, its use granted by the state and controlled under "expropriation policies."[31]

In the master plan that was then elaborated, to be implemented in accordance with Decreto-Lei no. 743/74, was issued by the provisional government of Rosa Coutinho and allowed for land expropriation of *musseques* and unused private land. The new Golfe would cover an area of 6.1 hectares (15.07 acres) and would be divided into four areas to accommodate 5,000 inhabitants each, with a civic center placed in the middle to cater to all the sections of the neighborhood. The streets separating the four areas would be thoroughfares lined with small shops, recreational clubs, and market areas for artisans; a hospital and pediatric clinic; a post office, a police station, and a fire station; and a project office for the People's Neighborhood Committee.[32]

The main concern in designing a neighborhood that would accommodate the new norms brought about by the new political dispensation, even if this dispensation was transitory, was not only how to build houses for the poor who were moving to the city from the countryside, as Troufa Real claimed; it was also how to address preservation of the way of life that people were used to. The underlying conceptualization was that the transformation of the shantytown should not destroy its existing "social and cultural patterns."[33] As a result, according to Troufa Real, careful attention was paid to the prevailing relationships between city blocks, houses, courts, and streets, and the habits and traditions of the communities that were tied to them.[34] Critically, the new planning approach attempted to take into account the nature of the *musseques* themselves. Since these inhabitants lacked so many things—employment security (for those who were employed), clean water, sewers, and electricity— planners thought that a way to deal with this was to shape spaces that would allow for the harnessing of particular social relations. As such, "convenient and rapid pedestrian access to work sites were [*sic*] provided"[35] through the building of alleyways between houses and plots. Marketplaces were integrated into the spatial planning, and small squares were designed for meetings and sports activities. The houses themselves were designed to look very similar to the ones in the *musseques*, with covered porches and open yards, to preserve the patterns of traditional family life.[36]

Even though these attempts at changing living conditions in the city might have been motivated by good intentions, one cannot fail to detect in them the continually recurring colonial desire to cluster the social by separating the various groups in their ascriptive *bairros*. Furthermore, if creating the semblance of proper and well-established *bairros* was intended to prevent residents from invading the parts of the city being progressively abandoned by the settlers, it did not work. The reason for this was not only that the understanding of culture permeating the plan was retrograde, seemingly out of the most basic colonial manual, but also that this approach at urban redress, so to speak, was unfolding during the most critical period of Angolan political history, a time when drastic changes were underway. This long discussion of the last attempt at slum upgrading shows the extent to which the project was still infused with a colonial vision and also how, more problematically, it created the canvas on which further attempts at upgrading would be reenacted in postcolonial times, as I will show in the following chapters.

The Turmoil of Independence

The colonial question was still at the heart of Portugal's politics after the April revolution, and the path to self-determination of the previously governed African territories was decided amid violence, protests, and threats of further coups. It was only with the promulgation of the Lei Constitucional (Constitutional Law) no. 7/74 (an appendix to the constitution) on July 27, 1974, by the Portuguese president, António de Spínola, that the road was opened to the independence of the Portuguese territories in Africa.[37] In the same solemn and dramatic communication to the country, Spínola also added that the Portuguese were ready to initiate negotiations for the transfer of power to the legitimate representatives of the colonized.

With Spínola's declaration and the promulgation of the new Portuguese Constitution, the destiny of Portugal and the colonies was sealed. Portugal engaged in negotiations with each of the colonies to determine the process of their path into formal independence. In the case of Angola, the Portuguese government met with representatives of the three nationalist movements, namely the MPLA, the FNLA (Frente Nacional for the Liberation of Angola [National Front for the Liberation of Angola]) and UNITA (União Nacional para a Independência de Angola [National Union for the Independence of Angola]), in Alvor, Portugal, to sign the Alvor Agreement, which put an end to the war for independence, discussed the preparations for the transfer of sovereignty, and decided on a date for independence: November 11, 1975. The nationalist forces also agreed to hold elections on October 31 and to govern through a transitional structure to be led by the Portuguese high commissioner, Admiral Rosa Coutinho, between January 1975 and the moment of independence. Under this agreement, contingents of these nationalist movements moved to Luanda, which led to the further deterioration of the political situation there.

Even though most of the MPLA's leaders had left Luanda in the early 1960s and made their political and clandestine careers outside the capital, the MPLA was the party with the highest number of supporters in Luanda. First, the MPLA that grew in the maquis, and in foreign countries such as the Belgian Congo and Zambia, had been formed in Luanda; and even after the failed attempt at liberation of political prisoners, in 1961, that had led to the harsh response of the Portuguese—who took the opportunity to eliminate all nationalist cells in Luanda—it still had a great deal of support in the city, particularly among those coming of age politically in the late 1960s and early 1970s.[38] Many youths growing up in the *musseques* during these times sympathized with the MPLA and were influential in helping the MPLA gain a foothold in Luanda in the period that followed.[39]

The negotiations for the independence of Angola and the arrival of contingents of the nationalist movements in the city dictated to a great extent the fate of most of Luanda's residents. The Portuguese settlers, in particular, felt themselves to be in quite a difficult situation, for they were now at the receiving end of much hatred and resentment. While settlers accused the government that took power in Lisbon of having abandoned them, the latter responded with recriminations that the settlers had exploited Africans, making a profit from their suffering and poverty. For most Angolans, particularly those attuned to the message of the nationalist movements, the Carnation Revolution had put an end to colonialism and, as such, Angolans thought settlers should leave the country. The postcolonial leadership on the verge of holding power was inclined to extend Angolan citizenship to those settlers who decided to stay. But the prevailing climate of recrimination and violence, and particularly the suspicion in the settler community that the Portuguese army was conspiring with the MPLA to surrender to the Angolan side settlers who were then to be tortured and even killed, helped many people to make up their minds.[40] Most settlers attempted to leave the country, taking with them all the belongings with which they had filled their houses and apartments.

The civil war that would later wreak havoc on the whole country for almost three decades was starting in Luanda, through skirmishes over territory that emerged between the nationalist movements soon after their arrival in the capital. Memoirs written by Portuguese settlers leaving Luanda during this time are vivid in their descriptions of the terror in the city caused by violent confrontations between the members of the various movements, which, according to the settlers, lay behind their decision to leave. As the settlers, who held a great many of the positions in the formal sector, were key to the proper functioning of the economy as whole, the greater the number of them leaving, the harder the living conditions of those staying behind. As such, early in 1975, the lack of water, electricity, and fuel became everyday realities. When Banco de Portugal chartered an airplane to remove its workers from Luanda, living conditions in the city deteriorated even further, for their departure made it difficult to conduct normal banking operations such as ordinary payments and money transfers.[41]

The flight from Angola, and particularly from Luanda, was, as many Portuguese have put it, the greatest exodus in African history.[42] For months, particularly after early 1975, in the various sawmills in the city, tonnes of logs were being cut into lumber to make wooden crates. The Polish journalist Ryszard Kapuscinski provided one of the most enduring images of independence in Angola in his description of a streetscape in downtown Luanda, full of crates that contained the belongings of Portuguese settlers who were leaving the country. "Everybody was busy building crates," he writes, "mountains of boards and plywood were brought in. Crates were the main topic of conversation—how to build them, what was the best thing to reinforce them with."[43] Those who left the city back then recall the nights they spent making wooden crates and hearing the sound of hammering nails interspersed with shots outside, until the city ran out of wood and nobody else could make containers anymore.[44] Although Kapuscinski has since been accused of fabricating facts and mixing reportage with fiction, he nonetheless captured something essential to grapple with the atmosphere in Luanda at the time when state power was being seized by the nationalist movements.[45] For he conveys the sense of desperation in the city that came about when those for whom it had been built decided to leave: "The city lived in an atmosphere of hysteria and trembled with dread."[46]

Millions of those crates were sent to Lisbon by plane and ship, up to the point at which workers' committees from Porto de Luanda had to organize to prevent such operations. By July 1975, the settler community had started to put pressure on the Junta Governativa de Angola (Governing Council of Angola), the governing body during the period of transition. In protests in front of the governor's palace, settlers and Angolans demanded their evacuation, the former to Portugal and the latter to other parts of Angola. There were hundreds of people camped in the garden of the palace, determined to stay put until conditions were created to enable their travel to Lisbon.[47] The airport had become the main site of concentration for settlers, to the extent that to onlookers it was as if the whole city's population had moved there. Thousands of people could be seen sleeping on the floor, surrounded by all the belongings they could salvage, in the long days of waiting to board the emergency flights.[48] In the end, more than 200,000 Portuguese left Angola, in 905 nonstop flights chartered by companies such as the Portuguese TAP (Transportes Aéreos Portugueses [Portuguese Air Transportation]) and TAAG (Transportes Aéreos de Angola [Angolan Air Transportation]), the Portuguese Air Force, Perfect Air Tours, Trans International Airlines, Union des Transports Aériens (Union for Air Transportation), World Airways, InterFlug, Swissair Martinair, Aeroflot, FratFlug, and the Royal Air Force.[49] While, in Kapucsinski's estimation, "the nomad city without roofs and walls, the city of refugees around the airport, gradually vanished from the earth,"[50] something else was emerging in Luanda. The abandoned city—the city of unclaimed crates and cars, the city of empty apartments full of colonial memorabilia, detective novels, and old magazines— would gradually be occupied by those who, during colonial times, languished in the *musseques*.

Righting the Right to the City

In his study on biopolitics, Roberto Esposito discusses the interplay between *immunitas* and community by highlighting the separation between both concepts. When threatened, the community may recoil for self-preservation. In this stage, violence and the law are key elements for policing the border between *immunitas* and community. For whereas, in the colonial situation, violence may allow land to be seized, law is that which determines and codifies what is "proper," or the regimes for conservation and transmission of property.[51] Since the colonial system in Angola had thrived through the dispossession of land from the Natives, and since such an order of things was being dismantled at the same time the settlers' community was leaving the country, the task of the colonial government was a simple one: it did not have to protect the concept of property per se but, rather, the rights of the masses and, more specifically, the right to housing. Or to put it differently, at the heart of property rights was more than a simple repossession of land by force and law that mimicked the ways in which the colonial state had used such means to dispossess the Native population. Of importance here is that the meaning of community itself, those whose interests merited protection from the law, was shifting. People—the Angolan people irrespective of race, ethnicity, or origin—were becoming the community, and under the banner *o mais importante é resolver os problemas do povo* (the most important thing is to solve the people's problems), the Angolan government embarked on one of the most radical land reforms the world has known. It was not so much a case of distribution of land, or property, as in many places in post–World War II Latin America. It was rather an annihilation of property rights altogether to the extent that the notion of squatting may not help much in understanding inhabitation in these years: everyone was a squatter, and nobody was a squatter. This redistribution of housing and land is what Luanda has been closer to asserting as the right to the city.

When the Portuguese left, the first Angolan government, led by Agostinho Neto, lost no time in seizing their assets. The industrial park that gave jobs to thousands of people and that provided a great many products for daily use was at the center of these preoccupations. But housing did not fall far behind. Professing Marxist-Leninist ideology—and pledging to bring an end to the "Exploração do homem pelo homem" (exploitation of man by man) through the practice of *partir os dentes à pequena burguesia* (breaking the teeth of the petty bourgeoisie)—this government promulgated the far-reaching Lei das Nacionalizações e Confiscos de Empresas e Outros Bens (Law for the Nationalization and Confiscation of Companies and Other Goods).[52] This piece of legislation defined the Angolan economy as an economy of resistance, geared toward the construction of a planned economy as a way to "responder firmemente ao bloqueio económico e a destruição do aparelho produtivo nacional que os inimigos do povo angolano tentam neste momento realizar" (firmly respond to the economic blockage and destruction of the fabric of national production that the enemies of the Angolan state are presently carrying out).[53] This came in the wake of an almost complete stagnation of the productive sector by virtue of the flight of its owners and managers from the country, as well as the flight of the skilled workers who operated it. Many of the reasons that the law gave for the confiscations of these industries were merely technical and managerial, such as the lack of capital or the lack of productivity. However, the government was also taking hold of many industries on political grounds, appropriating those factories whose owners had been accused of collaborating with the colonial forces of repression or who had given support to opposing nationalist movements. This is the thinking, I would like to suggest, that was expanded in the offshoot of Lei no. 43/76, which dealt exclusively with the real estate of those who were leaving the country.[54] Short, laconic, and lacking any preamble, the first article of the law reads: "revertem em benefício do estado, passando a constituir seu património e sem direito a qualquer indemnização, todos os prédios de habitação, ou parte deles, propriedade de cidadãos nacionais e estrangeiros, e cujos titulares se encontram injustificadamente ausentes do país há mais de quarenta e cinco dias" (it reverts to the state, becoming its property and without any compensation, all buildings for inhabitation, or parts thereof, belonging to Angolan citizens or foreigners, whose owners are absent from the country for more than forty-five days).[55] Previous owners were barred from claiming any compensation.[56] From there, the legal conditions were set in place for the occupation of the buildings and apartments in the city center by those Angolans who lived on the outskirts of the city or who were coming to Luanda from the provinces.

Property confiscation would work as follows: The Ministry for Public Works, Housing, and Transportation would initiate the reversion of property to the state, but the final order would be signed in conjunction with the Ministry of Justice. After the approval of the order, it was the task of the Ministry of Justice to register the buildings or apartments with the Office of Land Registry, "livres de qualquer ónus ou encargos" (with no charges to the state).[57] Meanwhile, the occupants of these buildings would continue to pay the monthly rents to the Ministry of Public Works, Housing, and Transportation, which was also given responsibility for "administrar e conservar os prédios" (administering and maintaining the buildings).[58]

However, the whole process of occupation and housing redistribution did not go as smoothly as the law might have anticipated. The Junta de Habitação, under the authority of the Ministry of Public Works, had the responsibility for overseeing housing redistribution. The plan, decided at the highest echelons of the ruling party, was to provide housing to those Angolans who had fought against Portuguese colonialism and who held prominent positions in the party, the state, or the army. Housing was allocated to them according to their rank.

The most prominent among them were given houses in the Alvalade or Mira-mar neighborhoods, whereas those who held lower positions were given houses and apartments in neighborhoods such as Maculusso or Ingombotas. Claudia Gastrow has also collected evidence that several Angolans who worked for the Portuguese and were aware at the time of their employers' preparation for de-parture, were able to secure keys for houses in the city center.[59] Embassies of the countries that were pledging recognition of Angolan sovereignty and es-tablishing diplomatic ties with the new government were likewise given houses in Alvalade and Miramar or buildings in other parts of the city. The Cubans, for instance—who rushed to Angola early in 1975, allegedly to prevent Luanda from being taken by the South African army alongside the other nationalist movements—occupied entire apartment buildings, some of them turned into authentic vertical military barracks, in various sections of the city.[60]

As for the rest of the population, Gastrow describes the ways in which hous-ing distribution produced its own disjunction because, on the one hand, hous-ing was allocated or occupied, but, on the other, the state was very slow in making these occupations legal. In my own research on this question, I was able to find out that up to the early 1980s, years after the promulgation of the law of confiscation, the matter was far from being settled. *Diário da República* (the official government gazette) was still full of reports on the *processo de con-fisco* (confiscation process), referring to those who had left the country for periods longer than forty-five days and whose property had been occupied, and summoning their occupants to the offices of the Delegação Provincial do Instituto de Habitação (Provincial Delegation of the Institute for Habitation) "no prazo de trinta dias a contar da data de publicação, a fim de manifestarem a sua ocupação" (within thirty days of the publication of the notice in order to demonstrate the occupation of the housing units).[61]

The Junta de Habitação initially did a remarkable job, not only in distribut-ing houses and collecting rents but also, and especially, in preventing empty houses from being occupied. Such was the case that by early 1978, there were still a considerable number of vacant houses in the city center. My father, for instance, who had returned to the city from the countryside—the whole family had left Luanda in July 1975 during the time that the Portuguese were also leaving—and was working as a driver for Constrói, a construction company, found a vacant apartment on Rua Missão. This apartment had been used as an office by a legal firm, Bastos & Irmãos, which provided services to Constrói. Tasked one day, in 1977, with collecting a safe from the lawyers' abandoned of-fice, my father made a decision. Since the apartment—on the second floor of a building in front of the then Comissariado Provincial de Luanda (Provincial

Commissariat of Luanda)—was spacious, my father decided not to return the keys and soon after brought in the whole family to live there: my mother and five children, including me. My mother told me that in the days after the occupation, two men tried to open the door with a key they had. But they could not do so because my father had already changed the lock. The lawyers, who were supposed to be looking after the property, did not bother us.

All of these occupations, invasions, and outright squatting taking place in those years were not producing any significant impact on the composition of the built environment. Besides the four- or five-story buildings the Cubans had erected in various *bairros* beyond the *fronteira*, little construction had taken place. However, in terms of its social makeup, the city could not have been more different. By that time, a great many of the occupants of the commercial buildings and houses in the city center had come from the *musseques* or even from the provinces. When people could no longer secure spaces for living in the city center or around the *musseques*, they started to build *bairros* of their own. The pressure on the services of a city that was meant to accommodate less than a half million people was reaching the breaking point. A few years after independence, services such as water, electricity, and regular garbage collection had been reduced in certain (less affluent) areas of the city. Living conditions for the next dozen years of so in Luanda would become the nightmare that has become the staple of novels such as Ondjaki's *Os transparentes*.

Houses as Machines to Live In

In terms of domestic architecture, the modernist Luanda that had emerged from the early 1950s until the mid-1970s was directly inspired by Le Corbusier's idea that "a house is a machine to live in."[62] Behind the agenda put forward through this dictum, Le Corbusier attempted to advance two outcomes. First, he operated under the necessity of addressing the housing scarcity that most countries in northern Europe faced in the period between the wars. The way to go, then, was to harness industrial methods so as to build houses on an industrial scale. Second, he also put forward the idea that urban living itself would take on machinelike operations occurring within the confines of apartment blocks: elevators could lift hundreds of kilograms up dozens of floors; water could flow through the simple gesture of turning on a tap; waste could be sent into the sewerage system at the press of a button.

More important, his fascination with machines informed more than his planning models, in that he imagined housing to be at the center of the interface between the city and industry. Most of his suggestions for zoning regulations stemmed from this idea. He thought working places and living places ought to be linked by large and functional thoroughfares. The automobile, then, a machine par excellence, would make the connection between housing and workplaces possible. Such a scheme would then allow urban planners to carve out functional interfaces within the downtrodden urban fabric. Unsurprisingly, Le Corbusier's modernist principles exerted a fascination on urban planners far beyond Paris. In Luanda, for instance, urban planners and architects of modernist persuasion devised in the machinic aspect of the house its Trojan Horse function.[63] In an urban environment where the colonized and destitute population languished in the *musseques,* and where settlers only constituted a minority, the apartment buildings, or a block of apartments, could constitute the last resort of colonial comfort and privilege.

In those days, one could make the case that the apartment building was supplanting all other forms of housing as the chief type of dwelling. The apartment buildings lodged a major portion of the hundreds and thousands of Portuguese who had moved to Luanda since the early 1950s. The reasons suggested by Sharon Marcus for the apartment building to become one of "the most dominant architectural elements" throughout much of Europe in the nineteenth century apply to Luanda's urban expansion of the mid-twentieth century. Apartment buildings could "provide spatially compact housing in a city with a rapidly increasing population" and offer the "expanding middle class opportunities for investing in relatively expanding and profitable properties."[64]

Following the precepts of developmental colonialism, the Portuguese increased public investment in Angola, particularly in Luanda, and from the 1940s onward, much infrastructure and countless facilities were added to the city. However, domestic architecture was for the most part promoted by what Mário Murteira has called "private economic power."[65] Throughout most of Angola's colonial history, there was a sometimes muted and sometimes open and vociferous conflict between the center of the empire, in Lisbon, and settlers' interests in the colonies. The empire could assert more dominance over the colonies, during, for instance, the tenure of Norton de Matos in Angola. In the 1930s, Salazar promulgated several laws that prevented the colonies from manufacturing various commodities so as to protect the economy and particularly employment in continental Portugal. Demand for manufactured products in the colonies was certainly keeping afloat countless businesses in continental Portugal. In the division of labor between the colony and the mother country, Angola was expected to contribute with the production of raw materials and Portugal the finished ones, a system that had tremendous repercussions on the tariff structure between the two territories.[66] For Portugal exported far more to the colonies that it received from them.[67] After the military skirmishes of 1961, and after the Portuguese in Angola threatened the mother country with secession, things started to change, and a colonial bourgeoisie, formed by the interests of 5,500 small- and medium-scale industries, started to consolidate.[68]

But the reforms of early 1961 gave more autonomy to the colonies, and the continental Portuguese who were moving to Angola at this time provided technical skills that supported such an expansion of the economy. The boom in construction, at an almost industrial scale, can be linked to the fact that Angola was becoming self-sufficient in producing numerous construction materials that no longer had to be imported from Portugal. Those materials, such as cement for concrete, were being supplied by sometimes brand-new factories installed in the satellite cities of Viana and Cacuaco. The construction of apartment buildings, then, became a hugely profitable business that attracted the investment of a growing number of construction companies in the hope that the demand for housing would not abate in the near future.

However, the boom in construction would not perhaps have taken place without the regulatory reforms implemented earlier by Estado Novo. In the 1950s, Portugal promulgated a law on the institutionalization of horizontal property, Decreto-Lei no. 40/333, of November 17, 1956, with far-reaching consequences, some of which still have a ripple effect on present-day Luanda, as we will see later. Defined as "propriedade por andares" (property by floors), horizontal property consisted of the regime of shared property that occurs in situations in which, for instance, "se uma casa for de dois senhores, de maneira que de um deles seja o sótão e de outro o sobrado" (a house belongs to two owners in a manner in which the basement is owned by one and the loft by the other).[69] To prevent these situations from falling into a legal void, this law intended to accommodate the "desejo compreensível manifestado a breve trecho por uma grande parte da população, de ver legalmente facultada a possibilidade de aquisição do domínio sobre casa uma das diversas fracções autónomas em que os grandes edifícios podem finalmente ser divididos, dada a impossibilidade económica que para a generalidade passou a representar a aquisicação da propriedade sobre todo o prédio" (understandable desire manifested by a great number of people to be legally given the possibility for the acquisition of autonomous fractions into which the buildings could be divided up, given the economic impossibility for almost everyone of purchasing an entire building).[70] In the long preamble to the law, one also learns that construction firms were lobbying for the approval of such a measure, since it would allow for the increase in the construction of apartment buildings. Furthermore, such a legal arrangement was expected to "se rasgam novas perspectivas ao comércio da propriedade predial urbana" (open up new perspectives for the commercializa-tion of urban building property).[71] Of critical importance for the effects this law had on urban development in Angola was that, from the late 1950s onward, there were powerful investors and construction firms who were able to put their resources into property. Furthermore, the law also allowed the middle class in Portugal and in the colonies to have access to urban property. One can even extend such as view to make the case that the prospect of owning property might have made moving to Luanda appealing to potential settlers. Seizing the opportunity, many settlers entered into cooperatives to finance the construc-tion of apartment buildings to be rented to those arriving from Portugal.

The architects of the so-called African generation, discussed in the previ-ous chapter, took an active role in this process. The likes of Vieira da Costa, in their capacity as urbanists at the Câmara Municipal de Luanda, approved the construction projects, and certified architects secured such projects for their own practices and for those close to them—especially those who shared their faith in modernist architecture. They were particularly well placed to navigate the incongruous and divergent interests that not rarely pit-ted the Portuguese colonial government against the interests of the colonial bourgeoisie. In 1944, when the minister of the colonies, Marcelo Caetano, cre-ated the Gabinete de Urbanização Colonial (GUC), under the oversight of his own ministry, the thinking was that urban planning in the colonies could be driven from offices in Lisbon. In fact, this office undertook several planning projects for public buildings in the colonial territories.[72] But with the reforms of the colonial structure in the 1960s, mentioned above, offices of the GUC, then rebaptized Gabinete de Urbanização Ultramarina, were installed in the colonies so that they could have more autonomy in planning and construction. Contrary to the view that "local architects" could then question "social and racial segregation," as Ana Tostões has put it, the more autonomy and control architects and public officials in Luanda had, the more they capitulated to the interests of the colonial bourgeoise.[73]

The outcome of such an influence of the colonial bourgeoisie over Portu-gal's colonial vision played a central role in Luanda's domestic architecture. For most settlers, the mindset was to make as much money as possible before returning to continental Portugal. Vieira da Costa himself admits that settlers in Angola were still too attached to Portugal, where they return to "onde se casa e onde a mulher regressa para dar à luz os seus filhos" (marry and where the wife returns to give birth).[74] Accordingly, investors favored, and pushed for, modes of construction that would allow for the delivery of housing in high numbers, and they wanted the planners and architects to design buildings that could be constructed en masse and through standardized processes so that these buildings could accommodate the greatest possible number of occupants.

Such a system of mass production of housing fitted regimes of urban land ownership in which much land was in the hands of very few, but, because of the radiocentric layout of Luanda, available land for construction was within the *fronteira do asfalto*. The greatest number of apartments had to be constructed on the land that was available. But apartment buildings provide a whole set of advantages, if compared with the single-family house. They are easier to secure than single-family houses, an advantage that, after 1961, became a powerful argument to convince metropolitan Portuguese to move to Luanda, since the war for independence was underway. Prices could be scaled up so that the higher the apartment was in the building, the more expensive it would become; for the logic was that the higher the apartment, the better off its owners would be in terms of reduced exposure to the noise from the streets and, especially, better protection against mosquitoes. Ultimately, the apartment building was expected to provide its residents with both security and comfort, even if the city around it was dysfunctional, as a great part of colonial Luanda was.

So, if during late colonial times these apartment buildings were the instantiations of machinelike operations, the question Luandans very soon learned to ask in the postindependence period was, What happens to a city when these machinelike processes no longer operate properly? At the height of the period of construction in Luanda, a great deal of what could happen to these buildings, from a leak to a structural break caused by moisture, could be easily and quickly repaired, not only because the construction industry was functional but also because skilled labor was available, not to mention the fact that the city was new, and more often than not, the architects and the builders were still working in Luanda. With independence, the flight of the settlers, and the occupation of most of these buildings by Angolans, the notion of the house as a machine for living had to be reexamined.

Originally, the apartments in these buildings had been built for young clerks who worked in Luanda for a couple of years before heading back to Portugal—even if the Portuguese government had intended them to settle in the colonies permanently. This group formed a youthful demographic made up of young couples and unmarried men and women, and the housing in Luanda's "urban consolidated core" reflected this lifestyle.[75] Hence, for the most part, apartments in the city center tended to be studios, one or two bedrooms, and very rarely three bedrooms.

What happened to Luanda then has been covered in various architectural analyses that deal with materials, and poetically described by the Portuguese architect Álvaro Siza: "Residents embark on their daily struggle to limit the damage inflicted by invasions of insects and rodents, the rot brought with fungal infestation and the corrosive effects of the elements. Rainwater drips through the roof where the wind has blown off a tile, feeding a mold that threatens and decomposes the timbers, the gutters are full of rotten leaves."[76] Even though Siza is referring to the life of a building and uses this description to make the point that the real life cycle of a building only starts when the occupants move in, it is still applicable to what happened to the majority of buildings in Luanda when their original occupants left the city and they were occupied by people who, for the most part, had never lived in a building constructed with concrete and with complex internal technical components. In a similar vein, AbdouMaliq Simone has famously written about the ways in which the absence of functioning infrastructure means that people in various parts of Africa must resort to collaboration to make things work.[77] In his assessment of urban life on the continent, it is precisely because of these repertoires of collaboration that infrastructure performs the function it is supposed to. Such an insight is useful to come to terms with the ways in which Luandans have given a second life to Le Corbusier's machines for living. In the absence of the formal infrastructure that created the conditions for the seamless functioning of these buildings as machines, people did not necessarily abandon them. Breakdown could always be averted, or fixed, so that the machine could work again.

After independence, when squatters reclaimed the city, these apartments came to be occupied by entire families, sometimes including as many as three generations. Living rooms and bedrooms were divided up into smaller compartments that could fit as many as twenty people. Many of these new residents, unpoliced by building managers and owners, and facing hardships unknown to the previous inhabitants, drew on practices they had used before moving to these buildings. The open corridors and galleries—imagined by modernist architects as passageways and means to provide air circulation—were transformed into common yards where neighbors cooked and even raised domestic animals.[78] When space was no longer available in the apartments and the corridors, residents built rooms on the terraces, using not only wood and corrugated iron but also bricks and cement. Thus, where the intention during the colonial period had been for these apartment buildings to segregate Portuguese from African city dwellers, and keep the latter outside the city center, the *musseque* struck back, so to speak, after independence.

The kinds of things the new urban dwellers did to accommodate the increasing number of people in their households is a case study in both the limits and the potential transformative power of architecture. The verandas, designed to allow sunlight to enter the rooms, were often transformed into extra rooms by constructing walls of brick or wood and corrugated iron. Complete apartments were built on top of nearly every rooftop, using the same kinds of materials. Cubicles intended to store janitors' cleaning materials were transformed into minuscule apartments, often shared by several people.

The first fatalities of the crumbling state of many buildings in central Luanda were perhaps the elevators. Since most of the buildings in the city center have more than five stories, elevators made life easier for their occupants during colonial times. With the flight of the Portuguese and the halt of production, there was a scarcity of technicians and more reliance on imports. The few Portuguese who came to work in Angola at that time alongside the Cubans and Soviets, as *cooperantes* (expatriate contract workers paid directly by their governments), and other technicians and engineers from socialist countries, were not enough to meet the demand. By the early 1980s, very few of the buildings in the whole city had working elevators. When the elevators stopped working, people used the shafts as garbage bins. When the garbage piled up to the higher floors of the buildings, residents often cleared out the garbage to brick up the entrances to the shaft. In many places, when original water pipes that were encased in the walls broke, they were not fixed but bypassed and replaced by exterior pipes. This meant that if they broke again, fixing them would not mean excavating the wall to replace them.

Together, these factors progressively worsened the living conditions in apartment buildings in Luanda. Buildings are physical structures designed to support a certain weight for a certain period of time. The excess weight to which these new uses subjected the buildings took a heavy toll on them. This coincided with a general breakdown of an already weakened infrastructure (especially in terms of the supply of water and electricity), without which these buildings could not "function" in the way they were intended to do. Today, most of the buildings no longer have running water. Residents can do two things to access water: they can pay one of the thousands of homeless boys to haul buckets of water to their apartments, or, if they have enough money, they can install a pump on the ground floor to pump water into a cistern installed in their apartment that then feeds their taps. Water leaking from walls and ceilings has had debilitating effects on the steel and concrete structures of these buildings, just as rising levels of humidity have corroded the cores of the foundations. An unreliable distribution of electricity has driven residents to seek solutions that, again, are threatening the integrity of these buildings. Candles and oil lamps used during the frequent power outages pose a serious risk of fire. Powerful generators acquired by the affluent cause intense vibrations that lead to cracks in the walls of the buildings.

Some of these architectural facilities have been granted a second life, on account of the economic moment the country experienced in the new millennium. The improved economic situation caused by the boom in oil exports, and the resultant influx of expatriate workers, has led to the refurbishment of a few of these apartment buildings—of which I will say more in the next chapter. In this way, the fragmentation of the city that many authors describe as a distinctive element of the postcolonial African city has reached the fabric of the buildings themselves.[79] In one and the same building, for instance, one can find apartments with electricity and others lit by candles. Some people have their own water pumps, and others carry buckets of water. Some owners display expensive carpets and hang tasteful paintings on the walls, while others live with broken floors and water leaking through their walls. Elevators have become an index of this disparity. In a situation where it is nearly impossible to convince all apartment owners in a given building to contribute to the maintenance costs of the elevators, it is very common that a few who can afford it will pay for the maintenance and running costs of the elevators and will access them with a special set of keys. Refurbished and equipped with the best modern amenities—bought overseas or purchased as imported goods in downtown Luanda, often at three or four times the original price—these apartments symbolize a different world. Satellite dishes and cable television connect the apartment dwellers with the world outside Angola. Yet these refurbished apartments abut others in bad repair, with neither water nor electricity, with walls eaten out by water leaks and the smoke of oil lamps, and often still belonging to people from the *musseques* who took them over after independence. In many an apartment block, affluent dwellers have to roll up their pants to walk through stagnant water leaking from ceilings and floors all the way through the corridors, staircases, and basements. In the face of this, one may agree with Lefebvre when he writes: "The worldwide does not abolish the local."[80] The apartment house has then become, for many owners in present-day Luanda, a cocoon against the dysfunctionality of the city.

Buildings in Luanda are at the heart of many doomsday tales, and I believe that what has driven the more recent transformations of the urban may be partially justified by the state of many of them. One can find many of these apocalyptic descriptions in Angolan novels, as Ondjaki's *Os transparentes*, but one can also draw on Benjamin's descriptions of Naples to make sense of the legacy of modernist architecture in Luanda.[81] For walking in certain sections of the city, in Kinaxixe or Maianga, evokes an experience of phantasmagoria akin to the one that Benjamin felt in the ruins of Naples, which he deemed a "transiency of empires."[82] For him, the decay of Naples held something allegorical because of its irreducibility to the architectural forms that were triumphing all over Europe. The decay of Luanda can be decoded in similarly allegorical terms: after all, the arcades of nineteenth-century Paris, to which Benjamin dedicated his most important work, were incorporated into the modernist design of Luandan buildings.[83] Likewise, the city's center was conceived to enable a vibrant commercial life. But in Luanda, the arcades were tropicalized and opened up to the city. The buildings constructed on *pilotis*, to form areas of shade that could protect passersby from the irradiating sun while also forming space for built-in stores, were used in the postindependence period to accommodate the thousands of operators of the informal economy who sold everything: food, electrical appliances, clothes, shoes. Today, most of these arcades simply showcase the infrastructural problems that afflict these buildings: leaking water pipes and structures on the verge of collapse.

. . .

With independence, the whole ideological and technical scaffolding system that sustained urban life in the ways it had been conceived during colonialism was upended. With the departure of those who owned the land, or property, and for those for whose comfort and security the city of Luanda had expanded beyond the historic center, the Angolan government was forced into nationalizing most of the urban stock. At stake here were the Marxist-Leninist leanings that most of the postindependence intelligentsia professed. Also, the government deemed such nationalizations necessary to supplement the machinelike operations that were no longer in place. By conflating the state and the population under the same entity, the Angolan government was then realizing the principle of the right to the city.

Those Angolans who had been forced to live in bairros indígenas, later on called populares, and in the *musseques* moved to the city center left by the Portuguese, alongside thousands of other Angolans who were abandoning the rural areas because of the ongoing civil war and the failure of the policy to revitalize the postcolonial economy. Neither the measures implemented in the period of transition, from the Carnation Revolution to independence, nor the attempts to control the occupation of houses by the Junta de Habitação could halt this process.

The city that came about after independence no longer determined occupation on the basis of race or class. There were other criteria for securing housing in the former city center, such as having a high position in the government, the party, or the military, but for the most part occupation was determined by cunning or by seizing property left by settlers. As such, the system of boundaries that arbitrates the differences between city and periphery, formal and informal, inside and outside, were no longer of use to come to terms with modes of habitation in postcolonial Luanda. The squatters, whom the border of the city had been created to repulse, had given to themselves a place to live within the city's frontier. However, this does not mean that the notion of skin as an analytic category loses critical purchase. It is rather the other way around.

As Marcus suggests, apartment houses constitute a very ambiguous urban architectural typology, for they provide only a thin separation between the "internal space of domesticity from the external space of the public or the street," becoming in this way an arbiter of the tension between "city and home, public and private, women and men."[84] This was a far cry from Luanda's colonial situation. The tension between the publicness of the street and the privacy of the apartment house could only be held as much as occupants of these properties formed a homogenous group, the settlers' society. There was of course some heterogeneity among the settlers, in terms of political leaning (i.e., if they were born in Angola or in continental Portugal) and in terms of their income and status in the colonial society. But for the most part this heterogeneity did not include Black Angolans. Accordingly, it was only through social immunization, or the expunging of the undesirable bodies from the city, that the expansion of the formal and urban grid could be posited. Or, to put it differently, the proliferation of apartment buildings as the predominant type of dwelling in the city went hand in hand with the thickening of the formal city's skin so that within its borders settlers could enjoy public life in a secure setting.

Postcolonial Luanda emerged at a time when the skin of the city receded. The line that separated those who belonged from those who did not belong no longer coincided with the *fronteira do asfalto*, or geographic demarcation of *bairros*, but now stood at the level of the apartment buildings, or even the apartment. However, for this, machinic operations had to be carved out within the apartment building and the apartment. The city, as an organized system of bundled infrastructure and service provision, also receded, and most occupants of the apartments in the city center were then forced into finding ways to provide for themselves services such as water and electricity. Consequently, the separation between the haves and the have-nots no longer stood at the level of the city, or the block, or even the apartment buildings, but at the level of the apartment itself. As such, it was not only the dismantling of colonial urbanism that was being uprooted in these years. It was also the notion of the colonial *fronteira do asfalto*, or the skin of the city.

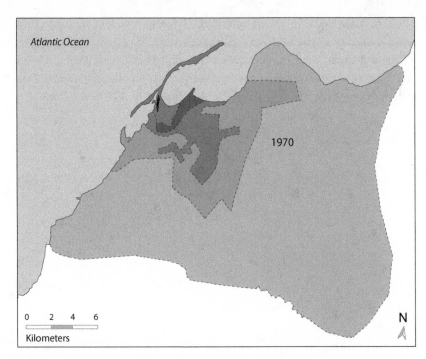

Map 4.1. Luanda in 1970.

4. A City Decentered

Is its excentricity a decentering?—Jacques Derrida, *Writing and Difference*, 2012

• • •

Porto de Luanda was conceived to occupy a very particular place not simply in the city but also in relation to the city. Contrary to the old port, which was located in the middle of the bay, the new one, built in the early 1940s, was pushed to the bay's northern edge. With time, this arrangement allowed for implementation of an ambitious urban renewal plan that involved land reclamation and the consolidation of the concrete wall to ward off the sea. This in turn opened the way for the construction of dozens of buildings, from the early 1950s onward, which later came to characterize Luanda's famous skyline, the Marginal de Luanda. As such, Porto de Luanda is the nodal point for two different categories of zones in the zoning system conceived by the colonial urbanists: the commercial and residential zones, and a zone dedicated to transport, logistics, and supporting industries for the port, since most shipping companies have their headquarters in its vicinity. This section of the city is not only the confluence of Porto de Luanda and the railway but also where the National Road 100 (EN 100), also known as Cacuaco Road, begins. It connects the city center to one of the satellite cities, Cacuaco, which was proposed by David Moreira da Silva and Étienne de Gröer in the first master plan for the city discussed in chapter 2. From the port into the periphery, the road is irregular, tricky, and dangerous, running almost parallel to the sea. On the one side of it lies the coast, and on the other, the abrupt escarpments, known as *barrocas*. The consolidation of these slopes, with concrete walls, allowed for the construction of a part of the affluent Bairro Miramar. But most of the vast track of land a few kilometers farther north of Miramar, and beyond Sambizanga, was left undeveloped and used during colonial times as the city's garbage dump. In the 1980s, when the harshest postindependence economic crisis Luandans had ever known hit the country, this section of the city became the densest zone in the whole nation, on account of the formation of the Roque Santeiro market.

The section of the city that falls within the area bounded by the EN100, N'Dunduma Street, and Senado da Câmara Street is like an informal *bairro*; it comprised Roque Santeiro and several other informal settlements, particularly Boavista. For a lack of a better word, I will be calling it a triangle to make sense of a sector of the city that, for its function, detaches itself from the whole and acquires a life of its own. It then produces gravitational forces with powerful effects on the city's form. Classical urban theory and various strands of contemporary urban theory, and their inability to address informality in its own terms, would call this triangle an edge city, as this term came about to make sense of the city sprawl. However, even though Roque Santeiro offered most amenities that edge cities offer, a "wider range of commercial and cultural facilities," as Mark Clapson has put it in relation to the British city Milton Keynes, it was of a particular nature.[1] It came about spontaneously as the byproduct of the severe economic crisis in the 1980s, becoming the heartbeat of the Angolan economy. Claudia Gastrow has succinctly shown the powerful effects that the informal economy had on the urban; as she puts it, "The informalization of the economy was paralleled by the informalization of the city."[2] After independence, the Angolan state was quick to bring many commercial and industrial activities under the purview of the planned economy. As people started to revert to *esquemas* (schemes—a wide range of informal strategies such as paying workers in kind rather than in cash so that they could trade these goods on the black market) to make ends meet, government officials would deem these practices parallel, in the strict geometric sense of the concept—lines that run in the same direction but never intersect—and criminalize them. The agents who came together in 1986 to create the Roque Santeiro market found in the triangle the only place where they could pursue their activities outside the regulatory environment of the planned economy. In the end, what came into being was an economy detached, even if entangled in many ways, from the formal economy.

Proponents of Southern urbanism would explain the emergence of this triangle, of which Roque Santeiro was a part, as a manifestation of the theoretical principle that the city-centric approach does not entirely capture the complex texture of the urban phenomenon and that critical urban theory should be attuned to an understanding of the urban that goes beyond the city-centric approach so as to successfully grapple with the intermingling between the rural and the urban. But I am also inclined to believe that the decentering I will discuss in this chapter can also be grasped through internal processes and dynamics.

Previous planning interventions in Luanda, particularly the modernist one, approached the city holistically. The city, according to them, could be conceived as a cohesive whole, and its outskirts a problem to be dealt with, in its time, through the expansion of the formal, urban grid. In the previous chapter, I attempted to provide a deconstructive reading of the transformation in the sociology of habitation from late colonialism to the early days of independence and onward. At stake is the question of how to come to terms with how the postcolonial aesthetics of living worked to radically transform the colonial city.

If Luanda of the 1970s was a modernist city, Luanda of the 1980s and 1990s was a profoundly postmodernist city. For the modernist architecture of Le Corbusier and the like has provided a great deal of the language for the consolidation of the urban grid, the alienation of history, and even the functional separation between *cidade* and *musseque*. In his reading of Kevin Lynch's *The Image of the City*, Fredric Jameson unveils Lynch's conformity with an Althusserian transparency (the correspondence between the real and the imaginary), in that Lynch's notion of cognitive mapping provides the tools for "disalienation in the traditional city," which "involves the practical reconquest of a sense of place and the construction or reconstruction of an articulated ensemble which can be retained in memory and which the individual subject can map and remap along the moments of mobile, alternative trajectories."[3] But for Jameson, this is an impossibility, for there is no place in the late-capitalist era for the realignment between the real and the imaginary, and such an elision is at the heart, for him, of the emergence of the postmodern condition. In this way, the postmodern lacks one of its referents, the modern. We are here at the realm of the commodity in its purest form, which for Marx is that which frees itself from the conditions of its production: labor. Or, for a more specific reference, we are confronted with the notion of the skin of the city as expressed by Ole, whose postmodernist reproductions freed themselves from his original photographs of *musseques* in the colonial era. As such, the Luanda of these years was post-modern in two fundamental ways. It was primarily postmodern in the sense in which modernism was no longer a structuring force, not even in the places where it emerged.[4] Second, as a postcolonial city, Luanda's search for new parameters for order and habitation was only starting in these years. It came first under the form of deconstruction, as I show in the previous chapter, and it will culminate with more aggressive ways, on the part of urban authorities, to find the correspondence between the real and the imaginary, which I will address in the next chapters.

The impossibility of the spatial and geographic orientation that Jameson discusses as one of the main ingredients for postmodernism is central in the sections I discuss below. But the focus will be on the street rather than the apartment, on the public space rather than the private space. The first Angolan government that took over in November 1975 struggled to manage the city in a way that was not very different from the last years of postcolonial times. The city center was still conceived as the catalyst for commercial and cultural activities, which was shown by the orientation of public transportation. It basically linked the city center to the peripheries. The demographic explosion from the early 1980s onward laid open these inconsistencies. There were then far more Luandans residing in the peripheries and newly formed *musseques* than in the city center. Consequently, there were also more residents living off the informal economy than residents whose main income was supplied by formal jobs. Since informal income-generating activities were frequently pursued in public spaces, the colonial and bourgeois notions of the distinction between public and private spaces were no longer of use. Colonial notions of frontier, or boundaries, were being turned inside out. As a result, the limit, the frontier, the skin of the city, was turned inside out. There was no longer any separation between interior and exterior, between the center—if we take this to mean the formal city center—and the periphery. In effect, the city center, the area where meaningful economic activities were taking place, was no longer at the center of the city but on the periphery. Those years might be represented as the time in which the squatters, those who had come too late to the city, had triumphed. As I show below, the effort at reordering the colonial city, by finding new referents through street-name change, was a gesture devoid of any significance. The city disassembled by independence could no longer be reassembled through the recomposition and resignification of its parts.

Postcolonial Reinscriptions

Independence shattered the colonial layout of the city that made possible the ascription of zones corresponding to races and classes. However, by the early 1980s, the city center accommodated a far greater racial and class diversity. Many Portuguese who had left the country in the period leading up to July 1975 came back once they knew that the Angolan government had expelled the other anticolonial movements, proclaimed independence, and kept its hold on the city, even if in most of the provinces military conflict was intense. Some buildings were also allocated to nationals of European countries, known as *cooperantes*, who had traveled to Angola in the first years of independence to replace the skilled labor force of settlers who had left. For the most part, they occupied entire buildings, which began to be known for their nationalities: Prédio dos Russos (Russian Building), Prédio dos Suecos (Swedish Building), Prédio dos Búlgaros (Bulgarian Building), and so on.

In chapter 3, I described the ways in which colonial city design was dealt with in Luanda in the aftermath of the Carnation Revolution through a genuine attempt at addressing how colonial racism dictated urban expansion. But after independence, perhaps on account of the many other vital concerns that preoccupied the Angolan government, addressing the legacy of colonial planning was not a top priority of the Angolan government. After all, the flight of the settlers had freed up a great deal of housing units, which allowed, albeit for a short amount of time, for the accommodation of hundreds of thousands of Angolans, who had previously lived in precarious accommodations. However, one of the few domains in which the government made an effort to uproot colonialism, or in which colonial ideology was inscribed in urban space, was in the manner in which topographic references were dealt with.

Many studies argue that revolutions are as ideological as they are spatial.[5] It is not uncommon for a political order that arises after a revolutionary process to invest a great deal of attention in the overhaul of cartographic and toponymic references of the places concerned.[6] Part of this focus comes from the realization that power (colonial power, for instance) is always about creating a space in which the oppressed feel themselves alienated.[7] The Portuguese had been conscious of this since the early days of the occupation.

When the Portuguese arrived in that part of Luanda that would later be called Cidade de São Paulo da Ascensão de Luanda, the territory, as I have shown, was scarcely populated and was used for the most part as an area for the extraction of zimbos, the currency used in the heyday of the Kingdom of Congo. As such, the Portuguese could name most of the places they encountered or established as they pleased, since they were not interfering with any other toponymic system. The rationale for the attribution of names to toponymic sites under Portuguese rule fluctuated over time, depending on the numeric size of the colonial contingent and the importance given to the colonial project. Early on, the Portuguese continued the tradition of naming certain places according to their Native designation in Kimbundu (the most commonly spoken language during much of the city's history), such as Maianga, Kinaxixe, or Mutamba. But the streets that were laid out to allow for the construction of the *sobrados* and other types of accommodation in the city center were given names of regions in Portugal, such as Serpa, Moura, Ourique, Loulé, Almada, Crato and Vila Viçosa, Penalfiel, Gaia, Monção, Mirandela, Almerim, Espinho, Estremadura, or Beiras.[8] With the design and redesign of new streets and avenues during the modernist intervention from the early 1950s onward, the choice fell either on "heroes" of the colonial occupation, such as João Teixeira Pinto and Alexandre de Serpa Pinto, or on colonial authorities, particularly governors of previous centuries, such as Conde do Lavradio and João Monteiro de Morais. By the early 1970s, the Portuguese had almost accomplished the task of creating a space that, from a toponymic perspective, would be more familiar to someone who was just arriving from Portugal than to a native of Angola.[9]

By the time the self-appointed government of Agostinho Neto took over, the composition of Luanda was changing drastically and, accordingly, streets and toponymic references had started to be given new names. This process was implemented in a rather ad hoc way, since no commission was formed to attend to this, nor did a formal process of naming take place. Reading these changes together, one arrives at the conclusion that behind them lay the imperative to translate the political trajectory the country was pursuing after independence into spatial references. The Roteiro Toponímico de Luanda (Toponymic Guide to Luanda), prepared in 1982 by the Ministério da Coordenação Provincial (Ministry for Provincial Coordination), states that 147 streets had been given new names since independence. Two groups of streets stand out in this process: on the one hand, the streets and other places that were named after the heroes of the anticolonial war, particularly those allegedly killed in combat, such as Hoji-ya-Henda and Lucrécia Paim;[10] on the other hand, the streets that were given names of prominent figures in the socialist universe, such as Karl Marx, Friedrich Engels, Vladimir Lenin, and Ho Chi Minh, or of champions from the developing world such as Kwame Nkrumah, Amílcar Cabral, Ahmed Ben Bella, and many others.

In the end, however, Luanda's new toponymic makeup was no less strange to those who lived there than before the renaming, since, for many residents,

Engels was as unfamiliar a referent as any Portuguese colonial governor. But it is important to recognize the new order of things emerging from these attempts at renaming. In this regard, it is useful to stress at the outset the disjunction between, on the one hand, the official domain in which names are given to streets and places and, on the other, how these very toponymic references percolate into people's perceptions. Part of the blame for this disjunction can be laid at the feet of the government, or the provincial authorities themselves, who, even if they were expedient in changing the names of streets in the *Diário da República*, dispensed with the need to ensure that municipal services swapped the old street signs for the ones with the new designations. In downtown Luanda, for instance, there are still various streets whose signs display colonial names. This partially explains why present-day Luandans still refer to many places by their colonial names, such as Praça Serpa Pinto—Serpa Pinto was a colonial commander during the scramble for Africa—although the official name of this square is Praça Amílcar Cabral, after the African nationalist who fought for the independence of Guinea-Bissau and Cape Verde. Another case in point is the Avenida dos Combatentes (Combatants Avenue). Built in the late 1960s and early 1970s and flanked by rows of modernist buildings, it was meant to be a celebration of the Portuguese heroes of World War I and was hence called Avenida dos Combatentes da Pátria (Combatants of the Fatherland Avenue). After independence this important artery became known as Avenida Commandante Valodia, but local residents still retain part of the older designation by calling it Avenida dos Ex-Combatentes, or ex–Avenida dos Combatentes, in an effort, perhaps, to retain the older designation, or to appeal to the new one that recalls those more recent combatants who fought for national liberation.

During colonial times the Portuguese tried to diminish the effects of the disorientation that the strange names could produce by keeping tabs on the new streets that came into existence with the expansion of the city. Mail could be delivered using these new names as addresses, and for the most part, people could call and remember streets by their official names. Even if colonial topographers attended to the relationship between the name and the referent—as the postcolonial government tried to do—they did so through the creation of referents, sometimes through architecture itself. In this scheme of things, squares, and particularly statues in the squares, played an important role in specifying a location. For instance, people would associate Praça Luiz de Camões with the statue of Luiz de Camões that was located there. When the statue was removed and the street was renamed Missão Street, people easily changed to the new designation, perhaps since Missão refers to the Methodist church situated nearby.[11] However, in many cases, finding these associations was not possible.

The difficulty of Luandans in postcolonial times to adopt the official names given to streets and places by the authorities might be explained by this way of orientation, through the evocation of relevant landmarks in the city. For instance, the street where the building of the old Angolan parliament was located was officially called Rua Primeiro Congresso do MPLA (First Congress of the MPLA Street), to mark the holding of the first ordinary congress of the MPLA, in December 1977. However, for most Luandans this street is simply called Rua da Assembleia (Parliament Street), because the old parliament building is there. Hence, people are less interested in the official name given to a particular square if they can refer to it by the name of an emblematic building standing there. Here I concur with the architect Ângela Mingas, who said that the destruction of monuments in the city was depriving residents of their geographic references.[12] Accordingly, it did not help that after independence the city removed all the colonial statues, without replacing them with statues of the people whose names were now being given to these places, destroying in this way the link between streets and squares.[13] It should be added, though, that the Angolan government has made some changes since the colonial era. For instance, in the early 1970s, the official name of Mutamba Square was Almirante Baptista de Andrade (Admiral Baptista de Andrade), which was seldom used outside the official sphere. After independence, this square was rebaptized with its old name, Mutamba.

These juxtapositions of references, names, and the politics behind street names have serious implications for how people orient themselves in and use the city. In present-day Luanda, this has become such an issue that from time to time the state-owned newspaper, *Jornal de Angola*, produces some writing on the topic. A decade ago for instance, *Jornal de Angola* published a story describing the case of Isabel Cassule, who works for an embassy in Miramar.[14] It explained how she gets by when, as part of her work, she needs to identify an address in the city. She told the journalist that on one particular day she had wasted an entire hour until she realized that the street name she was looking for was Presidente Houari Boumédiène, which is one of the most important streets in the whole city. It is not only the location of a number of embassies, such as the embassy of the United States, but also the location of the private residence of the then Angolan president, José Eduardo dos Santos. Cassule explained that the reason she did not know the names of the streets was because they were poorly signposted. Even though the reporter cited the position of the provincial government on this matter, acknowledging insufficient signposting in the city, he also used this vignette to criticize the city's residents for their ignorance of the official toponomy. In another example, the journalist reported that two informal vendors had failed to name the street on which they worked, even though it is one of the most important arteries in the city. They justified their ignorance by referring to their inability to read or write. In the closing section of the piece, the reporter made two points: first, that the inability of people to know street names might be linked to the fact that many residents refer to places by their popular names instead of the official ones; and second, that the state itself does not have the last word when it comes to naming places, since residents simply ignore official names or reject them.[15] In the last vignette in the article, the reporter referred to a woman who claimed to have lived for years on a street she knew as Roberto de Almeida Street, only to find out later that this was the street's colloquial name, given to it by virtue of the fact that it was in a part of the city inhabited by Roberto de Almeida, who was at the time one of the most prominent members of the ruling party.

In my wanderings through Luanda, I have often encountered this difficulty: when asking people about places, I have found that they do not seem to know the reasons why these places carry the names that they do. It is rare to find someone in the streets who can refer to them by their official names. Contrary to the *Jornal de Angola* reporter, I am not inclined to believe that ignorance is the explanation. The point is, rather, that the city that most people move in does not need names. To put this point in rather different terms, the city form to which street names are given no longer exists. As such, replacing street names with other names will not make any difference because something more complex is at work.[16]

Indeed, this is not simply an issue in Luanda as similar manifestations of it have been identified in other African cities. Niora Bigon and Ambe Njoh have argued that the proper naming of streets and places is "central to the orderly, systematic and semiotic construction of the city."[17] They locate the problem in the disjunction between what they call "descript" places, those that have names and can be located, and "nondescript" ones, those that do not have these features.[18] The former have their own histories, whereas the latter exist as a sort of exception, waiting for intervention so that they can also become descript. This designation made some sense for Luanda during colonial times, even if only in certain sections of the city, for these processes of designation, as I have tried to show in earlier chapters, cannot be disentangled from the colonial city-making project per se. The notion I want to propose in relation to postcolonial Luanda is that the city has become nondescript, in terms of the distinction made by Bigon and Njoh, because the institutions that were supposed to oversee and regulate these systems of orientation are no longer in place.

By the time the country became independent, and particularly in the following decade, the 1980s, these dualities, "descript" and "nondescript," "center" and "periphery," no longer had any critical purchase as the city Luandans came to inhabit was not the kind of city where these types of orientation made any sense. At the heart of this lay the disjunction between, on the one hand, the attempt at producing a proper city with its clearly delineated borders and, on the other, the city, or particularly, the city center, which was unable to exert an economic gravitational force on the periphery. There was no longer a place for the realignment between the real and the imaginary or between the physical city and the mental map of the city through which Luandans could orient themselves. My suggestion here is that part of the reason that topographic inscription became redundant was the decentering of Luanda that took place on the outskirts, by the area that later would be called Roque Santeiro. The whole new city, the informal city, was then closer to the mental city then the city built by the Portuguese.

Roque Santeiro: An Alternative to the City Center

One of the chief elements of colonial planning was centralization. Colonial cities, as many authors have shown, tended to be divided between, on the one hand, the center, designed mostly for the civilized population, and, on the other, the periphery, intended for the natives.[19] Colonial Luanda was not an exception in this regard, as has been clearly demonstrated in the previous chapter. Modernist intervention furthered this scheme by pushing the *musseques* farther and farther from the center. It was not by chance, then, that the masterpiece of modernist architecture in Luanda was Kinaxixe Marketplace. The intention that lay behind the location of the market in Kinaxixe, in the city center, was the furthering of the social clustering also discussed in the preceding chapter. After the construction of the market, residents of the city center no longer had to leave the consolidated urban core to obtain fresh produce. Traders could bring the produce to the city as long as they were in possession of their pass cards, and as long as they left the city before the curfew. And by the late 1960s, the white contingent in the city had increased to the extent that even menial labor, like taxi driving and shoe shining, was performed by whites, further entrenching the interplay between segregation and consumption patterns.

During colonial times, zoning was another name for the regulatory system that allowed for the separation of bodies according to race and class in the city. Colonial urbanists tried as much as possible to keep what they understood

Figure 4.1. View of Kinaxixe Square in 2015 after the destruction of Kinaxixe Marketplace. Source: Rui Sérgio Afonso.

as disorder out of the so-called consolidated urban core. Independence came with an urge to re-right the rights to the city in order to make any commitment at separation untenable. The processes I have described in the previous chapter at the level of the dwelling, or the apartment, will here be magnified so as to engage with the urban that was coming about in the first years of independence. Newcomers to the city were building everywhere. After they had occupied all vacant space in the city, they started to use every vacant space in the periphery.

In the early years after independence, the way in which the market operated did not differ from its manner of operating during the late colonial period. For there was still hope that the city would go unchanged after settlers moved elsewhere. But things changed drastically in the early 1980s, when UNITA recovered its strength and the country's security was in jeopardy. Since, simultaneously, agricultural collectivization programs were not yielding any success, the city center would no longer be supplied with fresh produce on a regular basis. I remember, for instance, visiting Kinaxixe Marketplace and seeing its stands that were almost empty and a butchery on the first floor that never had any meat to sell. With the economic crisis that hit the country in the early 1980s, the government decided to ration consumption. This was done by dividing the population up into categories with different political or social status (party members, government members, the military, and so on) for whom different stores were created. Those with access to US dollars could buy what they needed in the Lojas Francas (stores that only accepted payment in dollars). The people in general did not have any other choice but to use the Lojas do Povo (People's Stores), which for the most part only distributed basic items such as rice, beans, and sugar, in quantities that were far smaller than were needed to feed a family for a week or a month. From 1975 to 1985, those who had access to state-subsidized stores found business opportunities in the fact that they could buy products at fixed official prices and sell them at (black) market prices. Sometimes, the marginal gain in the diversion of products and services from one economy to the other could yield a profit of more than thirty times the original cost. Besides this simple subversion, a complex barter system was set in place to run parallel to the beleaguered official economy. People's stores, for instance, sold small portions of rice, beans, oil, sugar, and sometimes soap, but little more. Only in the "chiefs'" and the "directors'" stores could customers acquire beer, which then became the real currency in those years.[20] To buy clothes, those who were consumers at the people's stores had to exchange their rice and beans for beer and then sell the beer to finally buy clothes. So the selling points that started to sprout up in the concrete city, but more insistently in the *musseques*—with evocative names such as Ajuda Marido (Help Your Husband), and Cala-a-Boca (Shut Your Mouth)—were, in fact, what Arjun Appadurai has called in another context gateways to "paths for diversion."[21] Many of these selling points emerged spontaneously out of the aspiration of operators to create a sphere of exchange in which goods could attain value in the relation between demand and supply that the dynamic of the new economy was bringing forth.

In this context, a number of factories, and even some stores, paid their workers in kind. Those workers who were given, for instance, rice instead of a salary could then sell the rice to get what they needed. The so-called *economia paralela* (parallel economy) that was emerging should be seen not only as providing basic-income strategies for many Luandans to make ends meet but also as having powerful implications in the city form itself. For state control and unregulated economic activity were pushing the city's gravitational center to the periphery. The system of distribution of *bens de primeira necessidade* (essential goods) could only work when the population of Luanda was manageable and when, in one way or another, most residents had access to the central state's distribution schemes. However, the demographics of Luanda changed drastically in the early 1980s when groups of former refugees living in the Belgian Congo, who had left the country in the early 1960s, started to move back to Luanda. Most of them did not have any command of Portuguese, which was the main requirement for securing a job with the state, but they were bringing with them the skills needed to operate in the *economia paralela* and the networks for managing long-distance businesses.[22]

As far as I can recall, the *retornados* (returnees) were the first Angolan residents not only to sell goods openly on the streets but also to cook the food that they were selling on the street, such as the famous *micates* (cakes fried in oil, a very popular Congolese dish). In the mid-1980s these practices became ubiquitous, and even those Luandans who had formal jobs and needed to supplement their incomes one way or another did so with some kind of informal vending. By this time, the government started adopting a harder stance toward informal traders, who were put in jail, deprived of their goods, or simply chased from the streets.

In 1986, hundreds of these traders and informal operators set out their wares on the most undesirable plot of land in the whole city for trading their goods. This triangle, as I mentioned earlier, comprised the Porto de Luanda and had been used for the most part as the city's waste dump. The place was so secluded that it was there that the bodies of high-level members of the ruling party were dumped during the tragic events of 1977.[23] As a name for the market they chose Roque Santeiro, after a popular Brazilian soap opera aired by Angolan Public Television; Roque Santeiro was a sculptor who made statues of saints that failed to save the city when it was attacked by bandits and, instead, fled with valuables from the local church. In the next few years, Roque Santeiro would become a true savior for most Luandans.[24]

The strategic reason for the location of Roque Santeiro in that particular place, at the center of the triangle I referred to earlier, was the proximity of the Porto de Luanda. Since the country was increasingly relying on oil, and most of the goods for consumption were imported, such proximity allowed for products to be taken to Roque Santeiro as soon as ships arrived. Goods stolen from the Port of Luanda—or goods ransacked or recovered from the trucks that frequently crashed—found their way to the market. Over time, the market grew and diversified. Roque Santeiro came to perform the same role as Kinaxixe

Marketplace as a wholesale market for fresh produce; it soon became the heart-beat of the whole Luandan economy. Anything that could not be found in the formal commercial sector in Luanda was on display in Roque Santeiro, from produce and livestock—such as chickens, pigs, and goats—to alcohol and ciga-rettes, cars and car parts, foreign currencies such as US dollars, pirated Hol-lywood films in makeshift movie theaters, and women offering sex services, all arranged in sections across the fifty hectares (123.5 acres) of the grounds.

In the heyday of the marketplace, a great part of the city's commercial life happened in the vicinity of Roque Santeiro. With its more than 5,000 regis-tered traders and operators, Roque Santeiro received more than 20,000 sellers and 100,000 purchasers or visitors every day. The setup was basic: every busi-ness was conducted in the mud, and traders only had old sheets of corrugated iron and beaten canvas to protect them from the sun and rain.[25] As a wholesale market, Roque Santeiro would be visited by traders from other markets who wanted to buy products in bulk to sell elsewhere at a profit. Street traders from downtown Luanda would also replenish their stocks in Roque Santeiro. But, more important, many of Luanda's residents would visit the market in the after-noon when traders lowered their prices, hoping to go back home at the end of the day with fewer commodities to carry. The volume of transactions in Roque Santeiro was so important that it started to determine the prices of commodi-ties elsewhere in Luanda. Traders had the luxury of being able to lower their prices at times when they were receiving new commodities, which had ripple effects on prices in the city. And, for the same reason, Roque Santeiro also determined the exchange rate. This was particularly important in the context in which Angola, as an oil economy, was reliant on US dollars to purchase com-modities on the international markets.

By the late 1980s, Roque Santeiro became something more than a market-place, or a mixture between a marketplace and a refugee camp. Since thou-sands of people back then were leaving their houses in the countryside to find refuge in the city, and since the government did not have any policy regarding the provision of shelter for them, they had to somehow make ends meet. As such, Roque Santeiro became, for most people, a way to find their place in the city. Those who came with skills, such as mechanics, drivers, or tailors, easily found jobs in the many makeshift workshops and boutiques that abounded in the vicinity of the market. But even those who did not have any training could also find ways to make ends meet, by buying any sort of commodity wholesale to sell piecemeal. More important, the market created thousands of informal jobs, for there was a high demand for services to assist in the operation of the market. Traders needed people to carry their wares, and the hundreds of kitchens that served thousands of meals every day needed people to buy the produce, cut it up, cook and serve it, and clean the dishes.

Most of these operators did not live very far from the market. On the contrary, the heyday of Roque Santeiro went hand in hand with the significant expansion of old colonial *musseques* such as Sambizanga, Mota, and Lixeira, and the mushrooming of many other informal settlements. Some of these places later became *bairros* on their own terms. Most people built their houses in the vicinity of the market, to the extent that there was no longer any separation between the informal settlements and the market per se. Those houses were used as cinemas, restaurants, schools, and particularly as storage sites for the various tools that traders needed daily, such as stands, chairs, and tables, so that they did not have to take them back to their houses if they did not live close by.

For the most part, it was possible to build shacks by relying only on what was available in the marketplace. I have myself followed residents on journeys through the process of building or repairing their shacks. Cement was perhaps one of the few products manufactured in Angola, and there was a suspicion that a great proportion of the output of Cimangola—the main Angolan cement manufacturer—besides the quantity that had to be distributed to the government's public works, was ending up in Roque Santeiro. All other construction materials, such as corrugated iron, wood, nails, and so on could also be found there. Since building shacks was at this time an occupation that most people in these places were engaged in, it was not hard to find masons for hire and other professionals in the field of construction. When, by the late 1980s, almost no suitable land was available for construction, people started to build their houses in the most dangerous parts of Boavista. However, the problem with building on the slopes was not only the landslides that claimed lives during the rainy season but also the fact that most of the Boavista area had been used as a waste dump, particularly during colonial times. As a result, the many deaths every year from malaria and other diseases were certainly related to the insalubrious conditions there. I was also told that, paradoxically, there was a relationship between insalubrity and security as the places with more garbage had firmer soil and were therefore more secure for building houses. In this gamble, then, people were exposed to the danger of contracting diseases as the price for having a stable structure in which to live.

In terms of services such as water and electricity, even though the market was closed off from the city, the situation there was not much worse than in many places in the city center. Since that part of Luanda had never been fully urbanized, the government installed several fountains where residents could get water without being charged. And since there were not many fountains, fetching water required long walks for many people. The most reliable way to get water was to purchase it from the various trucks that were available for the greater part of the day. To obtain electricity, residents installed illegal connections or simply bought them from those who could link their dwellings to high-voltage poles and who knew people at the electricity company who could prevent these connections from being taken down. Over time, particularly during general elections, the electricity company would come and install proper connections from Roque Santeiro to the city's electrical grid.

As such, Roque Santeiro was decentering the city center, by pushing the economic activities beyond it. By the late 1980s, more and more people were relying on places outside the city center and outside the control of the formal distribution system for the satisfaction of their needs. The transformation of the system of public transportation is an instructive example of such a decentering. The formal public transportation system that had been introduced during the colonial period was organized in terms of a "lógica segregacionista" (logic of the segregationist system).[26] At that time, taxis were driven mostly by whites, and for the most part, they covered only the city center.[27] Most of the Black population used buses that operated throughout the city and also linked the center to the periphery; these buses served the unskilled labor force that lived in the *musseques*. However, there were very few options for those wanting to go from one point to another on the periphery. After independence the system did not change much, for the newly formed Empresa de Transportes Públicos (Public Transportation Company) operated under the same conditions. Mutamba was still the main stop from which most routes started.

However, when the economic crisis of the 1980s hit the country, the government was in a situation where new bus and car parts could not be imported, even if by then most of the buses operating on these routes were assembled largely in Angola. Things started to change in the mid-1980s, with the emergence of *candongueiros*—from *candonga*—which was the general term for any practice that was not formal. The drivers of the minibuses that started operating in the mid-1980s were referred to as *candongueiros*, and the name came to be used for the vehicles themselves. Of particular relevance for the formation of the alternative system of public transportation was the change in the demographics of Luanda. As I have discussed earlier, from the early 1980s onward, a wave of Angolans, most of them former refugees living in Zaire (the former Belgian Congo) or the offspring of refugees, started to arrive in Luanda. They spearheaded the initiatives for making money outside the formal sector. And they were also, for sure, the ones who started the practice of traveling abroad, particularly to France and Belgium, to buy finished goods of different kinds, putting everything into a shipping container and receiving it a month later in Luanda. They could engage in these practices because of the knowledge they had acquired in the places they came from and the networks of traders spanning countries and continents that they—or people they knew—were part of. The development of an alternative public transportation system in Luanda relied for the most part on these networks.[28]

It was through these international connections and goods-importation schemes that the cars that started to operate as *candongueiros* began to arrive.[29] The preferred car was the Toyota HiAce, manufactured in Japan and bought in Europe, particularly in Brussels. It is hard to think of any other vehicle that would better suit the purpose. The HiAce is a car that is easy to repair and can even function with an engine from another car manufacturer, such as Volkswagen. More important, it is so easy to fix that outside of the city center hundreds of workshops offering repair services were being set up. Parts for the car did not have to come from the original manufacturer; they could be produced in makeshift factories in Luanda or in other African cities such as Lagos and Dakar. The interior was easily dismantled and could be rearranged to accommodate benches so that more people could fit in.

The development of this alternative system of public transportation had powerful consequences for Luanda's city making in various ways. First, with the bankruptcy of the state's public transportation system, *candongueiros* became the main means of transportation for most people in the city, particularly workers on their daily commutes. Second, since Roque Santeiro became at this time an informal city center where more than 20,000 people would gather every day, the market replaced Mutamba as the main transportation hub in the city. For the first time, there was the possibility of going from one point on the periphery to another point on the periphery without stopping in the city center.[30] Third, the emergence of this system of transportation took place during the breakdown of infrastructure such as roads. The versatility of the HiAces meant that they could reach many places in the city that could not be reached by other vehicles, particularly during the rainy season. Last but not least, having a means of transportation that could reach every point in the city was surely an incentive for people to build houses farther and farther from the center. *Candongueiros*, then, pushed the limits of the city to the extent that what happened afterward, in terms of city planning, may be read as the state's trying to catch up with the reality of the decentering of the city center.

Luanda Inside-Out and Outside-In

By mid-1980s, only ten years into independence, it was as if those social practices that the Portuguese had been trying to confine to the *musseques* had simply descended on the city. What happened in Luanda back then was dissimilar to urban processes that are well documented in the literature, with many examples from places such as Detroit, or even Johannesburg, in which, when the poor move to the city, the well-to-do have the luxury of relocating to the suburbs.[31] Since Luanda did not have the option of the suburbs, and the city center was still the hub of the formal activities that had been spared by the economic crisis, the well-to-do did not have any other choice but to share the same space with the former residents of the *musseques*. Processes of social differentiation took place and became visible in two major ways: first, through the urban microfragmentation I discussed in the previous chapter, at the level of the apartment block, where it was common to have, in the same building and on the same floor, downtrodden apartments without electricity and with water leaking down the walls, and well-kept, well-functioning apartments. Second, urban fragmentation was visible at the level of the street because the newcomers to the city brought with them their own ways of engaging with and naming space. In these years, one can say, the skin of the city receded, and most of the differences between city and *musseques* with which colonial power operated ceased to have any critical purchase. If, on the one hand, the city was being decentered through informality and deregulation, on the other, the logic of the periphery was percolating into the city itself. This was taking place not only at the level of the apartment, as discussed before, but also, more profoundly, at the level of the street itself. Therefore, street naming was a simple manifestation of this broader issue.

In light of the mix of city and *musseques*, and the impossibility of separating the order from the disorder, or the urban from the peri-urban, we can ask a fundamental question: what if by disavowing postcolonial toponomy, Luandans were, for the most part, not simply appealing to an alternative cartography but pointing to a different way of dealing with space and distance? The Luanda that started to come about in the 1980s was less about movement per se. It involved a certain degree of stasis that comes with knowing where things are, finding the proper routes to these places. For many people, then, making ends meet was less about the capacity to know how to get from one place to another than about knowing where to be at the right time to have a chance of making an economic gain: hauling commodities, selling dollars, polishing shoes, and so on were only possible for those who had become part of these places.

By the time Luanda completed its first decade as the capital of Angola, in 1985, very few changes were of note, beyond those discussed in the previous chapter. Many streets were given new names, albeit formally, but the overall design of the city had not changed considerably. For the limits of the formal city, even if the informal city was growing, were still the same. However, at a deeper level, the decentering was taking place at the heart of the city center itself. The dichotomies, particularly the difference between center and periphery, that colonial urbanists so eagerly worked to establish were almost gone a few years into independence. This did not take place in a physical, or geographic, way. The city center, mostly built in concrete, occupied exactly the same area as before, even though the *musseques* were starting to grow to the extent that by 1990 they accommodated about 85 percent of the city's population. But in practice it was as if the logic of informality had taken over the formal city and Luanda was becoming two cities running in parallel, one formal and the other informal. It was as if, to put it differently, the rationale and logic of the informal had been superimposed onto the formal, to the extent that Luanda was turning into a sort of dystopian version of the city colonial planners had thought of and warned against.[32]

The formal city of Luanda, as I have been showing, was built to accommodate less than half a million inhabitants, which was Luanda's population by the time colonialism came to an end. Urban amenities such as parks, squares, boulevards, and generous sidewalks corresponded to these calculations. The colonial authorities could maintain the integrity of these places by means of several legal procedures that allowed, for instance, for people to circulate in specific sections of the city or through the creation of an entire political economy that made it financially impossible for Africans to live in most places in the city center. Furthermore, these forms of segregation were also maintained through custom. For instance, even if there were no specific rules governing admission of Blacks to the whites' movie theaters, Blacks knew that they should not go to these places.[33] It was through these written and unwritten procedures that the urban center had, for the most part, remained intact up until the time of independence.

After independence, in contrast, for those who could not find a formal job or did not have access to the opportunities provided by the socialist regime, the street was the place to make ends meet. For them, the street became far more than a series of intersecting nodes, as the tenets of urban planning have it.[34] Colonial urban planners might have imagined the streets of downtown Luanda as such nodes—as lines linking different points in the city; however, in postcolonial Luanda the entire meaning of the street for many residents changed. In the years of economic crisis, up to today, the street became not just a place of passage for most Luandans but precisely the place where things happen, to such an extent that several professional categories have emerged that are related to the work that people perform on the street. Some of the most resilient within such categories are the *kinguilas* and *zungueiras*. For example, a woman who exchanges dollars for the local kwanza currency is called a *kinguila*, "a person who waits," literally describing her activity of waiting on the street for customers. Similarly, a female street trader is not called after her trade but is called a *zungueira*, for the activity of walking that defines her trade.

Central to this appreciation of the street in Luanda is the culture of the private automobile that started to pick up by the late 1980s. At the time when the economic crisis hit the country and the formal system of public transportation was no longer reliable, *candongueiros* were introduced mostly to cater to the transportation needs of the poor. To provide means of transportation for the well-to-do at this time, the government was importing thousands of cars every year, to the extent that the private motor vehicle became a political weapon that the government and ruling party could use to impose discipline on its members.[35] The more the roads disintegrated, the more individual motor vehicles became near-residential cubicles in which most people started to spend a great part of their day. These elites became used to their new lifestyle, living as if they did not belong to the city, and their reality was quite separate from that of most Luandans. The imaginary city they created for themselves allowed them to move from one place to another without having to deal with, or even acknowledge, the harsh realities of life that most residents faced. They only saw extreme poverty from behind the darkened windshields of their cars, and they were protected from the inclemency of the tropical climate by the car's air-conditioning. Wastelands of misery were just thoroughfares they had to cross.[36]

The burgeoning elite did this to protect itself from the city that was emerging out of the collapse. It was as if the logic of Roque Santeiro was expanding into the formal city so that the formal and the informal economies were no longer running parallel to each other but had become superimposed. Luanda has, in some ways, begun to resemble a gigantic boulevard, with cars in perpetual traffic jams, and since there is an acute lack of parking spaces, drivers no longer exit their cars to purchase what they need in shops. Rather, the streets of Luanda themselves have become informal selling areas with a large variety of items on offer, ranging from food to clothes, cell phones to batteries, fans to rugs, and whatever else customers might require. The informal selling process is so well organized that when customers state what they desire, word passes from seller to seller until the item is found. Even if cars have to move forward and customers have already handed over payment, they know that they will be provided with the desired item a few hundred meters down the road.

In this context, the sidewalk and the road have become the points of contact for people coming from worlds apart. During the height of the oil boom, between 2000 and 2010, the social fabric of public spaces in Luanda, particularly the streets, became more complex. So now, on the one hand, there are those who are at home in a city that, year after year, is becoming the most expensive in the world, a city of banking institutions that deals with billions of dollars per day, a city of well-paid expatriates and nationals who pay small fortunes for their basic meals.[37] On the other hand, there are those who are at home in a city that is one of the poorest in the world. These two cities are dialectically linked: what makes the one wealthy is that which pushes the other into poverty. The street is where this encounter is operationalized.[38]

In a way, then, the whole city of Luanda has become an extension of Roque Santeiro, which, until the destruction of the market, was the provenance of most products sold in the streets. But it is also as if the logics of the *musseques* have contaminated the formal city. Sidewalks have become nearly off-limits for pedestrian traffic, not because they are unsafe, but because they have been completely neglected, their surfaces broken up by rain, soil erosion, extensive use, car accidents, and unfilled trenches after the repair of underground electric cables or water pipes. The city authorities ignore pedestrian circulation and leave it to those who have no other way to move about the city.

This neglect of public spaces in postindependence Luanda may be the product of social differentiation that was there from the start. On account of a predatory colonialism, most Luandans lived below the threshold of poverty until the 1980s, when a growing number of inhabitants started to accumulate wealth through various schemes commonly referred to at the time as "primitive accumulation." Those commuters could go without using the streets.

But others—such as the security guards who have grown to be crucial actors in the city, arbitrating between different worlds—do need the streets and take from them their means of subsistence. Violence is ubiquitous in Luanda, and when cell phones became an indispensable instrument of communication, they also became an object of greed: people were dying because they had exposed their cell phones to view on the street. Break-ins became common, and since the police were no longer interested in keeping the city safe, owners of property, businesses, and even family houses in most parts of the city had to hire private guards. The guards are visible outside every type of business: supermarkets, hotels, garages, and so on. This is one way in which the city deals with the problem of the enormous number of military operatives discharged with the ending of the wars.[39] Put differently, security companies, from their inception, were also a way to provide employment for those who had fought in the Angolan wars. And while some of these former soldiers work for well-established companies, a great number of them keep property safe for very little payment. For many owners, it is just a matter of having somebody standing in front of their property to discourage criminal activity.

Hence, almost an army of private guards occupies vast expanses of the city. As most of them work shifts of twenty-four hours, they mingle with the informal traders and sleep and eat and perform all other necessary activities in the places where they work: the streets. Their presence is so overwhelming that Luanda can appear to be one gigantic shelter: there they are, on the streets, not because they are saving money to invest in a life they have elsewhere, but, rather, because their jobs pay them too little to even cover their daily transportation costs back to their families. Since guards are hardly able to support themselves, let alone their families, it is not uncommon that their wives work as street traders to feed the children. Some guards do their work with great commitment, and it is not unusual that a private security guard is heroically killed trying to protect his place of work. But for most guards, this job is just an opportunity to make some extra money: often they will take on additional side jobs, such as carrying things for residents, washing cars, or performing other similar menial tasks.

The street, then, is the nodal point for different kinds of violence. It is marked by structural violence that is the by-product of an oil economy that excludes most Angolans by keeping them outside the circuits of distribution of the national rent. It is tarnished by the physical violence of unscrupulous thieves who do not hesitate to take people's lives to gain access to their belongings. But it is also stained by state-sanctioned violence exercised by the agents of the provincial authorities, or *fiscais* (tax inspectors), whose task it is to prevent traders, particularly female ones, from selling in the streets. For these traders, to sell is to be ready to run.

The informal city that lives on the streets subsists off the formal city. This life is less about how people come together to compensate for the nonexistent infrastructure and more about how they use the broken infrastructure—the ruins—and their knowledge to make the sorts of things that they need to live: people and infrastructure as hybrids for survival. Entrances and doorways of the apartment buildings have been converted into selling points, for they attract less attention from the *fiscais*, and these points allow the traders to more easily

Figure 4.2. An armed guard in Luanda during his work shift, 2017. Source: Rui Magalhães, @ rui_magalhaes.

combine trading with domestic activities. When traders do not live in that particular building, they come to an arrangement with the owner, or someone in the building, to use a space at the entrance for their activities.[40] An example from my wandering in the city may illustrate what I mean here. One day, I went to buy fruit at my regular seller. She was there, but she had no goods with her. She had spotted several *fiscais* and had hidden her goods inside an old building with the help of the building's security guards. I was surprised by this, as the governor of Luanda had issued a public announcement a few days earlier that the *fiscais* were forbidden to confiscate the wares of *zungueiras* (informal traders). She explained, however, that the *fiscais* were not interested in obeying the governor's request, for their concern was neither the law nor hygiene. In fact, their salaries were so meagre that they had to loot the traders' wares to obtain goods that they could sell for some additional income.[41] This example shows what the street has become for most Luandans: not just a means to connect two geographic points, but a thing, a space, in itself. It is the point where the city imagined as clean and orderly comes into contact with the city as a place of, or a tool for, survival.

These transformations have taken place against the backdrop of a demographic transition. In 1990, fifteen years into independence, the Luanda's population mushroomed to almost 3 million inhabitants. This was partly due to natural growth, but a great part of that number came from internal migration, particularly as a result of the failure of agricultural investment that had left thousands of people impoverished. A more important cause of this migration, however, was the war, although not always in the way in which it has been spoken about. Armed conflict had left hundreds of thousands of people looking for shelter in major cities, particularly Luanda, the seat of power and the safest place in the country. But the mushrooming of the Luandan population was also a tactical move, since, instead of moving the population to strategic hamlets, as military doctrines advise, army trucks were seen dumping people in Luanda so as to prepare the vacant territory for military actions. These people, then, were left in the city without any means to subsist and were forced to find their own ways to do so.

A number of these people saw in Roque Santeiro a way to make ends meet. They would buy goods to resell. As a result, places such as Boavista started to grow inordinately. Boavista operated as a sort of support structure for Roque Santeiro, in the sense that many of the people who sold in Roque Santeiro lived there. By the time the market closed at the end of the day, one could see half the goods on sale there, from fresh produce to animals, chairs, and so on, being transported to Boavista. With the emergence of Roque Santeiro, understanding Luanda through the distinction between the center and the periphery no longer had any critical purchase. Whereas economic activities, particularly in the retail sector, were moving to the periphery, and by this challenging the centrality of the city center, the former colonial city center was being taken over by the logics prevalent in the former peripheries. If the *fronteira do asfalto*, the skin of the city, was the most distinctive aspect of colonial urbanism, then, informal logic was instrumental for decolonizing Luanda.

• • •

As the informal economy emerged as a kind of supplement to the formal economy, or as a way to supplement those services and functions the formal could not provide, Roque Santeiro came about to play a similar role in relation to the formal urban. The dislocation of the organizing system of public transportation from the city center to Roque Santeiro is a symptom of such a process. The system of informal public transportation made it possible, for the first time, for commuters to move from one point to another on the periphery of the city without having to stop in the center. The informal economy thus became the nodal point between the urban center and the periphery as it presided over the emergence of social and urban fragmentation. More important, Roque Santeiro had powerful effects on the planning of the city, for in its heyday it became the city center par excellence—and not only for the kinds of people it brought together every day to trade; Roque Santeiro hosted music and book launches, even political rallies, and it also became the most important stop in the city for *candongueiros*.

The economic crisis of the 1980s brought the differentiation between the haves and the have-nots to the fore, between those who could satisfy their needs in the formal circuits of consumption and those who could not. The newcomers to the city did not have any option other than to partake in and sustain the informal economy that was emerging. Roque Santeiro was central to these transformations, because it concentrated a great number of these informal and illegal economic activities in one place, thereby enabling social differentiation to occur; for it was in this realm that so-called primitive accumulation was being practiced, making it possible for certain groups of people to generate financial resources for the first time, outside the strictures of the planned economy. But, more important, it allowed the hundreds of thousands of people coming from the countryside to find places where they could build a shack and to engage in some form of economic activity that yielded an income. These were the new squatters, the ones who could no longer find housing in the former colonial urban center but who would nonetheless change the city.

The decentering of Luanda's center through the emergence of Roque Santeiro laid bare two interlocked logics. On the one hand, there was the coming into being of an informal center, towered over by Roque Santeiro, which, emerging as an arbitrator of economic exchanges, allowed several vital urban activities to take place. All in all, these processes revealed the inadequacies of colonial planning in the postcolonial order. For the reading of the urban that was then available pertained to the mix between the formal and the informal. On the other hand, the city center, whose frontiers had come about to keep disorder and anomaly at bay, could no longer function without the same disorder and anomaly.

It was not the case that the periphery was evolving while the city center was kept intact. In a symbiotic process, changes in the periphery were having powerful effects in the city center to the extent that those categories were losing any critical purchase to grapple with the urban transformations of the time. There was no longer any correspondence between the real city, of colonial ruins, and the mental map, or how people interiorized the city. It was as if the logic of Roque Santeiro had contaminated the city itself, for Luanda became a gigantic boulevard. And it also contributed to the fragmentation of the city that had been happening as a way to accommodate those who, during those years, had embarked on a path of what was then called "primitive accumulation." Luanda changed to accommodate these processes of fragmentation. As such, the reinscriptions of urban toponomy were of little help, for it was the form of the city itself that was in transformation. Demographics are of crucial importance here. Because of the long civil war ravaging the country, Luanda was receiving daily thousands of internal displaced people, who, not finding any structure to help them settle in, navigated around Roque Santeiro and its subsidiary informal marketplaces, as traders or operators, as purchasers to sell at a profit in other markets or on the streets, and as consumers. Thus, the networked parallel economy was pushing the center of the city farther and farther from its original position because of the number of activities, resources, and savoir faire required to operate it. It was not only a matter of sellers, drivers, mechanics, and those professionals who were required to make these systems work. It was also a matter of other activities and systems that gravitated toward Roque Santeiro and toward the formal and informal systems—such as car imports, trade in car parts, car repairs, car theft, and the preparation of falsified documentation—needed to operate the transportation system.[42] In general, it was against this informal decentralization, produced by informalization as a response to the economic crisis, that the government would later act, not in an attempt at recentralization, but in an effort to explode the dichotomy between centralization and decentralization, through the creation of various *centralidades* (centralities). This process is the general topic for the next two chapters.

Part III.   Fragmentation

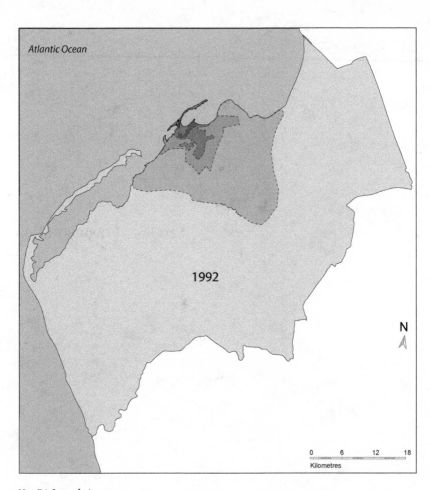

Atlantic Ocean

1992

N

0　　6　　12　　18
Kilometres

Map 5.1. Luanda in 1992.

5. Reversing (Urban) Composition

Today's urban question is the land question.—Ananya Roy, "What Is Urban about Critical Urban Theory," 2015

• • •

It might have started with the first step, when João Pedro rented an apartment in a ten-story apartment block in one of those old buildings in front of the Marginal, a dozen meters from the Igreja de Nossa Senhora da Nazaré, in Baixa de Luanda—one of the very first to be erected in the 1950s, only a few years after the construction of Port of Luanda. As was common practice in Luanda during the oil boom, in the early 2010s, he entered into an agreement with the owner of the apartment to pay a cheaper annual lease in exchange for the apartment's refurbishment. Aware of the government's intention to restore the Marginal de Luanda, and particularly the government's unrealistic and megalomanic desire to create three artificial islands in the Bay of Luanda, João Pedro launched himself into a quite daring business venture.[1] Convinced of the Marginal's value accrual over time and its potential to become a hub for

Luanda's burgeoning real estate market, he managed to convince some of his neighbors in the building to rent their apartments to him. The promise was that he would repair and, eventually, rent them to expatriate oil workers for a given amount of time. And one day down the line, the owner could move back into a brand-new apartment. Since the cheapest of these apartments would not cost less than US$3,000 per month, and as leases were paid in full for at least a year, João Pedro calculated that he could easily pay a part of these sums to the owners and still make a considerable profit. For prospective renters, it would cost obviously less than the thousands of dollars they paid daily in hotels such as Epic Sana—whose lobby João Pedro used to frequent to recruit tenants. Following a snowballing approach for such a scheme, he expected to be able to sublease as many apartments as he financially and logistically could, but by the time we met in Luanda, in 2013, he was managing only five apartments.[2] Most occupants he approached were reluctant to sign up for the deal, for fear they could lose possession of their apartment for good, since, for many occupants, it was impossible to demonstrate property ownership.

What surprised me the various times I visited this building and heard João Pedro's stories and learned of his projects were the discernible differences among the apartments. Whereas the apartments João Pedro had renovated were well resourced and well equipped with modern and imported appliances and could rely on a continuous and uninterrupted supply of water and electricity provided by state-of-the-art water pumps and generators, the others were worlds apart in terms of conservation and outfitting. There were tenants who could not afford to pay the exorbitant prices for electricity, and peering into their homes, one would see that they had regressed to using candles. There were also tenants, who, unable to install a water pump to service their apartments, provisioned their households with buckets of water that had to be brought up. Whereas most of the occupants used the stairs to move up and down, those in João Pedro's apartments could use the elevators that were made available to them through a key.

If one were to present this Marginal apartment block in cross-section, with the façade removed so as to reveal its interior (as Georges Perec famously did in his novel *Life: A User's Manual*), an interesting finding to contemplate would be how these apartments stood in relation to the city's infrastructure network—as some of them, by virtue of being equipped with generators and water pumps, were cut off from the grid, from the infrastructured urban fabric. As was the case throughout the city, such a metaphor would convey an image that is inimical to urban planning which, for the most part, strives for totality, or at least for the smoothness infrastructure can provide, which is on its own terms,

Figure 5.1. A man descending from his Luanda apartment to fetch water, 2018. Source: Rui Magalhães, @rui_magalhaes.

as Brian Larkin has put it, "the architecture of circulation."[3] Such was, at least historically, the cornerstone for the expansion of Luanda's urban grid, whose organizing principle, the *fronteira do asfalto*—the separation between the formal and the informal city—also set up the limits within which continuity of infrastructure provision could be attained. Accordingly, if one dubs such a process *urban composition*, or the way in which the urban can manifest through continuity or the fluidity of the architecture of circulation, the reverse should also be examined. As such, reverse urban composition, in the context of this chapter, will be evoked as the process through which the urban is fragmented, undone, and etiolated.

The holistic city that such a continuity implies, the horizon of modernist urban planning, has been in present-day urban situations cut through across variegated geographic locations, pierced and fragmented into a myriad of zones, enclaves, or "fortified networks," a term evoked by Dennis Rodgers to make sense, for instance, of the ways in which affluent inhabitants in Managua shield themselves against crime and insecurity in a limited number of heavily protected locations.[4] With some local and specific variants, such a framework fits into the most recent urban development in Luanda, as I will show below in this chapter. However, contrary to many other geographic settings glossed in contemporary urban theory, where the emergence of these enclaves is linked to the withdrawal of the state from the public sphere, urban transformation in Luanda begs a different interpretation. In Luanda, the emergence of these sorts of residential and commercial hubs is a direct consequence of the liberalization of the economy, and particularly the privatization of the real estate market, which came under the guise of the fractioning of property. To put it differently, private property was not an urban vector before the liberalization of the economy. It came, in fact, with the liberalization of the economy.

Key to understanding the enclaving in Luanda is land, a topic that tends to be overlooked in various trends of contemporary urban theory. One of the rare and worthwhile exceptions is the position of Ananya Roy, who, taking issue with Lefebvre's injunction that "we live in the age of an urban revolution" and that therefore the urban amounts to almost everything, argues that it is the urban question that is subsumed in the land question and not the other way round.[5] This is partly because "this land question very much encompasses regulations, registers and rights that are not urban and that are not simply making the way for the urban."[6] Such a formulation provides the framework through which, in this chapter, I will be examining the unfolding of Luanda's urban fragmentation in whose background lies seismic shifts occurring within the Angolan political-economic system in the early 1990s. The property rights being reconfigured in these times in the wake of the demise of the socialist order do not simply pertain to urban expansion. Their scope was broader, touching on the reconfiguration of state-society relations, which came through recalibrations of access to urban land. How these recalibrations relate to larger processes, such as constitutional arrangements, will be the topic of the next chapter.

It is from the mid-1990 onward that the shape and form of Luanda started to change at an unprecedented pace. The Brazilian consultants who pushed for the Programa Luanda Sul, discussed in this chapter, were aware of the incompleteness of postcolonial Luanda, which was still for the most part divided into the center and periphery. By proposing Luanda Sul as the third city, through suburbanization, one that would break the duality of colonial urbanism, their intention was primarily to provide the city with social facilities to cater to a more sophisticated and demanding class of consumers, which was emerging as a result of the shift to neoliberalism. So the economy took a major role in these transformations, but they were more strongly driven by politics. In the next chapter, I will discuss in more detail the political reconfiguration that allowed for urban expansion at an unprecedented scale, but now I will mention a crucial factor in this process, which I will call (for lack of a better term) the *perimetization* of Cidade Alta, the presidential precinct. By this, I mean the process through which the presidential palace and supporting services were progressively cut off from the rest of the city. More emphatically put, it was the possibility of these arrangements that allowed the presidential palace to move back and, in this way, play a central role in urban transformation. On the other, it created the condition for the Programa Luanda Sul, which was more than an experiment in the formation of a real estate market. It came also as an experiment in how to extract land from the public domain and build housing, infrastructure, and better services on this once public land, so as to produce these almost extraterritorial zones of privilege and comfort, free from the uncertainties of public services. In the case of Luanda, the enfolding of this process is at the core of the formation of the *condominium*, or gated community. These modes of extraction, of cutting pieces from the urban totality, is what goes in this chapter under the name of reversed urban composition.

From Public Ownership to Common *Dominium*

At a superficial glance, Luanda may come off as any other city in postcolonial Africa or in the Global South. All in all, its city center is still punctuated by the effects of the grandiloquent and totalizing intentions of modernist planning, which had strived for the seamless expansion of the urban grid but whose ultimate outcome was the enforcement of the distinction between *cidade* and *musseque*. Such a view of the city's "past futures" has obviously waned and, what has been going on now is the city's recomposition into a series of fragments. However, here, as well, the description of Luanda does not fit for the most part into the general picture that critical urban theorists have been putting forward on the forms of the contemporary urbanization process, in which the urban has become increasingly fragmented and punctuated by the emergence of enclaves, free zones, and enclosures. It is an undeniable fact now that Luanda boasts the existence of numerous, more or less exclusive gated residential communities, inside, or adjacent to, *centralidades* and *urbanizações*. However, the historical trajectory to be traced so as to explain the emergence of these urban outlets does not result from the withdrawal of the state from the public sphere, which is the obvious outcome for cities turned into hotspots of crime and violence, producing the flight of the well-to-do into fortified residential communities. Fragmentation in Luanda is a by-product of the reconfigurations of property rights.

I showed earlier that, with the flight of settlers and property owners in the mid-1970s, the socialist government had moved to nationalize the property left behind, distributing it to the citizenry. This moment was part of a broader process of uprooting the fundamentals of the colonial economy by privileging collectivization of property rather than property rights. Consequently, the state became a sort of landowner, which through Junta de Habitação was expected to regulate access to property and collect rental payments. Crucial to make sense of the new role the state came to play was the tacit understanding that state, or the party, and society formed a single body, codified in the dictum "O MPLA é o povo e o povo é o MPLA." (The MPLA is the people and the people is the MPLA). As for the housing question, however, given that state and society (or state through society) were the owners of urban property, there was no clear-cut protocol on how the housing stock should be managed. The value of the rent fixed at the time of independence—and the formal-informal exchange currency market, which produced its own exchange rated and did not significantly impact the formal one—has been considered the culprit for the limited financial resources available for urban authorities to use to properly maintain these apartment blocks.

It only took a few years from independence for the cracks and the signs of dereliction to reveal themselves on the façades and structures of the city center's apartment buildings. The deficiencies that were showing up cannot simply be explained through use or, to be more specific, deleterious use. The municipality was of no help in providing basic services. Infrastructure could not respond to increasing pressure on services because of Luanda's population growth. Power blackouts became irritatingly frequent and were caused sometimes by technical problems, but in many other instances these power outages, which could linger for weeks or months, were provoked by UNITA's subversive military operations, targeting the high-voltage poles that transported electricity from Cambambe to Luanda. Water provision was even more irregular. There were cuts that could go on for weeks and, of more concern, there were sections of the city in which water had stopped running from the taps.[7] Sometimes those shortages had technical issues behind them as well, but not infrequently the main cause was that services could not provide an optimal quantity of water. It was not uncommon that occupants of the lowest floors of a building had water running in their taps, whereas those who lived on the upper floors did not. It was to circumvent these difficulties that most Luandans, particularly those with the means, were resorting to generators for an alternative power supply and to water pumps that had to be refilled from time to time through cistern trucks, which, ironically, was a reminder of the problems of water distribution that the city had experienced in the early years of its foundation, as I mentioned in chapter 1.

To address these issues of conservation and maintenance, the Angolan government made the painful decision to start shedding property from its real estate portfolios. These measures of far-reaching consequence were coming in the wake of the peace agreement signed between the government and the armed opposition, in 1991, which brought to the table the imperative to start undoing the deleterious effects of the long internecine warfare. *Ordenamento do território* (land management) was then at the top of the governmental agenda, which included the resettlement of populations, particularly those that had languished in the recently formed informal settlements of Luanda. Furthermore, the fall of the socialist bloc was putting in disarray the macroeconomic doctrines that informed the centrally planned economy. As such, major steps started to be taken to recast the country's economy under the principles of neoliberalism. Privatization was central in the process, principally the privatization of property.

The question of the state-owned housing stock loomed large in these deliberations. The government's position on the previously nationalized property, and how to distribute the seized property among the citizenry, is addressed in the Lei Sobre a Venda do Património do Estado (Sale of State Property Act). The government itself recognized that "uma considerável parte dessa propriedade imobiliária encontra-se em acentuado estado de depreciação, não apenas por mau uso e fruição por parte dos seus inquilinos como também pelo decurso de muito tempo sem acções de manutenção e conservação pelas competentes autoridades públicas para isso vocacionadas" (a considerable part of the [government-controlled] real estate is in an advanced state of depreciation, due not only to the improper use by occupants but also to the amount of time that passed without any conservation action from the public authorities expected to provide it). The alienation of such property is then justified as a decision for, on the one hand, relievinging the state "das pesadas despesas com a manutenção dos imóveis" (of the onerous costs of upkeep for these buildings) and, on the other, allowing for the "participação de outros agentes na gestão mobiliária" (participation of other agents in the real estate management), which could constitute "uma substancial fonte de receitas necessárias ao atendimento de um agama enorme de solicitações financeiras e outras a que o Estado, na sua actividade normal, deve acudir" (a substantial source of needed revenue for servicing a whole array of financial and other demands that the state, in its normal activity, ought to provide for). However, such a transfer of property would come with some important caveats: only Angolan nationals could apply for the acquisition of property (Art. 5.1); occupants would be given priority for acquisition (Art. 5.2); and, to prevent urban speculation, individuals could only bid for "um imóvel unifamiliar ou uma só fracção autónoma" (single-family property or detached fraction) (Art. 7). And, more important, perhaps, those benefiting from the purchases could not put their property on the market within ten years (Art. 15).[8]

In hindsight, one wonders the extent to which such a step was also aiming to narrow the gap between the socialist economy, in which the state played an active distributive role, and the enclave economy, which was expanding at the pace of the proportion of crude oil extraction in the overall gross domestic product. We know from recent scholarship on Luanda's urbanism the extent to which oil extraction has been crucial for the city's expansion beyond the boundaries of the city center established by colonial urban authorities. For Ricardo Cardoso, for instance, it is crude oil that has fueled the "government's prospect for the capital [Luanda]."[9] To put it in different terms, access to petrodollars has propelled urban transformation in an unconceivable way. But, conversely, it is no less correct to say that it is petroleum itself that has prevented the emergence of a full-fledged and functional real estate market. Of note is that the role the economy of oil has played in the urban setting in Luanda goes deeper than what has been established by scholars. I will come to the point in the next chapter.

Responding to the provocative and seminal book by James Scott, *Seeing Like a State*, James Ferguson has attempted to shift the attention from the state to the "global corporation that performs the same homogenizing operation at the 'global level.'"[10] Having in mind oil companies as the most prominent types of those global corporations, he delves into the Angola case to extract a couple of examples. He is right when he ascertains that the "clearest case of extractive economy (and no doubt the most attractive for the foreign investor) is provided by offshore oil extraction, as in Angola, where neither the oil nor most of the money it brings in ever touches the Angolan soil."[11] He then proceeds to shed light on the organization of the extractive infrastructures, in territories such as Cabinda, in northern Angola, where oil workers live in "gated compounds" that are isolated from most of the surrounding area. Such a description, however, is not applicable to Luanda, where up to the end of the socialist era the enclave economy of oil did not produce the extraterritoriality African scholars have observed in many other locations.[12] For, if there was, as there has been, a sector of the economy where oil companies have generously splurged, it was in real estate.

Aware that the circuit of oil money is unabashedly capitalist, and working on the edification of a "workers' homeland," the Angolan government had since independence attempted, as much as possible, to isolate the unavoidable effects of the oil economy from the national and centrally planned economy. For the Angolan economist José Cerqueira, the thinking of the socialist government was to work through a contradiction. Whereas the overall intention was to create "um socialismo" (a socialist system), the reality was that "no sector petrolífero funciona o capitalismo" (the oil sector is controlled by capitalism). A way out of this imbroglio was to create a barrier between, on the one hand, "the capitalism of the oil sector" and, on the other, the project for making of a socialist society in which there should not be any ownership of the means of production.[13] The direct consequence was that since oil production was inevitably bringing in dollars, the country's economy bifurcated into, on the one hand, an economy in dollars, mostly for the expatriate community and, on the other, an economy in the national currency, kwanza, for nationals. Putting it in different terms, whereas the dollar was the currency that circulated within the oil economy, the overall Angolan economy could only use kwanza for most of its operations. The enclave of dollars that such a duality produced not only had enduring consequences for the country's monetary policies, as Cerqueira argues, but also constituted, I wish to add, a major force in the reconfiguring of housing policies.

Not having in place any legal framework that would allow oil companies to build "gated compounds" for their expatriate labor force, these companies had to resort to the available housing that the crumbling historic center could provide.[14] In these years leading into independence, urban property could not be claimed, but nothing prevented apartments from being transitioned, meaning that in most cases apartments could not be capitalized, for they lacked any economic leverage for their occupants, who could move in, move out, trade off, and even "sell" their apartment without any transfer of ownership in the proper sense of the word, for property itself remained with the state. Whereas most Luandans who had secured housing in the city center were expected to pay only a modicum of rent for their premises, oil companies circulated in a different economic dimension.

By the time oil production picked up in the late 1980s and throughout the 1990s, the international oil companies that operated in Angola were desperate to house their workers. Since the labor market in Angola could not provide the skilled manpower to operate the oil extraction plants, tens of thousands of expatriates were residing mostly in Luanda to support the sector.

When oil companies did not secure rental property directly for their workers, they were at least willing to pay salaries to meet the exceedingly expensive costs of rental housing in Luanda.

Since the cost of living (housing, food, and other commodities) for this international labor force was supported by the Angolan government, or paid indirectly by the government, the demand for accommodation in the city sky-rocketed.[15] By the late 1990s, Luanda had become one of the most expensive cities in the world. The renting of an old, decrepit one-bedroom apartment in the city center could cost more than US$5,000 a month, and rents were paid annually.[16] In the early 1990s, dilapidated apartments in downtrodden build-ings could cost millions of dollars. Many of those who were squatting in houses in the city center preferred to rent them to well-to-do newcomers and expatri-ates, moving back to the peripheries they had come from, or using the money to buy land and build houses outside the city center. Those who were lucky enough to occupy stand-alone houses in the city center had even better busi-ness prospects. Most of these houses were torn down, and in their place were erected a great number of the postmodernist architectural structures that have since come to define Luanda's skyline.

From the early 1990s onward, most apartment buildings in the city center were inhabited by a combination of occupants holding different relations to the property they occupied. While some of them belonged to the category of occupants who were the original squatters—in the process, or not, of legalizing ownership—many of them, such as João Pedro, were medium- or long-term renters. Whereas the act met its primary objective of allowing for private prop-erty, it fell short of living up to its second objective, which was to achieve the efficient maintenance of the buildings through private ownership. For even if the capitalization of the real estate allowed for the improvement of individual properties, the act is silent when it comes to the management and upkeep of the common areas.

The sudden revaluation of property taking place in the wake of this pro-found political-economic transformation from socialism to capitalism had a powerful impact on Luanda's real estate market. The sort of urban social frag-mentation that I described in the previous chapter was becoming dramatically evident at this time. Those who had acquired their apartments at a symbolic price from the state could now resell them at staggering prices. Here, it is per-haps useful to compare colonial and postcolonial legal systems in their effects on real estate. Whereas for the colonial legislator, this law was an instrument for capital creation, since it allowed a potential investor to put down savings in the property market, the assumptions of the postcolonial legislator were rather different. Those occupants, whose property relations the law was expected normalize, were for the most part squatters, and most of them did not have any other assets other than the property itself. So, whereas during colonial times the apartment became an entrée to the city, in the postindependence period it became for a number of people an exit from the city. As such, countless apartment occupants started renting out their accommodations at exorbitant prices, which then allowed them to rent houses in cheaper areas outside of the city center or even to buy property elsewhere, in Portugal or South Africa.

To address the idiosyncratic situation that the 1991 act had brought about, in which individual apartments could be privately owned even though the apartment buildings were still the property of the state (for the law prevented economic groups from purchasing entire buildings), the government issued the Law of Condominiums (Lei dos Condomínios) in 2004, or more specifically the law on the administration and maintenance of buildings. Behind its promulgation was perhaps the need to regulate the crumbling urban stock that had been passed to the hands of those who had squatted in it. This law aimed less at creating a legal framework for the construction of gated communities and more at regulating horizontal property, or the situation in which property was not a detached house but simply a fraction of an apartment building.[17] The precedent was the colonial law that permitted private investment in real estate, as I have shown earlier. The premise of the law was that owners of the sections of a particular building would come together as proprietors to deliberate on their share of responsibilities in terms of the cost of the upkeep of common areas, such as driveways, corridors, garages, and storage units, and the plumbing and electricity in the common areas. Assuming that all occupants of apartment buildings in Luanda were homeowners in their own right, the law attempted to convert squatters into associates. Article 1 of the new act stipulated, for example, that "em prédios com mais de um piso, constituídos e registados em propriedade horizontal e ou compropriedade, é obrigatória a constituição e reunião annual de Assembleia de Condóminos para a eleição das respectivas administrações das partes comuns" (in buildings with more than one floor, constituted and registered in horizontal ownership and/or co-ownership, it is mandatory to hold an annual meeting of the Co-owners Association to elect managers of the common areas).[18] However, private property can hardly be created by law, and the owners of the dilapidated sections of many buildings never felt that they had to contribute to their conservation. In most buildings, one could see on the walls notices, sometimes in very harsh language, reminding residents to pay their monthly condominium contributions. More often than not, the buildings continued to be afflicted by the same kinds of deficiencies as before, in particular because residents did not tend to recognize the places they lived in as belonging to them. The solution to the maintenance problem that followed in this situation did not address this, since what was privatized was not the property per se but the management of the buildings; as regulated by the Lei dos Condomínios, tenants had to constitute themselves as a collective to oversee security, sanitation, and the management of the building.[19]

So, for oil companies operating in Angola, or other companies under million-dollar contracts with the Angolan government, such as Odebrecht, there were only two ways for navigating housing in Luanda. Either they carved out spaces of functionality in the crumbling historic city by purchasing apartments, apartments floors, or even buildings, or they could build their own complexes that were increasingly being called condominiums, which only later started to emerge. The gated residential communities, which in the context of Angolan urban scholarship have almost exclusively been examined from the point of view of urban typology, are in fact a result of the reconfigurations of property rights. Sónia Frias and Cristina Udelsmann Rodrigues are right when they argue that, rather than "urban violence," as in South Africa or Latin America, it is "access to infrastructure" and "better living" that explain the proliferation of gated residential communities in Luanda.[20] However, I would like to suggest that such a proliferation is subsumed in a larger process related to the reconfiguration of land and property rights. In the end, the best image to capture how residential gated communities came into being is not the cutting off slices of the urban and the urban infrastructural network associated with it, but rather the fractioning, or fragmenting, of collective property (or, to put it differently, the separation between state and property).

Cidade Alta as a Powerscape

When the first Angolan president, Agostinho Neto, died unexpectedly in Moscow, on September 10, 1979, after being rushed to the Soviet Union's capital for medical treatment, the MPLA's Central Committee made a decision not to bury him, as is common practice in Angola, but instead to embalm and conserve the body in a "mausoleum para a eternidade" (mausoleum for eternity).[21] To fulfill this promise, the party unanimously decided on two lines of action. First, it enlisted Soviet specialists in the complex and delicate technique of body conservation from the moment Neto's remains returned to Luanda and were deposited in a room at the Comissariado Provincial de Luanda for public display. Second, it commissioned the Soviets to design an elaborate mausoleum to which the body of Neto would be transferred, after the location for the monumental endeavor had been determined. The architectural projects that were soon made public reveal that the Angolan socialist government was not simply aiming at providing Neto's embalmed body with a tomb, however expensive it might be. The ruling party was envisioning capitalizing on Neto's body so as to turn it into a unifying symbol, the body of the nation itself. This was to be achieved by building around the mausoleum the country's political-administrative district, Centro Político Administrativo.

Bairro Praia do Bispo, a residential area behind the presidential palace, was the site chosen to receive the mausoleum, whose construction started in 1982 but was halted a few years later on account of the worsening of the politico-military situation. For more than two decades, the rocket-shaped, unfinished obelisk-like building was both a symbol of the grandiloquent aspirations of Angolan's first government and an experiment with socialism in Africa that had gone wrong. For a city that was experiencing massive migration from the countryside, not even the surroundings of the presidential palace were spared from squatting. As everywhere in Luanda, hundreds of thousands of squatters built their houses on every available plot of land that they could find. When there were no longer any plots of land available, in the informal settlement of Chicala—a few meters from the mausoleum construction site—squatters dumped refuse in the water, or used the rubbish the government failed to collect and built their houses on top of it.[22] Many of those who built in this manner were themselves members of the Guarda Presidencial (Presidential Guard). As people would say in Luanda, the presidency was itself one of the causes for urban informalization: whenever the presidential palace was moved, the members of the presidential guard would erect shacks so as to live close to work.

The resurfacing of the mausoleum project, as well as the commitment to the construction of the Centro, was at the top of the political agenda in the late 1990s. Angola was then shedding the effects of socialist orthodoxy in the national economy and embracing the market-driven approach to the national economy and its modes of governance. I have shown already the extent to which the alleviation of the state's role in housing through the selling of the property controlled by the state was part of this transformation. At a more structural level, there started to emerge among the ruling elite the notion that in order to carry out privatization, a stronger political center (and, necessarily, on physical or architectural terms) had to come about—one able to arbitrate among the competing interests that would certainly emerge as a consequence of private capital accumulation.[23] The overlap between privatization and political control has been examined by many African scholars, particularly Achille

Mbembe, who pointedly indicates that "in the African context, privatizations fundamentally alter the processes whereby wealth is allocated, income distributed, and ethno-regional balances regulated, as well as the narrowly political notions of public good and general interest."[24] In the Angolan case, such a construct came about in many ways, particularly under the guise of what, again, Mbembe has called the "privatization of this sovereignty."[25] More to the point, such a reconfiguration of sovereignty did not take place along the lines the literature on the topic has suggested: by insisting on the uses of concepts such as "shadow networks."[26] In Angola sovereignty was enlarged within the state itself through the ways in which the presidency of the republic, or more specifically the president, usurped the prerogative from other branches (the judiciary and the legislative).[27] I will discuss this point with further details in the next chapter. Here it is enough to say that if sovereignty, or centralization of power so as to arbitrate divergent economic interests, has taken on a physical form, this form can certainly be examined through the ways in which the mausoleum to Neto, the Centro Político Administrativo, and the Cidade Alta were merged into one single entity.

In the previous chapter, I used the geometric figure of the triangle to discuss in topographical terms the emergence of Roque Santeiro. My intention was to demonstrate the ways in which Roque Santeiro could be seen as a fraction detaching itself from the whole city and taking on a life of its own. For it was more than a mere marketplace; with time it had simultaneously become both a wholesale and a retail market; a logistics, distribution, and transportation center; a camp for the construction several informal settlements; and a major force in decentering the city center, so to speak. It can be seen as an enclosure, of an informal nature, but one that allows us to grapple with not only the rationales for the emergence of those enclosures but also the effects they bear on the city. Taking stock of Roque Santeiro's formation, I think it is perhaps theoretically productive to trace an association between the market and Cidade Alta. For, first of all, it was because of places such as Roque Santeiro, outlets for wealth creation and the interests that emerged out of the process, that the concentration of power, or privatization of political prerogatives, sovereignty, started to occur. As such, with time Cidade Alta entered into a topographical trajectory of detaching itself from the whole, becoming through this a sort of powerscape of its own.

As with Roque Santeiro, it is possible to present Cidade Alta as a triangle that cuts through and stretches from the embassy of the United Kingdom, on the Rua 17 de Setembro, to the Imprensa Nacional, on Rua P. Furtado, and the Memorial Dr. António Agostinho Neto, on Rua Nova Marginal. I discussed

Figure 5.2. Memorial Dr. António Agostinho Neto, under construction, as viewed from Bairro da Samba, 2015. Source: Ngoi Salucombo.

previously the resilience of topographical referentiality in Luanda. Here it is interesting to notice that it did not take much time for Luanda to start to refer to Cidade Alta, and no longer Futungo de Belas, as the seat of power in Angola.[28] Cidade Alta is not a *bairro*, or a district, in the administrative sense of the term, for it straddles various *bairros*, or districts, such as Maianga, Ingombota, and Bairro Azul. Like Roque Santeiro, from an albeit different point of view, Cidade Alta came to exert the same kind, in nature if not in intensity, of gravitational force on the rest of the city.

Historically, it had always been from the slopes of Cidade Alta that colonial governors controlled the whole country. Initially built in 1607–11 as the Câmara de Luanda, it was around 1621–30, during the administration of Governor Fernão de Sousa, that the original building was rebuilt as a palace for the governor and the colony's administration. It was demolished and reconstructed in 1761 according to the Pombalino style, since Marquês de Pombal was then the prime minister of Portugal.[29] Major refurbishments were carried out between 1912 and 1915, during the time of High Commissioner Norton de Matos, and later on, in 1946, the complex was subjected to "novas alterações de acordo com mudanças da vida social, o que implicou ampliação, modernização e também conservação" (new alterations, according to changes in social life, which implied extension, modernization, and conservation). For instance, a tower built in 1855 was demolished, and the façade "was expanded in order to merge it to the adjoining buildings, namely the Paço Episcopal [Bishop's House]"[30] (e se unificou a fachada com os edifícios confinantes). The architect Fernando Batalha, whose work in Luanda I discussed in chapter 1, was commissioned to oversee the modernization of the palace, and it was at that time that the building was given that classic façade that it displays now.[31]

When Agostinho Neto, the first Angolan president, took office, he preferred to use the former colonial palace, in Cidade Alta, as the presidential office and to use the beach house of the colonial governor, in Futungo de Belas to the south of Luanda, as the official residence of the president of the republic. Later on, I was told, tired of the distance he had to travel, he started to transfer some of the presidential services to Futungo de Belas. By the time dos Santos became president, in September 1979, the transfer of the presidential office to Futungo de Belas was complete. Over the years, dos Santos would turn Futungo de Belas into the seat of Angolan politics.[32] Having his lodging outside the city certainly allowed dos Santos to refurbish and expand the Cidade Alta, particularly the presidential level. However, having less interference, and governing the country from Futungo de Belas—in a section controlled by his private army, the Guarda Presidencial—also explains how he managed to consolidate his power, as I will discuss in further detail in the next chapter.

During those years, the embalmed body of Agostinho Neto was put to rest in one of the rooms of the palace. The Soviets were occupied with its conservation and the construction of the definitive tomb for Neto's remains, the mausoleum. Foundations were laid in the early 1980s, and the construction of the brutalist structure in the shape of a spaceship, or inverted torch, was advancing in height at a steady pace. During this time, Soviet urbanists were also working on the plan for the surroundings of the mausoleum. They might have used the plans drawn up during the late colonial period for the development of that area, in Praia do Bispo.[33] But the closer architectural precedent the Soviets were using was Red Square in Moscow, which was apparent in the plans through the construction of a major square, the Praça das Manifestações (Manifestation Square), to host major public events, the ones common in socialist countries, such as well-rehearsed and prodigious military parades. Construction was permanently halted in the late 1980s because of the onerous burden it was having on the country's finances (Angola had to pay for all the construction costs, chief among them the thousands of Soviets workers who were involved in all aspects of the construction, from design, carpentry, foundation, and even decoration). The fact that the Soviet Union was collapsing by the end of the 1980s might also have been a cause for the interruption of the involvement of the Soviets in this construction work.

It was only one year after the signature of the first peace agreement—between the central government and UNITA, in May 1991, which ended the civil war—that the Ministers' Council approved the creation of the Grupo Técnico de Apoio à Comissão Interministerial de Supervisão do Programa do Novo Centro Político Administrativo (Technical Group for Support of the Interministerial Commission for Oversight of the New Political Administrative Center). It was also around this time that the Presidential Office moved back to Cidade Alta.[34] Without the Soviets, the scope and ambition of the whole project was more modest, for the government was no longer aiming at the construction of an independent and detached Centro Político Administrativo but at an alternative one, as it was designated. This would simply involve the construction of a few buildings for the transfer of the presidential palace to Cidade Alta, and, more important, it would revolve around the renovation of various already-existing buildings to accommodate the ever expanding auxiliary services of the presidency. Resumption of the construction of the mausoleum was also contemplated in these plans.[35]

To open up space for the construction of these facilities—or simply to further the function of Cidade Alta, as the site of power—so as "instalar condignamente os orgãos de soberania" (to install with dignity the bodies of sovereignty), the government invited residents to find accommodations elsewhere in the city.[36] Some of those residents were financially compensated, and others accepted trading their houses for single-family detached houses in the new gated communities that were starting to sprout in the city. But a large majority of the residents in that part of the city, particularly those who had squatted in the houses they were living in and could not therefore produce title deeds, were removed by force. Residents of a section of Praia do Bispo called Saneamento, including, ironically, members of former president Agostinho Neto's entourage, were evicted and their houses were destroyed or rebuilt. The same fate was suffered by the inhabitants of the adjacent Chicala, whose land was then used either for the security perimeter of the president of the republic (defining how near to the presidential abode citizens were allowed to live) or for beautification projects.

The perimetization of Cidade Alta is of crucial importance for grappling with urban transformation, since it constituted an experiment in moving populations out of certain areas for political or aesthetics reasons, a practice that would later become normalized, as I show in the next chapter. For in order to do so, the nature of power itself needed to undergo profound changes. Rather than allowing bodies of the state to do the work they were expected to perform, the presidency was invested in creating organs of government under the control of Cidade Alta. One such organ is the Gabinete de Obras Especiais (Office of Special Works; GOE). Created by Decreto no. 24/98, published on August 7, 1998, its legal scope was only made public three years later, in 2001, with the publication of its status in the national gazette. Since the GOE was under direct control of the president himself, to whom the GOE's director reported, and since the GOE was tasked with pursuing the necessary work for the implementation of the Centro—alongside the unspecified "desempenhar outras tarefas que lhe forem incumbidas pelo Presidente da República, ou determinadas por lei" (to carry out other tasks requested by the President of the Republic or determined by law),[37] including the resettlement of former residents—one can arguably infer from such an arrangement that the administration of Cidade Alta had been subtracted from the management portfolio of the Provincial Government of Luanda.

The GOE then was called to take an active role in the presidential oversight of the construction, renovation, or refurbishment of dozens of houses, parking lots, and streets and to produce a study on the feasibility of converting Bairro do Saneamento, adjacent to the palace, into a complex for the presidential services in charge of travel and ceremonial activities.[38] Alongside these interventions, the GOE was also expected to carry on some specified or unspecified operations, at the personal whim of the president, such as the construction of thirty single-family units in Luanda Sul and the Residência Protocolar no. 3 (a residence for visiting foreign dignitaries) in Morro da Luz, which was in fact the house of dos Santos's mother. Among the other tasks bestowed on the agency were the conceptualization of master plans and the participation in negotiations regarding the finances of the Centro Político Administrativo, particularly those that involved compensation for relocation.[39] In this context, the Departamento de Realojamento (Rehousing Department) is introduced as a service "promover a mobilização e organização de famílias e instituições a realojar no âmbito do Programa do Centro Político Administrativo" (to promote the mobilization of families and institutions within the scope of the Program of the Centro Político Administrativo).[40]

By imposing the vague and ill-conceived plan of the Centro Politico Administrativo onto the Cidade Alta/Praia do Bispo, to carve out a space of power in Luanda's urban landscape, the presidency was not simply moving back to the city center so as to govern the city and the country from a central position. It was, more importantly, reconfiguring Luanda's powerscape, or the relationship between power and the urban. Both the Portuguese, who were planning to develop the section of the city adjacent to it, and the Soviets, who came to erect the mausoleum, agreed that Cidade Alta should preserve its architectural style, which was distinct from the rest of the city. The Lebanese firm Dar Al-Handasah, which had been involved in various projects of planning and construction in Cidade Alta, also pushed for a similar vision, by making a strong case for the preservation and restoration of the historical-political center, suggesting that the "nature and extent of the existing heritage establishes a strong physical character composed of lower rise buildings" and that "the strongly Portuguese style of many of the buildings with their pastel colouring, characteristic fenestration and unifying materials need[s] to be sympathetically addressed when new development is proposed." Since "each historical period established a strong empathy with its setting, a new development should abide by the same principles." The plan thus proposed that "the historical part of Luanda will be subject to specific building standards to ensure protection of its unique heritage assets. All new developments will have to comply with these standards."[41] Many of the new buildings, and particularly the renovations in these areas, followed this recommendation.

Dar Al-Handasah's vision is visible in the conceptual framework for the refurbishment and design of a couple of buildings in Cidade Alta, particularly the Angolan National Assembly, whose construction started in 2010 and which was dedicated on November 10, 2015. Although a new building for the parliament, or Assembleia do Povo (People's Assembly), had been part of the initial plan for the Centro Político Administrativo under the previous dispensation, the Angolan parliament had, since independence, occupied the building of the gigantic Cinema Restauração (Restoration Cinema), a multistory building that was a commercial cinema during colonial times, designed, in 1956, by the architect brothers João Garcia de Castilho and Luís Garcia de Castilho. The new National Assembly building was constructed by the Portuguese firm Teixeira Duarte Engenharia e Construções, and many Luandans were surprised to see that in terms of architectural style, it followed neither the style of most of the buildings in that area, the Pombalino and its derivatives, which had been destroyed, nor the architectural modernism of downtown Luanda; instead, it was a replica of the Banco Nacional de Angola (National Bank of Angola; BNA). Designed by the Portuguese architect Vasco Regaleira and built in 1956 as "the most significant monument of Portuguese architecture," the BNA emulated the iconic order of classical architecture, with façades, ionic columns, domes, a pediment, and arcades that stretched out in an L shape along the Avenida Marginal and Rua Serqueira Lukoki in downtown Luanda.[42] With its adorning frescoes that depicted various historical moments, the building came to act as a monument to the history of Portugal.[43] For the Angolan architect Ângela Mingas, the similarities between the new Assembleia and the existing BNA represent a reenactment of the colonial style, Português Suave, which for her should not have had a place in contemporary Luanda.[44]

While the new building for the National Assembly clearly took its cue from the BNA, its scale was far more ambitious. The central part of the building consists of a circular structure with a metallic dome that houses the main hall used for plenary meetings. This is flanked by four six-story wings (each including two underground levels) that house the offices of the president of parliament, the administrative council, and various parliamentary groups, and that provide rooms for the press, meeting areas, and restaurants.[45] Journalistic accounts have not failed to describe the building as "majestic architecture" and to make reference to the scale of the resources and finances used to build it: in total, the state disbursed over US$320 million for a building with an area of 60,000 square meters (645,835 square feet) that used 75,000 cubic meters (2,648,600 cubic feet) of concrete and 10,500 tonnes of steel.[46]

With reconstructions, removals, and particularly the construction of buildings such as the National Assembly, Cidade Alta affirms itself as the gravitational center of the country's political life. It does so through the perimetization of power. Administratively, Cidade Alta is under the purview of the Provincial Government of Luanda, but it is in fact controlled by the auxiliary services of the presidency. The detachment of Cidade Alta from Luanda has taken place in two major ways, through architecture and through a physical separation from the rest of the city. Cidade Alta is the zone of the city with the highest number of old buildings, the kind of buildings that were destroyed in downtown Luanda, as I discussed in chapter 1. Premodernist building typologies have been enforced as much as possible, even if some of these buildings are not the original ones but replicas of *sobrados*, or even if they follow the Pombalino style and its derivatives, as the presidential palace does. The variants of pastel as the main coloration for these buildings dominate in Cidade Alta, ranging from a saturated brick color to a lighter color that is closer to pink. In terms of the physical separation, since Cidade Alta is the abode of one of the most well-guarded powers in Angola, it has become a no-go zone for most residents. Roads and accesses have been blocked, or even closed off, to prevent pedestrian and automotive circulation. Moreover, very few services have remained there after the removals. Some of the city's facilities, such as the rebaptized Jardim da Cidade Alta (Garden of Cidade Alta), have also been closed off from the public.

Figure 5.3. View from the Marginal de Luanda, with the domed Banco Nacional de Angola by the waterfront and the dome of the National Assembly in the background, 2016. Source: Ferreira de Almeida Arquitectos.

Expanding the Urban Southward

The experimentation with the urban refurbishment of Cidade Alta, as discussed earlier, revealed above all the penchant of the presidency—particularly that of the president himself—for urban renewal, which came to be subsumed in the Programme of National Reconstruction. In the next chapter, I will show the extent and scale of such a reconstruction, which came to affect directly hundreds and thousands of Luandans. In the remainder of this chapter, I will discuss one of the earliest urban developments and how it opened the way for things to come, furthering urban fragmentation in Luanda.

With the relocation of the office of the president of the republic to Cidade Alta, the vast and highly militarized area it occupied in Futungo de Belas was left vacant. The services of the presidency that had been left behind, the units of the Presidential Guard as well as the few generals close to the presidency who were allowed to build their houses there, made the area out of reach for potential squatters. This zone was then earmarked to receive the first public-private partnership in urban development, the Programa Luanda Sul, which would allow the city to expand only in its almost hinterland to the south. Programa Luanda Sul would allow the construction of dozens of condominiums, which would bring to the city a new way of living.

In the early 1990s, frustrated by the limited high-class accommodation in Luanda, oil companies started to consider other ways to shelter their highly paid labor force. Odebrecht was the first international conglomerate operating in Angola that saw saw in the construction of housing to shelter expatriates a way to decrease operational costs. Operating in Angola since the mid-1980s, Odebrecht had built up an impressive conglomerate whose portfolio ranged from oil and diamonds to the construction of infrastructure and real estate.[47] They were the ones who in 1986 had built the first gated residential condominium to house Brazilian expatriate workers involved in various construction projects, chief among them the Cambambe Dam in the province of Kwanza Norte. Brazilian construction companies took this as an impulse to involve themselves in the building of similar developments.

But what Odebrecht would then propose as the Programa Luanda Sul was not simply expansion of its business portfolio into the burgeoning sector of urban development. Odebrecht lobbied the government to undertake such a redevelopment program by making the case that since Luanda was formed by two cities, the city center and the *musseques*, it was time to add a third one, so as to break the dichotomy of colonial planning and jumpstart Luanda's housing market, and, most important, to reduce the demographic pressure on the city center. Conceived as an innovative urban strategy, "a foundational urbanization scheme," the program unapologetically intended to blend, as Ricardo Cardoso has put it, capitalism and democracy in urban planning.[48]

Its inception dates to 1992, the year in which the country held its first democratic elections, but it was only in 1994, after "lengthy negotiations,"[49] that Odebrecht's concessionaire, Odebrecht Serviços no Exterior (Odebrecht Services Abroad; OSEL), signed a contract with Luanda's provincial government to carry out urban development in the city. Resolution 30/94, which rendered the endeavor legal, in terms of the problem of the "ocupação desordenada do solo urbano" (disorderly occupation of urban land), cast it as a way to prevent such "disorderly occupation of urban land" and to provide a solution for the "lack of infrastructure."[50] The Provincial Government of Luanda, or GPL, in partnership with Odebrecht, was then tasked with initiating, "with urgency," a program to address the dire situation Luanda was falling in.[51]

Luanda Sul was conceived as a scheme and turned into urban policy to foster land development in Luanda, and thus enabled the Provincial Government of Luanda to raise funds to be eventually invested back in infrastructure. Since back then the country was shedding its ties with the socialist orthodoxy, and as there were no legal instruments available to provide a regulatory framework for such an undertaking, colonial legislation was mobilized. During the time up to independence, the Lei dos Direitos de Superfície (Law of Surface Rights) was the legal framework that allowed the colonial government, municipalities, and legal persons of administrative public utilities "podem constituir o direito de superfície sobre terrenos de que sejam proprietários a favor de pessoas singulares e colectivas" (to constitute surface rights on land under their jurisdiction, in favor of individuals and legal persons).[52] In its postcolonial rendition—and according to the framework signed between the Provincial Government of Luanda and Odebrecht's subsidiary OSEL for the implementation of the Programa Piloto Luanda Sul—the granting of surface rights was conceived as a "definitive deed, for the terms of concession and transmissible to a third party," and it was intended to ameliorate land tenure in the city, for it would allow agents to acquire rights to the use of land.[53]

In practice, the project was implemented through the creation of a public-private partnership between Odebrecht and a recently constituted public company, Companhia de Desenvolvimento Urbano (Company for Urban Development; EDURB), which became the administrative vehicle of the program, representing the provincial government.[54] This land-concession scheme was supposed to work as follows: the government would make land available, at no cost, to public-private ventures for the purpose of developing it—which would involve the clearing of the area, the construction of access roads, the subdivision of the land into plots, and the installation of connections to municipal services. Once these tasks had been accomplished, EDURB would return the land to the provincial government. The company would be paid for its services at a rate "calculated as the cost of the installed infrastructure plus a social contribution."[55] In the next stage, the government would put these mixed-used developed plots on the market according to the legal terms of surface rights, which meant that the plots were transferable, and their leases could be renewed and mortgaged.[56] The land would be available to investors, or to the public in general, in two ways: either through cash sales, which would grant the purchasers immediate and full access to infrastructure (sewerage, electricity, and water), or by selling it first to developers, who would first pay for the land and only at a later stage pay for access to infrastructure in proportion to the payment already made. The aim of such a scheme, it was then announced, was to allow the government to levy taxes and tariffs on the municipal services provided on these plots, so as to raise funds to invest in social programs such as health and education and especially housing.[57]

Critics of the program were quick to point out that "while some land has been provided at no charge in the [first] category for re-located families, no land has yet been made available in the second category."[58] For them, this was either because the regulation was unclear or because the whole procedure was impractical. As such, they concluded, it was clear that the state was more interested in providing resources to its clients than in addressing the dire situation of urban poverty.[59] The concerns of the critics were not misplaced, given the ways in which the program subsequently unfolded. The approximately 4,046 hectares (10,000 acres) under the direct control of the program in Luanda Sul were divided into three sectors. Talatona was for upper-class residents, Novos Bairros for the middle class, and Morar for low-income residents. As such, the type and the quality of infrastructure and social services available to residents varied accordingly. For the upper class, Talatona was to be fully developed, and clients received their plots with "complete infrastructure."[60] In Novos Bairros, clients would be allowed to pay in instalments, but infrastructure was only provided piecemeal, if and when the buyers were able to pay for it. In Morar, where the social component of the program was implemented, EDURB was expected to install "evolving and basic infrastructure," financed by the state.[61] In other words, in these last two places the provincial government would only install infrastructure services when financial resources were available or when there was a pressing need to do so.

It is no coincidence that the oil companies were the first to jump on this bandwagon, attracted by the possibility of not having to pay high rents for the accommodation of their employees (particularly expatriates) in the city center through short- and medium-term leases. Their involvement was not only as renters or purchasers of housing but, more important, as developers. The state-owned oil company, Sonangol, formed a real estate firm, Sonangol Imobiliária e Propriedades (Sonangol Estate Company; SONIP), to work exclusively on housing projects for its employees, which ended up subcontracting the construction of dozens of condominiums in Talatona. In 1995, SONIP and the Cabinda Gulf Oil Company (CABGOC), an international oil consortium, pledged US$30 million for the construction of condominiums for their workers. Many of these buildings were built by OSEL, through the Brazilian engineer Prado Valladares, who was already attached to EDURB. The services company not only installed the infrastructure but also built the condominiums on land acquired for free from the government. It was on this basis, for instance, that Chevron commissioned OSEL and the local firm Sakus Empreendimentos e Participações (Sakus Ventures and Participations) to build the Monte Belo apartment building for its employees, at a total cost of US$250 million.[62]

The emergence of the Luanda Sul program had a staggering impact on Luanda's urban transformation. It was for the most part sequestered and used as a device for personal enrichment since it benefited Odebrecht as well as the companies it was associated with, particularly those controlled by people in the central government and those who had close business relationships with them. According to Odebrecht, the company invested about US$800 million in the construction of fourteen commercial and residential ventures, including shopping malls, such as the Belas Shopping Mall (2007), Angola's first ever shopping center, as well as later ones such as Brisas (2007) and Conchas (2010); business parks, such as Belas Business Park (2009); and condominiums, such as Arte Yetu (2009), Mirantes, Vereda das Flores (2003), Brisas (2005), Luar (2008), Atlântico Sul (2008), Pérolas (2009), Conchas (2009), and Diamantes (2012).[63] Once finished, these units in upscale housing developments were put on the real estate market, at prices ranging from US$600,000 for a three-bedroom apartment to US$900,000 for a four-bedroom apartment.[64] Needless to say, the state was the main client involved in the purchase of these residences. In fact, the state, the very institution that had made the serviced land available, also became the principal client in these schemes by purchasing a great many of the apartment buildings put on the market in order to distribute them as rental property to members of the burgeoning middle class.[65]

Whereas Luanda Sul allowed the many privileged inhabitants of Luanda to move to their mansions in the suburbs while renting out their accommodations in the city, it failed to do anything significant to house the poor. One reason for this, perhaps, was that the company involved in this program, EDURB, did not have a mandate to provide housing as such; it only serviced land. Moreover, the Luanda Sul program was also caught up in the administrative riddle that marred city planning in general.[66] The central government, the presidency, and the provincial government were all vying with each other to further their own interests. Each state agency proposed different plans with wide-ranging and sometimes contradictory aims, even if they failed to be implemented. For instance, the oversight of the whole development project was first given to Odebrecht, but the presidency of the republic took over the control of Luanda Sul through the GOE, before eventually the Governo Provincial de Luanda was given the same task.[67]

Moreover, Luanda Sul, as the city center, was not immune to *construções anárquicas* (unplanned construction) and encroachment. The urban development company did not have ways to prevent land from being occupied by squatters who did not pay for the services offered. Some of these squatters could not be considered part of the urban poor; they were well-established professionals or members of the Angolan army who did not have the means to join, or who refused to take part in, the payment schemes. Most of these people built their own infrastructure. Overall, then, whereas Talatona has indeed been developed, to the extent that nowadays Luandans identify the entire Luanda Sul area with it, the implementation of Novos Bairros and Morar is a far cry from the 17,000 plots envisioned. The program failed because the availability of serviced land was not matched by the formation of a sophisticated real estate market.

The appeal of Luanda Sul as a development project was initially the possibility that this sector of the city could provide a way out of the collapse of the city center. In terms of urban typology, it has succeeded. Luanda Sul is still by all accounts a distinctive form of urbanization compared with both the city center and the *musseques*. Conceived above all as a residential area, it offered limited commercial services, and residents had to commute to central Luanda for work and school. Planners expected that expanding the network of freeways linking Luanda to Luanda Sul would solve the problem, but it later became clear that access was not the only problem besetting the scheme. Luanda's roads were too narrow and quickly congested, so traffic jams became endemic. This led to a complete reconceptualization of Luanda Sul's layout, to make space for better road and freeway access and to expand its commercial and educational services so that residents did not have to go to Luanda every day. In Talatona, a great deal of effort went into the construction of roads, hotels, sport and leisure facilities, shopping malls, and convention centers. Yet no public spaces were included. The only open spaces are wide, often one-way, avenues that are uncomfortable and alienating for pedestrians. The housing type introduced in Talatona was inspired neither by the apartment blocks and single-family residences in the concrete city of the colonial period and early independence years nor by the shacks in the *musseques*; rather, it introduced the radical innovation of the gated community, or the condominium, protected from the outside by barbed wire and private security firms, in a more dramatic way than one would see in the city center. Inside, residents could enjoy urban amenities that the city center no longer offered, such as gardens and parks, and sometimes even swimming pools, tennis courts, fully equipped gyms, and even spas.

With Luanda Sul, the formal city of Luanda started to expand southward. Whereas Luanda Sul may have constituted a pole for urban development out of the historical city in the early beginning, successive waves of internal migration encroached in the space in between. In the emergence of Luanda Sul, one can see the coming together of the forces that have driven the southern expansion of the urban grid and the unbinding of infrastructure. We will see in the next chapter how the postwar reconstruction government has approached the question of redevelopment.

It is undisputable that the proliferation of gated communities in Luanda does not diverge, at least physically, from the patterns identified by scholars in other locations such as Latin America and other African countries. But in Luanda more specifically the emergence of the gated community as urban typology was predicated on the confluence of several factors—namely, the economy, particularly the oil economy, for whose operations the country depended on expatriate workers; the collapse of public services such as water, electricity, and sanitation; and particularly the shift in the property law.

• • •

Colonial urban authorities and designers may have conceived of Luanda as a whole so as to maintain the tension between the city and the *musseques*, through the coming to terms with a notion of *fronteira do asfalto* that was malleable and flexible, and in constant expansion by integrating more land into the city. With independence, this model for urban expansion was no longer workable. Whereas the city was being informally decentered, the city center was also being informalized to such an extent that in more recent times the putative separation of city center and *musseques* no longer made sense. Central to understanding the obliteration of this category is the preoccupation with Luanda's fate that urban authorities started to show from the mid-1990 onward. The expansion of the urban core to the south of the city center, whose principal aim was to provide more housing, ended up creating the conditions for urban fragmentation, or the reversal of urban composition.

From the standpoint of property and homeownership, the city of Luanda by the 1980s was an immense totality in which the state was almost the absolute owner of all built property. As such, the alienation of this property through what later came to be known as condominiums is important, for this removed housing from state control. To put it in slightly different terms, the condominium, then, being an apartment building or a section of detached single-family homes, was conceived as an excision, or a separation of property out of what was considered to be common (controlled by the state). The vignettes with which I started this chapter illustrate these acts of separation through the formal and informal ways in which apartment dwellers started to close off their premises by erecting walls and installing gates. The collapse of public services that pushed dwellers into finding ways to provide water and electricity for their houses further fractured the city's wholeness.

Whereas the Sale of State Property Act of 1991 intended to transfer the burden of conservation to the users, the Condominium Act of 2004 was drafted so as to force these users into association. This blueprint, through which neighbors come together to solve a common challenge, was transferred onto the condominiums as an urban housing typology. The condominium that in Luanda is for the most part understood in its physical component, as an independent complex of buildings, was also being deployed by the government as a legal tool intended to cut off sets of housing units, buildings, or even floors within the building as a means by which to deal with the disorderly occupation of housing in the city and beyond—a far cry from what the Portuguese had in mind when they sketched the condominium principle in the 1950s, as described earlier. For this time, without the anchor of market forces, the government could only enforce the condominium principle on the housing units that were being built as such.

The perimeterization of Cidade Alta and the parceling out of the land that came under the jurisdiction of Luanda Sul, such as Talatona, will become the major focus of Luanda's future expansion, as I will discuss in the next chapter. Practices that were taking place at a more modest scale, such as the relocation of residents in the zones adjacent to the presidential palace, later became the tools through which the city procured land for expansion. Central in this process is not simply the brute force that goes hand in hand with the removals but the reconfiguration of the political that reinforces the figure of the president of the republic as the main conveyor of urban transformation. In a nutshell, the approach followed for the renewal and beautification of the presidential premises are taken up at a broader scale in order to usher in transformation. However, for this process to unfold, larger questions about land, and not just urban land, had to reassessed. Reservas, then, became the tool at the government's disposal for circumventing the bureaucratic and legal hindrances to the removal of populations.

6. The Urban Yet to Come

Far from being marginal to contemporary processes of scalar recomposition and the reimagination of political communities, African cities can be seen as a frontier for a wide range of diffuse experimentation with the reconfiguration of bodies, territories, and social arrangements necessary to recalibrate technologies of control.—AbdouMaliq Simone, *For the City Yet to Come*, 2004

. . .

Luanda, so to speak, started with Ilha de Luanda. It was there that the Portuguese founders of the city established themselves in 1576, before moving inland. As almost everywhere in the Portuguese empire, the act of possession was sealed through the construction of a church, in homage to Nossa Senhora do Cabo. Most Luandans would like to believe that the election of such a patron for the first Catholic temple in the colonial settlement was internally motivated, but, in fact, the Portuguese were extending to the African soil the manifestations of popular religiosity that the saint had inspired in medieval Portugal. Throughout the few centuries of Portuguese presence, the natives, the Ilhéus,

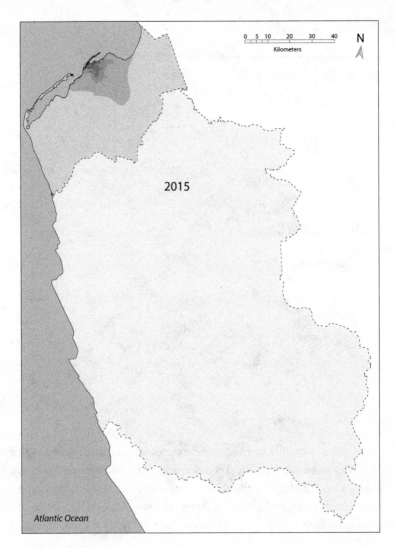

Map 6.1. Luanda in 2015.

were able to create their own refined systems of faith and worship, a syncretism between Catholicism and animism. Portuguese religious authorities might have believed that the natives praying in their church were devotees of Nossa Senhora do Cabo when they were, possibly, worshipping their own divinity, Kianda, the spirit of the water. From the 1950s onward, with the exponential growth of the settlers' population, Ilha de Luanda was turned into a recreational zone, without major disturbance to the Native population. Colonial authorities managed to build a few fishermen's villages alongside the houses built by the natives themselves using their own materials and techniques of construction. The success of such a coexistence was partially due to the Estado Novo's protection of folklore as cultural manifestations (in continental Portugal and in the colonies), and in Ilha de Luanda, the Portuguese attempted as much as possible to integrate the locals' cosmogony into everyday practices. For instance, violent tides, called *calemas*, have always been a common event, and the Portuguese, despite the work of land reclamation that was being carried out, did not actively oppose the gift-giving celebrations in which fishermen rowed out into the bay to throw food into the water to, it was believed, feed the Kianda.

With independence, in 1975, the attitude toward popular religious practices changed drastically. The self-proclaimed socialist government led by Agostinho Neto started to crack down on most forms of religion because they promoted superstition, which was then considered a hindrance to the construction of the new (socialist) man. The Kianda celebrations did not disappear, but their organizers and practitioners were forced into finding a secular language for these ceremonies, calling them Festas da Ilha de Luanda, or Festas da Ilha do Cabo (Feasts of Ilha de Luanda, or Feasts of Ilha do Cabo).[1] With the renouncing of the socialist orthodoxy, religion was reinstated and the Festas da Nossa Senhora do Cabo came back onto the city's official calendar. However, when the *calemas* violently swept across Ilha de Luanda in 2009, destroying hundreds of houses, the Provincial Government of Luanda did not contemplate the integrity of these communities and their practices but saw in the tragedy an opportunity to justify the evacuation of residents living on the Avenida Murtala Mohammed, the main road running the length of the island. To soothe the popular uproar, the authorities insisted that those moved out of Ilha were not part of the original community and had come to Luanda as refugees to squat on the state's land.

According to *Novo Jornal*'s reporter Sebastião Vemba, in less than twenty-four hours the Provincial Government organized a convoy of trucks from the Casa Militar (the military office in the presidency) and forced everyone on board. A woman whose baby had just died was forced to embark on one of the trucks with her baby's corpse. Alongside her were thousands of adults and children with all the belongings they were able to salvage not only from the destruction of the tides but also from the destruction of their homes by the brigades of the Casa Militar. The island's inhabitants were moved to Zango, a drive of about two hours to the southeast of the city, and placed in a camp with tents, in the rain, with no schools for the children and far removed from their places of work.[2] A few months after the relocation, the then governor of Luanda, Francisca do Espírito Santo, announced that the cleared area on Ilha de Luanda would form part of a larger project to create a variety of leisure facilities for the city. Since then, a vast sidewalk has been built to accommodate restaurants, bars, and other ventures catering to Luanda's nightlife. Part of the area cleared was later claimed by the redevelopment of the Bay of Luanda, discussed in chapter 1. In total, 700 families were moved out of the area. Only in 2016 did a group of around 100 families "receive plots of land for self-help building in an area that is managed by the Provincial Government, referred to by locals as *Ilha Seca* ('dry island'),"[3] while the vast majority remained in tents, a provisional situation that has now become permanent. In this manner, the response to a "natural disaster" became an alibi for forced relocation.[4]

I have shown since the beginning of this book that there has never been anything extraordinary about forced removals, and that those traumatic events have been conceived, before and after independence, as a mundane technique for *ordenamento do território* (land management). But those that started around 2005 were of a different nature. It was not simply a matter of removing squatters, or residents who in the eyes of urban authorities were illegally occupying land. Nor was it a way to consolidate the urban grid as during the height of the modernist interventions. Those removals were part of a major urban upheaval through which a reconstruction-oriented government was attempting to undo the marks of the civil war and poor management of the city. But to do so, urban solutions such as the implementation of master plans as a mechanism and tools for urban management would not be enough. Politics would have to come in; and it did, taking the form of a total reconfiguration of state-society relations.

In 1992, Angola shed ties with the communist orthodoxy and embraced neoliberalism. In 2010, a new constitution that anointed absolute presidentialism was approved. The two decades between these landmark events are crucial in understanding not only the overcoming of colonial urbanization, caught up in the divide between the center and the periphery, but also the coming into being of a new form of urbanism. Urban theorists have come up with several concepts to make sense of similar formations, such as "bypass-implant urbanism," "splintering urbanism," or the "urbanism of exception,"[5] but

Figure 6.I. Aerial view of Luanda, 1992. Source: John Liebenberg.

none of them provides a theoretical framework that encompasses those urban transformations occurring in Luanda.

Urban transformation in Luanda was of an eminent political nature because it went hand in hand with the increasing interference of the presidency of the republic, and the president himself, in the city's matters, through the creation of numerous organs to compete with the provincial urban authorities. A significant part of the urban upheaval, more specifically the construction of housing and infrastructure, was put under the Programa de Reconstrução Nacional, which was controlled by entities under the direct supervision of the president of the republic. The formation and insertion of those organs into the fabric of the state is the by-product of sweeping reconfigurations of political power, particularly the role of the president of the republic in relation to other branches of the government and the administration. This was achieved through the reconfirmation of formal and informal presidentialism, which allowed the president of the republic to claim prerogatives that should have been distributed among other bodies of the state, such as the Ministry of Finance and the Provincial Government of Luanda.

The Luanda that emerged out of these interventions is now a far cry from the one with the center-periphery divide of the 1970s. The construction of

centralidades and *urbanizações*—such as Nova Vida, Zango, and Kilamba—
changed Luanda's geometry dramatically. Luanda is no longer a city encircled by *musseques* but a historic center encircled by other centers, which are
still encircled by informal settlements. These transformations came about
with a major corollary. One the one hand, there has been the emergence
of a sort of bifurcated urbanism, in which the well-to do and the middle
class partake and engage in market-based relations (they can buy and sell
land, for instance), which, as I showed earlier, was the motivation for the
emergence of Luanda Sul. On the other, places such as Zango came about,
with houses—mostly devoid of formal market value—given to removed populations. My argument is not that these two categories are frozen, or even
interchangeable. The point is rather that these societal arrangements, the
bifurcation of the urban, are the by-product of the inscription of power on
space: the more the urban expanded, through the emergence of *centralidades*
and *urbanizações*, the more power tended to gravitate around the central
government. This is for the most part how the urban has been unraveling in
present-day Luanda.

Figure 6.2. A Chinese worker taking a break during the construction of Kilamba, 1992.
Source: Michael MacGarry.

Bifurcating the Urban

During the electoral campaign for the first elections since the end of the civil war, in 2008, the then president of the Republic of Angola, José Eduardo dos Santos, pledged the construction of one million houses in Luanda.[6] The ruling party won these elections in a landslide, and dos Santos reiterated the promise at various other events, particularly in October 2008, during the visit to Luanda of Anna Kamujulo Tibaijuka, who at the time was the undersecretary-general and executive director of the United Nations Human Settlements Programme (UN-Habitat). In a speech prepared for the occasion, dos Santos added some more detail on the government's urban renewal and housing strategy, whose scope and shape were up to that point unknown to the general public. For dos Santos, such a critical overhaul of Luanda's urban landscape would be delivered in the form of the implementation of policies, relying on the contribution of "capitais públicos e privados" (public and private capital), whose ultimate objective was the production of "espaços públicos de qualidade, na requalificação e revitalização dos centros urbanos: com inclusão social" (public spaces of quality, in the requalification and renewal of urban centers with social inclusion), through the elaboration of master and municipal plans, that "compreendendo e definindo uma estratégia deste territórios e da rede urbana, não só nas suas vertentes social e económica, mas também na sua interacção com os sectores agrícola, industrial, de logística, turismo e infraestruturas aeroportuárias, ferroviárias, e outras" (comprehend and define a strategy of these territories and the urban network, not only on this social and economic aspect, but also in its interaction with the agricultural, industrial, logistic, touristic and infrastructural sectors). These sets of interventions were, among others, buttressed by "da maximização da utilização do transporte públicos e serão incentivas politica que diminuam a circulação automóvel nos centros dos aglomerados urbanos, em especial nas áreas notáveis do ponto de vista histórico-cultural ou ambiental" (the maximization of the utilization of public transport so as to diminish automobile use in the urban centers, especially in those areas of historic-cultural and environmental interest).[7] For the materialization of such a vision, dos Santos offered the calculation that his government was willing to disburse US$50 million at the average of US$50,000 per house, in the next four years, until 2012. In the following years, the government embarked on a construction frenzy to reach its objectives.

It was with the purpose of making room for the construction of housing, partly to fulfill this electoral promise, that the government was undertaking the massive clearings, an example of which I discussed earlier in this chapter. Of note in this spate of evictions was that informal settlements were being cleared to allow for the construction not simply of high-end condominiums but also of social housing, whose beneficiaries were in similar economic circumstances as those who were being moved out. I call this process the bifurcation of the urban. To understand the impact of this process on urban transformation, one needs to engage with the reconfiguration of the political system. This system is, in part, reminiscent of what Partha Chatterjee has called "the politics of the governed" to make sense of the surplus society that capitalism in India has produced, a society whose members struggle to find their place in the market-driven economy and who are for the most part administered through governmental agencies.[8]

One of the most important axioms of the socialist regime was the interchangeability of the state and the citizenry. Ownership of housing during these years was buttressed by these principles in the sense that what belonged to the state belonged to the people, and the state properly speaking, with its apparatus and resources, was merely a custodian of the people's property. Squatters who had moved to the city center in the 1970s were not conscious of the fact that they were tenants of the state, but the larger mindset was that they were simply occupying houses left behind by the *colonos* (colonizers). This order of things started to change with the shift to neoliberalism, particularly when it came to the land question. The neoliberal, market-driven constitution approved in 1992 introduced the conceptual split between the state and the people by stating strongly that land belongs to the state (Art. 12). The Lei dos Direitos de Superfície (Law of Surface Rights), discussed in the previous chapter, which created the legal and regulatory framework for the emergence of Luanda Sul, was a translation of this constitutional principle in that it formalized the conditions by which citizens, and particularly investors, could have access to land. They could only benefit from land for a given amount of time stipulated by the state, which could repossess it if those users failed to render it profitable.

However, at the end of the civil war, in 2002, there was a shift into authoritarianism with strong implications for the ways in which land was accessed and how people had access to it. Angola held the first multiparty elections, in 1992, as a semipresidential regime in which the president of the republic was the head of the state, while the prime minister was the head of the government. These elections did not produce a winner, and the country was soon immersed in a more destructive cycle of civil war. To more effectively and expeditiously end to the war, the president of the republic, dos Santos, abolished the office of the prime minister in 1998 and became both head of the state and head of the government. With the end of the civil war, the political system did not enter into a process of democratic normalization, but dos Santos would use his accrued powers to formalize a state of emergency as a way to put the country onto the path of progress.

It was under this framework that the murky and constitutionally questionable Programa de Reconstrução Nacional (Program for National Reconstruction) was devised. Devasted by the long civil war, the Angolan government approached international donors for funding to rebuild infrastructure that had been destroyed by the conflict. International donors conditioned the loans on the democratization of the country. The government then turned to China, which was at that point upping the sophistication of its model of loaning money for infrastructure rehabilitation.[9] In 2004, Angola and China signed the framework agreement for a strategic public-private partnership, which became law under the Resolução 31/04. Under this partnership, Angola supplied oil to China, and the oil was converted into lines of credit to finance the operations of Chinese companies in Angola involved in the voluminous dossier on reconstruction.[10]

But there is far more to it. Whereas this oil-backed loan was facilitated by the Export-Import Bank of China and managed in Angola by the Ministry of Finance, the Angolan government, more specifically the presidency of the republic, opened another credit line of over US$10 billion through the China International Fund (CIF), which was directly managed by the Gabinete de Reconstrução Nacional (Office for National Reconstruction, GRN), under the direct oversight of the president of the republic.[11] The head of the GRN was General Hélder Vieira Dias, also known as Kopelipa, who was a member of dos Santos's inner circle, minister of state, and head of the Casa Civil da Presidência. The GRN has never publicly shared any information on the funds it received and used, but it has been calculated that at the height of program activity the GRN could have been managing a portfolio of around US$15 billion.[12]

Having this shadow war chest at his disposal allowed dos Santos to insulate himself from the government and implement his own semiprivate political agenda. It is worth noting, in this regard, that the same year that the framework agreement was signed with China and that the GRN was constituted, 2004, is also the year the Lei de Terras de Angola was approved. One cannot overstate how these three legal arrangements are imbricated and related to each other. For the implementation of the Programa de Reconstrução Nacional was buttressed by the existence of not only an authoritarian mindset to drive it but also one that could produce its legal and regulatory conditions. The Lei de Terras de Angola was received with enormous excitement on the part of the civil society and NGOs working on land issues because of the expectation that it would finally clarify the various blind spots, not only across different legal regimes (the constitutional law and the Civil Code) but also in the gap between the letter of the law and the practice of urban authorities. Unlike previous acts, either colonial or postcolonial, it was the first land act to specifically address urban land. But, this legal formulation, which crystalizes various other documents, procedures, and intentions and painstakingly defines land ownership, would soon became a matter of concern for civic organizations involved with the land question.

On the one hand, the Lei de Terras de Angola reaffirmed the primordial right of the state over land and establishes and formalizes the conditions under which private individuals and investors can access land. On the other hand, and more important, it created a sort of bifurcation of the land structure. Parallel to the domain of marketable land, there was another domain of land being extricated from market relations, which took the name Reservas Fundiárias do Estado. Article 27, on land reserves, establishes that "são havidos como terrenos reservados ou reservas os terrenos excluídos do regime geral de ocupação, uso ou fruição por pessoas singulares singulares ou colectivas, em função da sua afectação, total or parcial, à realização de fins especiais que determinam a sua constituição" (reserved land or reserves are those tracts of land excluded from the general regime of occupation, use or fruition, by individuals or legal persons, by virtue of its affectation, total or partial, to the realization of the ends that their constitution determines).[13] Included in this regime are stretches of maritime land; the protection of land for dams; the land in the vicinity of infrastructure, such as railways, roads, and bridges, as well as airports; and land confined within military bases and other structures for the protection of the state.[14]

As the juridical system in Angola is aligned with Roman jurisprudence, it is the Anglo-Saxon juridical figure of eminent domain—which allows authorities to transfer private land to the public domain, subject to compensation—that bears closer resemblance to the Reservas, although with notable caveats. With land already being public, by virtue of the constitution, Reservas were conceived as the legal instrument that allowed for the transfer of land from the public domain of the state to the private domain of the state, which came with two fundamental corollaries. On the one hand, the government was free to pursue removals and relocations of those using the state's private land and, on the other, the government could cut off land, divert it from public use, to realize projects of national interest, such as the construction of housing and infrastructure. These political-legal transformations allowed the government to claim an unprecedented hold on urban land, and they were at the heart of the state-led transformation reviewed below.

None of the above-mentioned legal articulations seem outrageous, or even specific, and one would find parts of it, in various iterations, in most legal systems in the world. The particularity of the scope of this disposition of

the law is that most Reservas have been determined after the fact so as to justify clearing the land from informal housing and subsistence farms. Through
the decree 87/08 by which the government has decided to "implementar um
conjunto de investimentos públicos e estruturantes" (implement an array of
strategic and structuring public investment), it transferred "do domínio público para o domínio do Estado" (from the public to the private domain of the
state) various urban plots, for the purpose of building housing projects. Those
tracts of land comprised areas from urban districts such as Sambizanga, Cazenga, Benfica, Bairro Operário, and Boavista. It is difficult to determine the
exact amount of land transferred to the private domain of the state in Luanda,
more so as the area and limits of the city have changed over time and the city
has been absorbing land from its surrounding semiurban and rural areas since
independence. However, by 2009-10 the overall area of Luanda was about 116
square kilometers, with the metropolitan area comprising a territory of about
18,000 square kilometers. From this it is safe to infer that whereas from the
Cidade de Luanda only a small fraction was added to the Reservas—namely,
the section of Bairro Operário Boavista, in Sambizanga—the overall area of the
Reservas combined, most of which lies outside Cidade de Luanda, occupies an
area three times larger than Luanda's historic center (map. 6.2).[15]

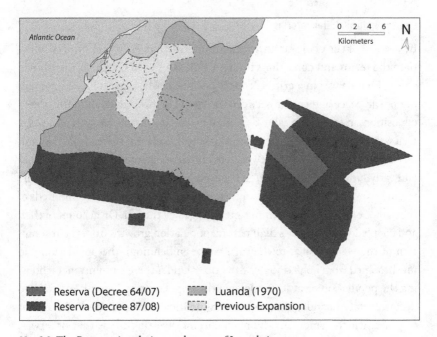

Map 6.2. The Reservas in relation to the area of Luanda in 1970.

Since the Reservas are an instrument that allows the state to transfer plots of land from its public to its private domain, or to withdraw land from circulation, they have contributed to the bifurcation of the urban. For instance, whereas Article 7 puts an emphasis on the "não exércicio ou pela inobservância dos indíces the aproveitamento útil e efectivo (lack of use and disregard for the utilitarian and effective use of the land), whose lack of observation is considered a reason for dispossession to the benefit of the state, other sections of the law seem to allow the state to demonetize land.[16] However, this land bifurcation does not necessarily produce a bifurcation of citizenship, or a sort of citizen-subject split as famously theorized by Mahmood Mamdani.[17] For social regimes and repertoires that preside over the transfer and circulation of land are too complex to be cast under these categories. I have met Luandans who have been given houses in Zango, who then sold them so as to purchase shacks in Boavista, precisely the place they had been removed from, so as to be given another house in Zango.[18] The rationale for this architecture of power, as Sylvia Croese has persuasively argued, is the reliance of the ruling power on the poor, not for "tax collection or labor" but for "political legitimacy and social stability."[19] This produces a system in which the ruling party expects the loyalty of the population in exchange for the houses and other amenities directly given to the population.

Centering through Decentering

By the end of the civil war, in 2002, around the time Angola started to negotiate the terms and conditions for a possible loan with China, as mentioned above, Luanda was in a critical condition. The clashes that followed the failure of the peace agreement between the Angolan government and the armed opposition, in 1992, were more destructive than any other moment of the long civil war. As was the case since independence, Luanda was spared from the military destruction, beyond the few days of military confrontation in late October and early November. However, the consequences of the war were profoundly felt in Luanda, as the capital became the country's main shelter for hundreds of thousands of people fleeing from zones ravaged by the war. On account of that, and coupled with the city's high natural population growth, from the resumption of the war, in 1992, to the turn of the millennium, the population had mushroomed from 1,698,000 to 2,829,000.[20] Under these circumstances, housing the population or at least allowing the population to house itself, so as to deconcentrate Luanda, became a crucial political endeavor. With the advent of peace, which came with the possibility of diverting funds that otherwise would be spent in the war effort, the *ordenamento do território* became a priority among urban authorities. Since early on, there was the firm conviction among urban authorities that the most deleterious effects of land management could be addressed through the elaboration of a master plan to tackle pressing issues such as infrastructure, improving electricity distribution and circulation, and housing. None of the planning initiatives I discuss below have ever been even partially implemented as I have demonstrated earlier. But the way they have come to be conceived, the agencies they involve, the rifts among agencies they stir, says much about the messiness of planning that has been addressed in African urban scholarship. Vanessa Watson and Richard Satgé, for instance, have used the term "conflicting rationalities" to make the case for the "divergence between state and community positions" in regard to planning implementation.[21] For the case of Luanda, it reveals the depth of political reconfiguration and the instruments that were deemed necessary for the implementation of the Programa de Reconstrução Nacional. Ultimately, it shows the increasing grip on the city from which dos Santos's entourage came to benefit.

In the mid-1990s, the Lebanese firm Dar Al-Handasah, also registered in Angola as the Dar Group, was approached to produce a study on urban growth. The team of consultants that Dar assembled for the task was asked to establish the ground rules and procedures to control, discipline, and manage the expansion of the city. In the various documents and reports they produced, they paid particular attention to the urban land question, for they seemed to be convinced that land ownership was the main culprit for the failure of the various planning initiatives the city had entertained. It was common that land targeted for development was progressively occupied by emerging *musseques*, an issue that could only be solved with the improvement of land regulatory regimes.[22] Taking further urban population growth as inevitable, the consultants proposed an approach that would consist of, on the one hand, the reordering of the city center and, on the other, the upgrading of the *musseques*.

To accommodate Luanda's growing population, Dar's consultants suggested the creation of a zone of urban expansion in the hinterland to the north of the city, integrating parts of the neighboring province of Bengo into Luanda's metropolitan area. While the central government was promoting the expansion of the city to the south, as seen in the previous chapter, Dar was making an alternative case for the opening of the northern sectors of Luanda to urbanization, and Dar even pushed for the construction of three satellite cities there: Sassa Bengo for 1,800,000 inhabitants, and Coastal City and Catete for 100,000 people each. Yet, taking up another tip from the French OTAM (Ominium Technique d'Aménagement [Technical Consortium for Planning]) plan prepared for the colonial authorities in 1973, Dar's *Integrated Plans* suggested limiting the expansion of the city to 17 million hectares (about 42 million acres, or a density of one hundred persons per hectare for a population of 1.7 million) and proposed to accommodate the growth of the city in three new cities, Viana, Cacuaco, and Camama.[23] Undeveloped land for agricultural and leisure purposes should enclose the city, so as to improve its environment and protect it against the mushrooming of informal settlements. Having this expansion as a guiding principle, Dar's planners analyzed three major scenarios, or alternatives, that would be better suited to address urban growth. The first one was called "Concentrated New Development Independent of the Existing Urban Center of Luanda" and was based on the plan for the new city of Kilamba, which was already being designed through the planning firm Shanghai Tongji Planning and Design Institute. The objective of this scenario was to allow for the emergence of other central nodes that would not only deconcentrate Luanda's historical center but also provide more services to the population, particularly those who lived outside the center. This was also the scenario that the firm was more sympathetic toward, for the area concerned was confined between two major rivers, the Kwanza and the Bengo, which created physical limits for expansion. The second scenario analyzed, "Concentric Peripheral Growth Pattern," was meant to take advantage of the circular highway, the Via Expressa, opened in 2008, which was about 60 kilometers (37 miles) long. One of the merits of this scenario was that it put brakes on the growth of the city center by restricting physical growth to the outskirts of town, "by limiting the outward physical spread."[24] The third scenario, called "Outward Growth and Optimization of Land Occupation," emphasized the reordering of the city through the construction of key connections and an integrated transportation system that would better link the peripheries to the center.

Looking closely into Dar's massive document, one easily glimpses the difficulty of its application. The consultants' work was being done under the auspices of the Provincial Government, but the scope of planning transcended the limits of the province itself. They were pushing for the reorganization of the entire province by recommending the superseding of the then current administrative division, one in which the city was divided up into *bairros*, for one in which Luanda was composed of nine districts. They were perhaps trying to come to terms with a representation of Luanda in which all the new and informal settlements would be comprised within the scope of a formal urban plan. The key for the functioning of the order they were proposing was decentering the city center through the emergence of other centers that would strive for autonomy. They correctly diagnosed that the poor implementation of planning in Luanda was caused by an ineffective municipal structure, which was broken up into six municipal areas rather than a single citywide government body with the power to make strategic citywide decisions," insofar as "it is clear that the scale of growth has outpaced the development of related infrastructure, and with growth set to continue at 6% per annum, [it] will continue to require infrastructure, with related services and facilities."[25] To overcome the capacity insufficiency, Dar Al-Handasah consultants recommended the establishment of an Urban Development Commission by the GPL, with the participation of central government ministries and consultant partners. Referred to as the Luanda Urban Development Commission (CUDL) this body would have responsibility for policy, planning, administration, infrastructure rehabilitation/maintenance, and service delivery.[26] For this to happen, Dar recognized that the scale of the interventions it was proposing went beyond the capacity of Luanda's Provincial Government, and one of the recommendations of the plans was the "creation of [an] Institutional Framework capable of managing an Urban Sector Development Strategy [USDS]," through "the establishment of an Urban Development Renewal Board (UDRB) or equivalent, provided with the powers to implement the USDS and the development of urban development and renewal regulations."[27] The UDRB should be a "Central Government Body responsible for the coordination and execution of construction projects within Luanda," and only directly accountable to the Council of Ministers. Furthermore, the *Integrated Plans* considered that the head of this body should have ministerial status, and that the UDRB's budget should be independent from both the Ministry of Public Works and the Provincial Government.[28] In other words, Dar was suggesting a more centralized process, preferably out of the hands of the city's regulatory body, to control the city's administration.

Presented in the form of a thousand-odd-page document, *Integrated Plans of Urban and Infrastructure Expansion of Luanda/Bengo* was approved by the Council of Ministers in 2011.[29] However, this plan was sidelined, and the main reason was not simply the rift between the Provincial and the National Government, or which institution should conduct the process, as Ricardo Cardoso seems to argue.[30] Such a stance is not incorrect, but it needs to be put in a larger context that takes into account the transformations of the fabric of the state itself. Some of them have been already discussed earlier in this chapter, particularly the ones that refer to the land question and how it relates to the institutional reforms of 2004, with the approval of the China loan and the GRN. But others are of a deeply political nature and speak to the ways in which the president of the republic, dos Santos, came to have such a command over the city's transformation. Here again one needs to backtrack so as to grasp the political configurations from 1998 onward that I mentioned before.

The presidentialism that was coming into being was sanctified by the constitution of 2010, a document produced by dos Santos's entourage and approved by the National Assembly, rubberstamped by the majority MPLA National Assembly members. Even though the new constitution enshrined fundamental civic rights, such as the right to protest, it formalized the prerogatives that since 1998 dos Santos had been taking over from other institutions of the state apparatus. It also drastically changed the voting system, creating a system in which elected presidents governed like medieval monarchs but were not directly elected by voters. Rather, they automatically became the president of the republic by virtue of having their name on top of the list of the winning political party. What the Angolan constitutionalists had in mind was the South African model, where the president of the republic is elected along the same lines. The particularity of the Angolan case, as many critics have voiced, is the lack of a system of checks and balances.[31] Even though presidents govern almost single-handedly, they are not accountable and cannot be brought to justice or demoted. More alarmingly is that not having a system of local power in place (Angola has never held local elections), and with provincial and local authorities being appointed by the president of the republic—or appointed by those appointed by the president—deprives the provincial and local administrations from constituting a counterweight to central power. In this context, the rift that may pit the central against the Provincial Government does not have any significance. Major government portfolios, in the iteration of the 2010 constitution, are approved by the presidency of the republic as presidential decrees. Of importance is this regard is the frequent use of the term *Executivo* (Executive) to make sense of the separation between the central government and the presidency of the republic.

In this context, building the one million houses was conceived as a task that only the Executivo could perform, as it required the simplification of the tender system and the protection of an opacity that was deemed necessary for the implementation of the Programa de Reconstrução Nacional. It was, simply put, the institutionalization of the state of emergency, the one that came into being so as to put an end to the civil war. In this regard, Dar Group had accomplished a major task, which was an invitation to imagine what a decentralized expansion of urban Luanda could look like. But even if the legal framework the consultants proposed as the managerial apparatus of the master plan followed the lines of the neoliberal doctrine—in which public prerogatives are transferred to private institutions—they still conceived the Provincial Government of Luanda as the epicenter of the operations. However, as in many other aspects of Angolan political life in which vital administrative portfolios were being transferred to the presidency of the republic, Cidade Alta became the purveyor of urban transformation.

None of these events unfolded overnight and all were part of dos Santos's strategy to encompass power, which, as I have sketched in the previous chapter, consisted, first of all, of the creation of parallel organizations to duplicate the work that the formal ones were performing and, eventually, replace the formal ones by the parallel ones. For even though the Ministry of Territorial Administration had published an executive decree in 2004 (Executive Decree 102/04) giving the provincial government "the responsibility for ensuring and controlling the development of Luanda in all sectors,"[32] in the same year the central government once again demoted a provincial governor and appointed an administrative commission as replacement. Moreover, in the following year, the central government created two parallel organisms, namely the Comissão para o Desenvolvimento de Luanda (Luanda Urban Development Commission) and, later, the Grupo Técnico (GATEC), which took over some of the responsibilities of the GPL, such as the "rehousing of the communities living in the areas scheduled for projects of social impact."[33]

It is under these all-encompassing political reconfigurations that one may more positively grasp the scope and dimensions of the urban transformation ushered in from the first decade of the twenty-first century onward. With changes in the electoral system and the redistribution of power and prerogatives among the various branches of the government, dos Santos and his Executive were then free to approve the most outrageous pieces of legislation and conduct the most criminal evictions with no concern that such moves would hinder dos Santos's prospect of being reelected. Furthermore, dos Santos was also given free rein to do things the way it pleased him. He deemed the GPL unsuited and incapable of managing the city's urban planning process, and, bringing this task to the Executive, he appointed his own daughter, Isabel dos Santos, as the head of the master planning consortium. Dubbed the richest woman in Africa, Isabel dos Santos assembled, through her real estate company, Urbinvest, a conglomerate of firms and entities to produce the Plano Director Geral Metropolitano de Luanda (Metropolitan Plan for Luanda; PDGML). These entities included the British architectural firm Broadway Malyan and the South African consulting engineering company Aurecon, and for data collection, the planning effort relied on researchers affiliated with the Portuguese Universidade Nova de Lisboa (New University of Lisbon).

Any doubt about who was in control of Luanda's urban overhaul was dispelled by the official presentation of the master plan, which, in itself, was an enactment of the theater of power behind the new constitutional order. The venue for the launch, on December 15, 2015, was not the headquarters of the Council of Ministers or any venue in the presidential palace, nor a convention center, but the noble room of the Provincial Government of Luanda itself. This gesture is of more significance as it occurred by the time another governor of Luanda had been sacked by dos Santos and replaced by an administrative commission led by a lawyer, Graciano Domingos, whose presence in the act was not as a representative of Luandans but as a facilitator of the transfer of planning oversight to Urbinvest and its associates. The ceremony, part of a two-day meeting, was chaired by the president of the republic himself and attended by all his staff members. In a city where the governor had just been dismissed, it was an indication that the central government was in charge. The new rules of articulation between the national and the Provincial Government were unsurprisingly introduced by Carlos Feijó, an advisor to the president, who has been credited not only as the main architect of the "atypical" constitution of 2010 but also as a broker of the expansion of presidential power in the city.[34] Feijó is also behind the formation of several technical groups and commissions that came to usurp the powers of the Provincial Government. On this occasion, Feijó said once again that it was the position of the national government that the province of Luanda did not have the capacity to solve the innumerable technical problems it faced and that the city should rather be governed by a technical commission. This view was consistent with the positions taken in the plans of both Dar and dos Santos, which argued for a model of governance outside the purview of the local government. The way was thus paved for Isabel dos Santos to introduce her own program for saving Luanda. Unsurprisingly, the vision of Luanda Isabel dos Santos expounded in front of her father's cabinet was strikingly similar to the broad strokes of Luanda's transformation that President dos Santos had elaborated in the meeting with the UN-Habitat representative Anna Tibaijuka. It was not simply that Isabel dos Santos was voicing her father's vision of Luanda's future. It was also that "fantasy urbanism" was an ubiquitous resource that any authoritarian regime could appropriate.[35] Giving substance to these fantasies, Isabel dos Santos spelled out that Luanda's urban transformation would be anchored in three pillars. The first one, "Livable Luanda," pertained to the provision of the services and facilities that the city needed. Accordingly, a habitable city should include neighborhoods that enabled people to live close to their workplaces so that they could get there on foot or by using public transport. The second pillar was called "Beautiful Luanda," and here the priority lay with "protecting and enhancing the city's natural resources."[36] This was also explained as a way of linking the past with the future, for Luanda was once considered "one of the most beautiful cities in the world." The third pillar, called "Strategic Luanda," was concerned with promoting economic growth and diversification of the economy. Here, the point was to turn Luanda into a dynamic city, a city for the youth, located in the center of Africa and the world.[37]

The PDGML acknowledged the importance of the *Integrated Plans* proposed by Dar and used it as an "initial base standard" but chastised it for its lack of ambition and "reserve[d] the right to elevate this (at times) modest target to something more appropriate to a key world capital city."[38] To drive this urban agenda of uncompromising scope, the organigram behind the planning initiative was substantially altered. Master planning managers would no longer report to the Provincial Government of Luanda but to the presidency of the republic. In that sense, Dar's consultants were right when they suggested that the Provincial Government of Luanda did not have technical capacity to meet the challenges of implementing a master plan on the scale of the province of Luanda. Whereas the *Integrated Plans* introduced for the first time the notion of Luanda's metropolitan area, which consisted of the province of Luanda and a few municipalities of the neighboring province, Bengo, the PDGML practically fused the provinces of Luanda and Bengo, which together occupied an area of about 522.1 hectares (1290.13 acres). Planning at such a scale also meant that details would be subsumed into the larger vision that the master plan strived to achieve.

But the presidency of republic did not have the technical capacity to implement a plan on such a scale. The upshot of the master plan was that by the time the PDGML was introduced to Luandans, the presidency of the republic was already in control of the technical instruments for assembling structures for the refurbishment of Cidade Alta, which could be easily amplified so as to transform Luanda. Whereas for Dar's consultants, the core of planning inaction was fundamentally the land question, which signals that Dar's intervention was still limited to the realm of the urban, the PDGML made a different assessment, less urban and more fundamentally political, in tandem with the political reconfigurations discussed above. In reviewing the institutional framework of the province of Luanda, the PDGML's consultants came to the conclusion that the reason for inaction was the "number of competing entities . . . charged with implementing different elements of the presidential decree 59/11, although no single government body was implicitly empowered to command and manage the process," which, "given the scope and scale of the task at hand," needed to change.[39] The PDGML's consultants also recommended the creation of an independent institution to manage the implementation of the master plan, the Regeneration and Urban Authority of Luanda.[40] However, contrary to Dar's position, in the PDGML, this institution reported directly to the presidency of the republic, more specifically the Casa Civil, rather than the Provincial Government of Luanda.

Further arguments for the similarities of José Eduardo dos Santos's vision and Isabel dos Santos's plan were the political scope of the intervention they each proposed. Nepotism does not single-handedly explain such a communion of interests, but it explains the channels of communication between José Eduardo's philosophy of power and Isabel's acumen for turning an abstract vision into business opportunities or, in this case, practical realizations. For at stake here was no longer planning for land use or infrastructure provision. Instead, the PDGML was attempting to plan society itself. Isabel dos Santos may have often insisted that the PDGML was the outcome of a thorough process of public consultation, but it relies heavily on the availability of previous documentation that supersedes the technical domain of planning itself and takes stock of the discussions among political strategists on how to assemble society in a way that consolidates the undisputed rule of the ruling party for at least the next four decades.[41] Not surprisingly, the document states that the plan "covers all matters relating to housing, transport, education, health and environment. It delivers centrally managed and funded initiatives undertaken in liaison with the National Government institutions for each discipline."[42] It does this in many ways, particularly by integrating suggestions and recommendations from previous planning interventions and by drawing on reports commissioned by the government on how to bring about social change, in particular the voluminous *Angola Strategy 2025* report (also known as Angola Horizon 2025).[43] The plan admits that these documents, and many others, such as the Angolan Development Plan 2013–2017 and the Provincial Development Plan 2013–2017, "were integrated into a unique vision for the local development of the province until 2030."[44]

It is through the lenses of these political and social arrangements that the land question, under the formulation proposed through the reserves, should be revisited. Dar's plans carefully mention the possibility of "expropriation by a public utility."[45] Conversely, by the time Isabel dos Santos presented her vision on the urban yet to come, the political terrain in which institutions operated had already shifted. For by December 2015, all the shenanigans regarding land use that could require negotiation had already been superseded. If, prior to 2010, the Angolan government was concerned with removing squatters and illegals from the city under the constraints of the land-related legal regime that allowed those with tenure to claim compensation, after 2010 this was for the most part not the case. For the plan unceremoniously contemplated the "removal of unlicensed developments from open land,"[46] and it stated that "displaced households will be subsumed into areas licensed for new residential centralities, established with appropriate service provision."[47] Planning could then take place after the fact: "Where future roads and utility infrastructure is planned existing residents will need to be relocated and rehoused."[48] This only furthered the bifurcation of the urban, in that it created the conditions for more removal and more groups of the population under the whim of the government in order to access habitation.

Urban Intentions: The Conditions for Things to Come

The critique of grandiloquent planning initiatives in the Global South has been undertaken by a number of scholars who have located such gestures in an urban theorization in which local democratic process, or the idea of the state as the purveyor of the common good, is superseded, and the process of urban transformation is taken over by international coalitions—for instance, by global consultancy firms.[49] More specifically, the vision that President dos Santos was intimating for Luanda's geographic expansion on that day of October 2008, and that was corroborated more assertively in Isabel dos Santos's master plan, could easily have been plucked from the modernist master plans Watson has derogatorily called, "African urban fantasies."[50] Tailored for the tastes of an emerging middle and upper class in Africa, these fantasy plans are, according to Watson, dreams that offer "environments that are (hyper) modern, high status, clean and well-serviced."[51] Furthermore, even though many of these anticipations of urban futures "may or may not materialize or may be implemented in part,"[52] as Watson suggests, the result is the unevenness they produce on the urban, epitomized by urban fragmentation and urban discontinuity, in the form of enclaves, fortifications, and enclosures. The urban formations that have been extensively examined in the urban literature and given concepts such as "splintered urbanism" or "urbanism of exception" may effortlessly be deployed to describe Luanda's fragmentation through the emergence of *urbanizações* and *centralidades* such as Talatona. However, to fully grasp the unfolding of these sorts of fragmentation in the context of Luanda, precepts of a critical urban theory unable to grapple with local contingencies may not be of use. More than the urban properly speaking per se, urban transformation in Luanda is anchored in political transformation, and particularly in shifts in state-society relations.

Even though the planning initiatives discussed above have not been implemented, they nonetheless have left enduring effects. On a more practical and expedient level, both the Dar Group and Isabel dos Santos's conglomerates were awarded tenders to construction of infrastructure or housing in the plans they were elaborating.[53] As such, I would like to suggest that the accuracy in reading the expansion of present-day Luanda, from the first decade of the twenty-first century onward, can only be understood through that which was proposed and not concretized, the same way I have earlier in this book made the case that one can only understand Luanda's modernization, in the early 1940s, through that which was proposed by de Gröer and Moreira da Silva. But what may be of even greater importance is engaging with the process that accompanied these planning initiatives, for they speak of mechanisms of power, the functioning of the institutions they mobilize, and the necessary shifting in regulatory frameworks. In sum, despite the lack of technical capacity to implement the proposed initiatives, they nonetheless are shaped by and create the conditions for things to come.

Even if these plans did not directly anticipate the emergence of some of the most famous *centralidades* and *urbanizações*, such Nova Vida, Kilamba, and Zango, the ideas and concepts they represented, and the institutions and resources they mobilized, certainly created the conditions for the expansion of the city far beyond the historic center. Their coming into being is caught up with, intersected by, and produced by the interplay of the institutions and the repertoires I have discussed in this chapter

When the construction of the development project Projecto Nova Vida (New Life Project) started in 1999, it was announced as the implementation of a new philosophy of urbanization. Nova Vida took the form of a gigantic gated community located about 18 kilometers (11 miles) to the south of the city center and between two major roads, the Estrada do Camama-Talatona and Comandante Loy. Covering an area of about 182 hectares (450 acres), the whole project involved the construction of 10,000 units, in various phases. In the first phase, which took place from 2001 to 2005, 2,000 units—single-family dwellings and apartment buildings—were built. In the second phase, up to 2007, 1,862 units were added to Nova Vida.[54] But the agreement with China was not yet on the government agenda, and the focus was the implementation of an urban development project along the lines of neoliberal precepts. For whereas the project was initially intended to accommodate civil servants and war veterans, it was the first time the government was coming to terms with a rent-to-purchase scheme, which would allow renters to claim property ownership after twenty years of regular rental payments.[55] However, signs of presidential interference into urban issues were already creeping in. The construction of this *urbanização* was managed by the Brigada de Construções e Obras Militares (Brigade for Construction of Military Works), directly controlled by the presidency of the republic.

Figure: 6.3. A street in Kilamba, 2004. Source: Sylvia Croese.

The construction of Zango shows more emphatically not only the planning anxiety that was permeating the city's expansion but also, because of the time it spans, the shift in urban policies from autoconstruction to forced accommodation. It shows more forcefully what I have earlier called the bifurcation of the urban. Whereas Nova Vida was driven by the forces of the market, Zango was initially conceived as a zone of relocation, where those taken forcefully from various parts of Luanda, such as Ilha de Luanda, as I mentioned at the start of this chapter, were sent to. By the time three children died in Boavista, after heavy rains produced landslides, in September 2000, authorities started to resettle Boavista's residents to Zango, which was later declared a Reserva. Zango, which covers an area of 90 square kilometers (about 60 square miles), is situated 30 kilometers (18 miles) southeast of Luanda.[56] In the following months, a few thousand more of Luanda's residents would be forcefully relocated to Zango.

By the time the first relocated residents arrived in Zango, in early 2003, there were several hundred recently built houses. During these early phases, urban authorities were hopeful that Zango could become a full-fledged *centralidade*, by the sheer effort of its newly relocated residents, according to the urban upgrading policies. The role of the government consisted in dividing up the plots and installing infrastructure, and the locals were expected to build their own houses.[57] Accordingly, the initial plan was to distribute plots of land to those relocated from the city and to allow them to build their own houses. However, because of the slow pace of the construction and the climate of popular insubordination these relocations were generating, the government commissioned Dar Al-Handasah to produce a master plan for the new *urbanização*, which would consist of four clusters of houses, referred to as Zango 1, 2, 3, and 4, "including all infrastructure and services necessary to turn Zango into a small city."[58] A Brazilian construction firm was also asked to build and install infrastructure for 10,000 residents.[59] Once developed, these areas passed to the control of the Provincial Government of Luanda, under the auspices of the Programa de Habitação Social (Program of Social Housing).[60]

Contrary to the intentions behind the inception of Talatona and to a lesser degree Nova Vida, Zango came into being as a scheme to relocate and provide housing for Luanda's poor residents, who were prevented by law from using these houses as an economic asset in that they could not sell or transfer them.[61] This interdiction did not obviously prevent the emergence of an active and robust informal housing market in Zango. But the success of the Zango experiment—that a considerable number of those relocated managed to rebuild their lives in the relocation zones—may have encouraged the government to use Zango as a sort of repository for those removed from the city center. It was in Zango, for instance, that houses were offered to those residents in the buildings in the city center at risk of collapse, such as the Cuca building.[62]

If the construction of Nova Vida was market-oriented, and if Zango can be considered a social housing project, it is the construction of Kilamba that bears more strongly the mark of the new political and urban order inaugurated with the constitution of 2010—particularly because Kilamba was only possible through the China financing scheme. In this regard, Kilamba is unapologetically an offspring, or the material rendition, of the formalization of the state of emergency. Kilamba was built outside the framework of any city's master plan or outside the control and oversight of any locally based institution. The implementation of such a *centralidade* was a surprise even for those working on taming the city's disorderly urban growth, such as Dar's consultants. For they did not pass up the opportunity to address the construction of Kilamba toward the end of their study on Luanda's predicaments, which they deemed, "unrealistic, inadequate, unsustainable and possibly anti-constitutional."[63]

The intentions behind the conception of Kilamba and the role it was expected to play in Luanda's expansion are discernable in the choice of the name. The name Cidade do Kilamba (and not Cidade *de* Kilamba: in English Kilamba's City instead of City of Kilamba or Kilamba City) was given in homage to the first Angolan president, Agostinho Neto, who, by virtue of being a medical doctor, was given the nom de guerre Kilamba, which means "doctor" in the Angolan language Kimbundu. Perhaps in homage to his predecessor, himself a president, Kilamba became the urban project dos Santos and his Executive were more seriously involved with. With Kilamba, dos Santos intended not only to showcase the urban philosophy his government espoused but also to set the terms of his legacy, or how he wanted his intervention in the city to be remembered.[64]

Showcased as the epitome of the one million houses promised by the president, Kilamba was a central project in the immense portfolio of the construction of infrastructure and housing managed by the GRN, and it was by far the most complex and ambitious urban project built under the framework signed by Angola and China in 2004. The entire residential project was meant to house a population of 200,000, covering an area of 52 square kilometers (32 square miles), amounting to 900 hectares (2,223 acres), which, according to Viegas, was the area of Luanda's city center in the 1980s.[65] Constituting the largest urban project ever built from scratch, it was expected to add 20,000 residential apartments and 246 business units to Luanda's urban stock. The first cornerstone of the new city was laid in April 2008, and the first phase of the project was inaugurated by President dos Santos himself on July 11, 2011. Once completed, Kilamba was intended to be a fully-fledged district with twenty-four preschools, numerous primary schools, and eight high schools. It was also to be equipped with two electrical substations, seventy-seven transformer stations, water supply stations, a sewage treatment plant, and infrastructure for drainage.

A further proof of the personal investment of dos Santos in the construction and management of Kilamba is the controversy surrounding its occupation. Soon after the city's inauguration, the government tasked Delta Imobiliária, a private company, with administering the sale of the housing stock that was being made available in the real estate market. Delta Imobiliária then announced that the prices of the two- to four-bedroom apartments would range from US$150,000 to US$200,000. Initially, Kilamba failed to elicit the interest of potential buyers, to the extent that by June 2013, only 300 of the more than 3,000 available apartments had been sold. In the international press, Kilamba was being described as a ghost town and was compared with many others, particularly in China, that were scantly inhabited. This prompted a visit by President dos Santos himself, who ordered the decrease of prices for the units with immediate effect.[66] According to an executive decree published subsequently, the prices of the three-bedroom apartments were reduced to about US$70,000. Building on the Nova Vida Project, the government also announced a state-backed mortgage scheme, called at the time Renda Resolúvel (the possibility given to occupants to turn the payment of their rents into contributions toward acquiring the units), to be administered by the Fundo de Fomento Habitacional (Housing Development Fund), which allowed residents to pay for their apartments over a thirty-year period at a 3 percent fixed interest rate.[67] In practice, a family occupying a three-bedroom apartment would have to pay about US$300 a month, which was affordable for most middle-class families in Luanda.[68] To obtain units, prospective buyers would have to apply to SONIP's offices—the firm that took over the management of commercialization of property in Kilamba from GNR in 2013—to have their names placed on waiting lists that were published from time to time. Since thousands of people had spent days in the long queue to find that their names were not on the lists, accusations of lack of transparency and favoritism soon emerged.[69] Nonetheless, by September 2013, SONIP had concluded the selling process and announced that all the units had been sold. Yet thousands of people who had applied did not receive any units, even though they had met all the requirements. For many days, protesters gathered in front of the SONIP office, but to no avail.[70]

Nova Vida, Zango, and Kilamba are presented in this chapter as instantiations of the ways in which the urban, and particularly the housing question, has been dealt with. They show the gap between dream and reality in the sense that these urban developments were not part of any of the plans analyzed in this chapter. And yet it is undeniable that they have emerged and gained a life of their own. As I have mentioned earlier, despite the lack of technical capacity to implement the proposed plans, the plans were nonetheless shaped by, and created the conditions for, things to come. And vice versa: these specific housing projects did not result from overall master plans but were only possible and shaped by the same conditions that resulted in those plans. But they also show the extent to which the urban, particularly in relation to ownership, has been bifurcated. There are, on the one hand, those who have access to property through their own investments and savings, particularly those who can afford to buy land and acquire their title deeds. On the other hand, there are those for whom the only prospect for formal housing is social, through the various schemes fashioned by the government. These ways of living in the city are not static, as I have shown. But the social, or the social access to housing, is not simply reserved for the urban poor, for a considerable amount of housing in places such as Kilamba was distributed under various state-supported schemes.

. . .

At the height of the construction frenzy, which for obvious reasons coincided with the boom in the production of oil, with ups and downs from 2002 to 2014, Angolan urban authorities used to say that Luanda was a construction site. The Programa de Reconstrução Nacional was on the news regularly, and President dos Santos was always seen groundbreaking or dedicating infrastructure or facilities such hospitals and schools. For his preoccupation with overhauling the urban transformation, and, consequently, leaving his mark on the process, dos Santos has become known as as the Arquitecto da Paz (Architect of Peace). This descriptor points to two important features of dos Santos's legacy: as the one who ended the long civil war by pursuing Jonas Savimbi until his death, and as the one who played a critical role in urban transformation. For he certainly used the war machine he built over the years for the sake of the infrastructure and housing overhaul. It was not only his gigantic compound, the Futungo de Belas, that was given over for urban development (see chapter 5); it was also units of the military that were remobilized to build housing, or more expediently, to remove urban dwellers from areas targeted for renovation.

For populist and electoral reasons, these public ceremonies did not have to wait until the completion of construction, for construction projects were inaugurated in phases to allow the president to dedicate the same project on multiple occasions. For several major construction projects, such as Kilamba, only the first phase was dedicated, as there was no serious commitment to conclude the other phases. Furthermore, on account of the rashness and carelessness with which several projected constructions were implemented, and the lack of independent oversight, the quality of these projects has been called into question and has alarmed countless workers and residents. For instance, the Chinese-built Central Hospital of Luanda had to be evacuated when an imminent collapse was suspected, forcing the building's demolition in 2010.[71] A day does not pass without Kilamba residents complaining about the advancing degradation of their apartments because of leaks, fissures in the walls, and other structural problems. Just as there are several unfinished buildings in the city center, whose construction halted with the depreciation of oil prices, in the mid-2010s, a no less important and worrying number of urban projects will not be completed until an indeterminate date. Overall, Luanda as a construction site, which was meant to be transitory and a phase leading to a better urban future, has become for residents a permanent condition for inhabiting the city.

However, the incompleteness of infrastructure and construction projects does not hide the completeness of the overhaul of the urban form. Luanda today is postcolonial in the sense that urban categories such as city and periphery, which corresponded to the social categories of colonizer and colonized, no longer capture the breadth and the depth of what Luanda has become. The scale and the dimension of the urban expansion is such that colonial administrative categories such *bairros* are no longer of use for making sense of the city's geography and are superseded by *centralidades* and *urbanizações*, some of them, such as Zango and Kilamba, housing hundreds of thousands of residents.

It does not mean that the city has decentralized around the lines proposed by the planning interventions discussed in this chapter. Both master plans have made the case that job opportunity had to be created outside the city center so that residents of the *centralidades* and *urbanizações* did not have to constantly commute. There is a great deal of economic activity occurring in the new places, but the major hindrance to decentralization is not the economy but the political system, as I have shown in this chapter. Whereas the city has been geographically decentralized, decision-making processes have been centralized. The position of the president for the administrative council of *centralidades* such as Kilamba is deliberated and appointed by the presidency and the ruling party.

All in all, with its urban interventions, particularly the legal and regulatory reforms, the government has accomplished something worthy of the most insensitive colonial regime: the split between citizenship and land. Millions of Luandans now have access to social housing, either in the city center or in new *centralidades* and *urbanizações*. But this does not mean they own the land their houses are built on. There is an informal real estate market through which houses in the *urbanizações* and *centralidades* are bought and sold. The problem here is not only that these pieces of property do not constitute a permanent economic asset, as Hernando de Soto has famously made the case for, but that this property is seen as ephemeral.[72] For there is the expectation that the state eventually will give them houses. This work may still be incomplete, but it creates a particular condition of citizenship, one deprived of effective political rights and at the mercy of the ruling party. It is a whole nation that has been reduced to a quasi-squatter condition, which, in times of authoritarian rule, provides new meaning to Casa Luandense. In the end, for the average Luandan, things are not so different from colonial times, as discussed earlier in this book, particularly in chapters 1 and 2. The right to residence is for the most part not accompanied by the right to own land, which can be formally transferred or purchased. This renders the condition of inhabiting ephemeral, and in many cases fraught with dangers (e.g., the potential for removal), which is exactly what life on the skin of a city looks like.

Coda: *Is Luanda Not Paris?*

Still not dark until ten-thirty or a quarter to eleven at night, and the pleasure of simply wandering through the streets, of being lost and yet never fully lost, as in the streets of the Village in New York, but now an entire city was like the Village, with no grid and few right angles in the neighborhood they went to as one sinuous, cobbled path wound around and flowed into another. . . .—Paul Auster, *4321*, 2017

• • •

In late 2016, I was visiting Paris to attend an international conference. One evening, after the conclusion of the proceedings for the day, I went out for a stroll. I have been consistent in my habit of exploring cities through walking and have tried doing so in many cities I have visited, whether Paris, New York, Kampala, or Barcelona. Lacking a reliable sense of orientation, I often struggle to find my way back if I take convoluted routes. I thus tend to walk in straight lines. That late afternoon in Paris, I set out from my accommodation in the Boulevard Raspail and headed towards the Rue de Fleurus. Turning right into the Rue de Sèvres, I continued onto the Rue du Four until I reached the Boulevard Saint-Germain. Here I stopped for a while to appreciate the quintessential Parisian street life: people walking or running as if rushing to catch the train out of town, others peering into store windows, and many crowding into cafés on both sides of the boulevard. I continued in the direction of the Boulevard Saint-Michel, turning into the Rue Racine and the Rue Rotrou to reach the Rue de Vaugirard, which took me up to the Musée du Luxembourg. Here I made a stop to observe the scene and sort through my notes. What impressed me, and still impresses me, about Paris is the sense of continuity from one place to the other. If one walks there mindlessly, one hardly feels the changes from one street to another, from one neighborhood to the next. Parisians, I believe, would ascribe particular identities to particular parts of the city, such as the Marais or the Oberkampf. Those more interested in their city would be able to account for these differences and particularities by addressing issues of architectural style, zoning laws, regulations, materials, and ornamentation. Yet despite these local shifts and historicities, there is continuity across them reflected in the sidewalks: it is possible to walk from the Marais to the Oberkampf without encountering any major obstacles.

It was not the first time I had visited or walked in Paris. However, in this particular late afternoon and early evening I was doing so when my memories of walking in Luanda as a method of inquiry were still fresh. Like a flâneur, I had drifted through Luanda, sometimes mindlessly and at other times more purposefully. I was then following, or at least trying to find a practical use for, the growing body of literature that experiments with walking as a methodology, a means of acquiring knowledge of the urban.[1] The method is, as Christopher Prendergast writes, "based on that characteristic denizen of the literature of nineteenth-century Paris, the *Flaneur*, and the corresponding notion of the city as a special kind of visual field, peculiarly open to the mobile gaze and unforeseen encounter."[2] However, since Luanda is not as walkable as Paris—as the various discussions in this book have shown—I only use this approach with caution. Nonetheless, two techniques emerged from these exercises. First, wandering through Luanda exposed me to countless uncoordinated encounters that provided me with a number of fortuitous experiences and episodes that fill this book. Putting it differently, a number of situations described in the previous chapters are less the product of deliberate attempts to know the city than the outcome of my wanderings in it. My fragmented analysis is apt for approaching Luanda's urban fragmentation. Second, these drifting walks allowed me to come to terms with the analytics of tracing associations, as I discussed in the introduction. For instance, as I was conducting fieldwork in Roque Santeiro market one day in 2008, I heard that the Direcção Nacional de Investigação Criminal (National Directorate for Criminal Investigation; DNIC) prison had just collapsed, killing dozens of people. Walking there not only drew my attention to the conditions of naked deprivation in which most Angolans live (Roque Santeiro was the means through which most Luandans fended off poverty, while the DNIC incarcerated people who had committed petty crimes) but also allowed me to understand the economy of expenditure in Angola, particularly in Luanda. In this economy, the value ascribed to human life was inversely proportional to the value of oil in international markets.

My intention here is not to compare Paris with Luanda, even if I give plenty of credit to the comparative framework and to how this has been useful for putting the conditions that exist in particular cities in perspective. In fact, comparative analyses have become a mainstay in urban studies, even if the question of what specific units and categories to compare, and on which rationale to base the comparison, is far from settled.[3] To be precise, then, I am not evoking Paris here to determine what it has in common with Luanda, or the extent to which the two cities diverge. I am, rather, mentioning Paris for how it "invites reflection" or serves as a device that is useful for thinking through cities elsewhere, as Jennifer Robinson has put it.[4]

The aspect of the comparatist framework I am more wary about is the one that significantly pervades urban theory. Southern urbanism theorists, as discussed in the introduction, have positioned themselves against this by asserting that the tenets of the theories that produced knowledge of cities in the North, such as Paris, New York, or London, are not applicable to cities of the South. Cities in the South are radically different from these Northern cities, and the processes that have brought them into existence and that sustain life there are likewise radically different. One wonders whether such an articulation of theory by difference does not share conceptual fundamentals with some precepts of the social sciences such as anthropology. Bronisław Malinowski set the parameters for this way of thinking in his famous *Argonauts of the Western Pacific*, in which, from the outset, he conceives of the reader as alien from the reality he is describing: "Imagine yourself suddenly set down surrounded by all your gear, alone on a tropical beach close to a native village, while the launch or dinghy which has brought you sails away out of sight."[5] In this manner Malinowski not only invites his reader to imagine what happens when civilization sails away, out of sight, but also offers a functionalist portrayal of culture, which for the most part is still ingrained in the ways in which we deal with, and try to make sense of, life in the rest of the world. Participant observation was, in a way, an invitation to the methodological othering of the uncivilized: of finding new ways to comprehend it, as if the traditional methods of Western social sciences, such as political science and sociology, were not applicable.

Southern urbanism, a brainchild of development studies, proceeds from the same predicament. Cities in the South are too bustling and too precarious, it is argued, and life there is always too contingent, to be understood in these conventional ways. Part of the problem is the functionalism that is ingrained in these approaches, which expects cities to behave in particular ways so that they may be explicable in certain ways.[6] Such renditions, however, denounce an old school of critical urban studies, characterized by a certain ecumenism championed by writers such as Lewis Mumford.[7] More contemporary efforts in this direction attempt to distill the main characteristics of urban life by providing a general discussion of discrete topics applicable across the board, such as the "dynamic of agglomeration and polarization" and the "unfolding of an associated nexus of location, land use and human interactions."[8]

Countering this tendency is the growing body of literature that strives to assert particularity, singularity, or uniqueness—a topic discussed in the introduction of this book. Such a gesture invites us to think in terms not of sameness but of difference. Filip de Boeck, who has given the most poignant descriptions of life in African cities, has done so in ways that emphasize the surreal to such an extent that most of the experiences he describes are hardly reproducible in other African locales.[9] Ato Quayson has provided a timely corrective to this, urging Africanist scholars to separate the ephemeral from processes and structures. In criticizing Jean Comaroff, John Comaroff, Rem Koolhaas, and others, he is less concerned with the ways in which "their models are afflicted by a measure of romanticism regarding the inventiveness of African urban dwellers" than with their conclusions that do not "derive from an understanding of the relationship between ephemera, process and structure in the formation of the African Urban."[10] In other words, he concludes, the analysis of ephemerality and provisionality should go hand in hand with the historicization of the conditions that make these ephemeral engagements operational.

The specter of comparativism that haunts urban studies can be aptly described by an illustration provided by Italo Calvino, in his famous novel *Invisible Cities*. There is a moment in his story when the monarch, Kublai Khan, becomes suspicious of the stories he is being told by Marco Polo and asks the explorer the reason for the striking similarities between all the fantastic cities he is describing. Apologetically, Polo explains that because Venice was the first city he saw, he describes all other cities he sees in comparison to it; in this manner all other cities bear the original mark of Venice: "Every time I describe a city I am saying something about Venice."[11] The implication of Marco Polo's observation is that certain cities come to be taken as palimpsests through which to understand the contemporary urban.

The point I am attempting to make here is not that an engagement with Paris is irrelevant to an understanding of Luanda's formation but the contrary. In fact, Paris, dubbed by Walter Benjamin as the capital of the nineteenth century, comes to condense a great part of urban theory. And because of this overrepresentation in theory, Paris gets to be referred to when we are not explicitly referring to it. It is now an incontestable fact that cities learn from each other through practices of transmission, contamination, and diffusion that are at the heart of the planning endeavor, as several scholars have shown.[12] In the case of Paris, there is a robust body of literature that shows how Haussmann's renewal served as a blueprint for similar processes in other cities around the world. David Pinkney has written of the ways in which Northern cities such as Barcelona and Brussels, or even Washington, Chicago, and Philadelphia, but also cities such as Cairo or Buenos Aires in the colonial world or the New World, emulated what was then considered the cutting-edge plan for Paris.[13] In the case of Luanda, there were several reasons why the city's plan emulated Paris's solutions. In fact, as discussed in chapter 2, one of the authors of the first plan for Luanda, Étienne de Gröer, was French. The radial solution that he suggested to ease circulation outward from the city center was not very different from proposals put forward in later plans for Paris, particularly in terms of how to connect the city's center to its burgeoning peripheries. Subsequent colonial architects and planners of Luanda, such as Vasco Vieira da Costa, were enamored of Le Corbusier's architectural experiments and propositions; many completed internships in his Paris atelier. The solutions they developed for Luanda were very close to the ones they saw or heard of in Paris. And just like Paris, Luanda was not a blank slate when modernist architecture arrived; by that time it had already existed for more than three hundred years. To build the vertical and symmetrical architecture of modernism in the city meant the destruction of several landmarks, for the most part of religious and military nature.

The point I have been trying to make throughout this book concerns the understanding of borders and frontiers implicit in the process of city making. I have done so by using the metaphor of the skin to speak not only of separation but also more forcefully of the interstices, or lines of demarcation, which are the symbolic place where I situate the squatter as a pivotal element for grasping the city's transformation. Here, specifically, I am trying to make a case that concerns urban theory in general. My argument is that the flâneur is not only a device to unmask capitalism, and particularly consumption, as Benjamin would have it. The flâneur is also a yardstick for measuring the level of cityness itself. The more the city is walkable for a flâneur, as Paris is, the more the urban process is accomplished.

But before moving on to discuss such a theoretical leap, the production of the continuity of Paris set against the fragmentation of most cities in the Global South deserves some further explanation. Paris's resilience and permanence has become a major trope in journalism, literature, and film. For instance, commenting for the *New York Times* in the aftermath of the deadly terrorist attacks on Paris on November 13, 2015, Alex Toledano describes a postcard of Rue Bichat during the Belle Époque to assert that Paris has not changed much since then. For this he gives credit to Louis Napoleon and his "efficient prefect," Haussmann, as well as to "conscious urban preservation and respectful wartime enemies."[14] However, it was not by accident that Paris achieved this celebrated resilience, permanence, and continuity. Pinkney, who was already writing on the urban in the 1950s, seems to concur, arguing that the city of Paris has not changed much over the past hundred years: "[The] boundaries, [the] wards and [the] names have remained exactly the same. Even [the] streets and houses are little different from a century ago. Their appearance is an astonishing survival from the past that is unique among the centers of the cities of northern Europe."[15]

Reading present-day Luanda against the historical Paris, one is tempted to agree with Mike Davis and many others who find present-day African cities plagued by the same kinds of ills that characterized urban life in most Northern cities by the time of the industrial revolution.[16] Streets were irregular and ill lit, discouraging mobility. Misery, hunger, and, above all, unemployment loomed large over Paris, as David Harvey has described, for "class quarters did exist in Paris at mid-century, and the poorest of them were dismal slums. In the crowded center of the city eastward from the Church of Sainte-Eustache and the Rue Montmartre rose a mass of ancient and decaying tenements, ordinarily five or more stories high, without courtyards, and with frontages of only twenty feet. The streets were narrow and winding. Many had no sidewalks, and they were usually wet from the open sewers that ran in the gutters."[17]

Transformation in Paris, as many authors have argued, was complex and protracted. Thoughts, ideas, and plans for how the city should change were already circulating, and even being implemented on a piecemeal basis, by the time Emperor Napoleon III appointed Haussmann as prefect of the Seine on June 29, 1853. The emperor had such a passion for urban questions that he personally handed the maps and plans for the transformation of Paris to his prefect. Obsessed with detail, Haussmann added to the wishes of the emperor his own intentions for the width of streets and the location of bridges and even urinals. To bring order and symmetry to Paris, Haussmann envisaged the construction of the most important avenues and streets, such as the Rue de Saint Antoine, as well as the enlargement and broadening of many others. Vacant spaces that were opened up through the destruction of buildings, and sometimes of entire blocks, were given to developers for the construction of five-story apartment buildings. This led to increased speculation in the city and pushed the urban poor farther from the city center. To achieve his vision of rectilinear organization and symmetry, Haussmann ordered the demolition of everything that stood in the way. His goal was to make Paris not just the representation of imperial power but also the capital of modernity, as Harvey argues in his book on Paris.[18] To realize such a vision, Haussmann spared not even monuments and churches.

Several commentators, including Benjamin, have reasoned that Napoleon and Haussmann were motivated by a desire to prevent popular uprisings from taking place in the city by making the building of barricades more difficult. The redesigned streets not only gave the army easier access to any section of the city but also allowed it to maneuver more freely and thus outflank any resisting group. However, Paris's enduring legacy is perhaps the way in which capital was enshrined in the fabric of the city itself. I agree with Harvey when he writes that "it was, however, a storm he [Haussmann] neither created nor tamed, but a deep turbulence in the evolution of French economy, politics and culture, that in the end threw him as mercilessly to the dogs as he threw medieval Paris to the *demolisseurs* (demolishers). In the process the city achieved an aura of capitalist modernity, in both its physical and its administrative infrastructures, that has lasted to this day."[19]

When Haussmann was demoted from his position in January 1870, and even by the time the emperor surrendered nine months later, their work was still unfinished. The Avenue de l'Opéra, the Avenue de la République, the Boulevard Saint-Germain, and the Boulevard Raspail were only completed at a later stage.[20] Remarkably, the city's overhaul continued even after the withdrawal of its main instigators from the public scene; this can be attributed to the fact that the ideas and rationale for the city's transformation were already there by the time these two individuals intervened. However, their intervention set in motion very specific historical dynamics. It was not that Haussmann disliked Paris's past architectural forms, such as churches and medieval buildings, but rather that he was convinced that the past should not stand in the way of the future, or of modernity. To memorialize the past, Haussmann championed the creation of a number of institutions, such as museums, whose practical benefit, as Pinkney writes, was to make the demolitions of ancient houses more tolerable.[21] However, all of this backfired: "The museums, the historical works, the engravings and the maps whose production Haussmann did so much to encourage were to help in slowly turning public opinion against him."[22] For while these gestures encouraged people to think of the benefits of the demolitions, they ended up creating the conditions for the emergence of a nostalgic or revivalist movement. While what had been destroyed could not be brought back to life, these movements could at least prevent the destruction of other landmarks. Ironically, what was produced during the Second Empire as the new and the modern has prevailed in today's city fabric as the old and historical.

In Luanda, these lessons from Paris on how to modernize and still preserve old architecture were not taken seriously, as I discussed in chapter 1. Colonial architects were more interested in the proposals made by Le Corbusier, which they drew on to argue for the demolition of complete city blocks (many of them containing architectural landmarks) to make space for rectilinear avenues and tall buildings, for the sake of symmetry. Then, in the postindependence period, and particularly after 2008, a new layer of edifices was imposed on the city. When postmodern skyscrapers were erected in Luanda, most residents marveled that they could be seen from all over town. Most Luandans were happy that the sections of the city they lived in could be compared with neighborhoods in other highly advanced cities in the world. This is reminiscent of Sarah Nuttall and Achille Mbembe's contention, in their study of Johannesburg, that the dichotomy between Northern and Southern cities is irrelevant, since some of the latter contain infrastructure and forms of fragmentation that resemble spaces in the Global North.[23] They argue against their critics, in particular Michael Watts, that the notion that slums mark urbanization in the South is misleading, as there are places in the North, such as parts of Los Angeles or even of Paris, that are marred by the same dysfunctionality as places in the South.[24]

It is almost inevitable, then, that those whose awareness of the formation of Paris and other cities in the North has been shaped by urban theory do not approach cities in the South, such as Luanda, using the same theoretical lens. But if they do so, they are simply focusing on that which in the South does not conform to the formation of cities in the North. This is part of the reason why, throughout this book, I have invited the reader to see Luanda through the perspective of the squatter. For while the presence of the flâneur is about continuity and permanence in the city, that of the squatter is about its discontinuity and fragmentation.

In this book I have presented this insight in many ways, particularly through the ways in which one navigates the city. To say that Luanda is not a walkable city amounts to an understatement. This was the case in the past, particularly in certain sections of downtown Luanda, as the previous chapters have shown. During the heyday of modernist architecture, the city center had well-kept and intact sidewalks, with most buildings in Luiz de Camões Street, Avenida Serpa Pinto, and Avenida dos Antigos Combatentes equipped with built-in areas of shade to protect walkers from the burning tropical sun. But independence brought drastic changes to the walkability of Luanda. New buildings have taken over the space of the sidewalks. It is nearly impossible to find an intact sidewalk; heavy rains have destroyed those sections that still exist. Maintenance teams fixing water pipes and electricity wires do not backfill their excavations along the sides of the roads. Even if there has been a concerted effort lately to change this, with some of the city's famous potholes being filled, there are still many more that need to be closed up, with the garbage decomposing in them indicating the length of time they have been adorning the city. The walker in Luanda does not have, or cannot have, the same kind of mindlessness one finds in the illustrations and descriptions of the flâneur in Paris.

It is, rather, the contrary. In Luanda, a walker's senses have to be actively mobilized. Care needs to be taken not to step in animal and even human feces. The walker needs to show readiness to jump over potholes or weave between cars whenever sidewalks end abruptly or cars use them for parking. New neighborhoods eliminate sidewalks altogether: walking in these parts of the town is beyond contemplation for most city dwellers. It is as if roads and sidewalks were made for the purpose of discouraging walking. Coffee shops and other locations of interest are placed at such long distances from each other that people are discouraged from walking.

As such, the city has had to be repurposed so as to fit in with the ways in which it is used by the squatter, the one who uses it as a tool for survival, in most cases against the law. Sidewalks, for instance, have become less places to walk, or paths of transition from one place to another, than places in which to be and to stay put. For a great number of Luandans, sidewalks offer the opportunity to cut a deal. First-time visitors to Luanda will notice the thousands of people who spend most of their time on the street. These are not homeless people, but people who sell goods, keep and protect property, cook, sleep, converse, or haul things to the upper stories in the adjacent buildings. Incredibly, they demonstrate loyalty to the places where they work. The shoe shiner who works in the entrance lobby of the building in which I grew up, and where I spend most of my time when in Luanda, has been there for about eight years. He knows me; he knows my family; he knows when I am in the country and when I am traveling. The woman who pretends to sell recharged cards for cellular phones, but who actually exchanges currencies, has also occupied the same position for more than five years. Both are part of the eyes of the city, the ones who keep the streets safer, as Jane Jacobs would have it.[25]

My interest in Paris might perhaps have been sparked by my training in cultural anthropology at Columbia University, with an approach that placed more emphasis on a critique of capitalism than on urban studies. Benjamin's writings on the codification of commodity fetishism in the Parisian arcades of the nineteenth century were central to the debates held there.[26] In hindsight I can see that when I moved back to Luanda to begin my fieldwork, my gaze upon the city was significantly shaped by these conceptualizations. Paris was in my mind when I approached Luanda ethnographically, and Benjamin's arcades formed a sort of palimpsest for me. My naïve engagement with Roque

Santeiro, for instance, was motivated by an effort to find in Luanda the correspondence, or lack thereof, that spoke to the relationship between the physical form and the political-economic conditions in Luanda. However, the removal of Roque Santeiro, one of whose most enduring consequences was the increase in informal trade, pushed me to engage with the city from a different perspective. As such, this book has been an attempt to rewrite urban theory from the perspective of the squatter, or the one who uses the city, and to focus on how the squatter's position in relation to the city, on its margins, incites the authorities to come up with ways in which borders, social or physical, can be reinforced.

Throughout this book I have used the image of the skin to shed some light on cities that are not like Paris, in this case Luanda. For skin, as a thin membrane, helps us to conceive of separations that do not effectively separate. My use of the metaphor of the skin, then, is akin to what the Angolan novelist Ondjaki has evoked in his novel Os transparentes to allude to a city that is made up of visible and invisible lines of circulation and intersection, lines that sometimes divide and fragment.[27] Pier Vittorio Aureli traces such a genealogy in the architecture of the urban, which he calls absolute architecture, through the use of a number of components such as the villa and the skyscraper as envelopes to protect the inside and insiders against disorder and to create a boundary against the world.[28] In her attempt to make sense of the contemporary penchant for enclosure, in the form of the gated community, for instance, Teresa Caldeira dubs São Paulo the "city of walls."[29] In Luanda, Kilamba and many other urban developments touched on in this book could be taken to provide fodder for this theory.

In this book, I have tried to place the emphasis elsewhere. I am less interested in the divide between interior and exterior than in the line, or edge, that creates this divide. Furthermore, a division such as center and periphery, morphologically or historically speaking, is something that obscures more than it illuminates the urban process in Luanda. Roque Santeiro, for instance, was at the periphery of the city for much of the period of modernist intervention. It then enjoyed a central position in relation to the city at the time of the severe economic crisis in the country, during which a number of vital economic operations such as wholesale trade and transportation moved to the periphery and were mostly organized by agents without a place in the central economy. As such, the idea of the city that I have pursued is less about that which stands inside or outside—through the various dichotomies that urban studies has offered to us, such as formal/informal, or city/slum—and more about the modalities that make up such exclusions. The city lies, then, in this thin membrane, the skin, that is constantly growing and expanding, or contracting, receding.

ANGOLENSE	what the natives of Angola, particularly around Luanda, called themselves in the nineteen century
AXILUANDA	literally those of the net, fishermen
BAIRRO	neighborhood
BAIXA	*see* Cidade Baixa
BARROCA	escarpment
CACIMBA	well
CALEMA	tide
CÂMARA MUNICIPAL DE LUANDA	Municipal Chamber of Luanda
CANDONGA	informal business
CANDONGUEIRO	those who practice informal business
CASA LUANDENSE	typical house of colonial Luanda
CASA MILITAR	the military office in the presidency
CENTRALIDADE	centrality
CIDADE	city
CIDADE ALTA	Higher City
CIDADE BAIXA	Lower City, or downtown
CIDADE DE CIMENTO	cement city
COLONO	settler or colonizer
COMITÉ POPULAR	people's committee

CONDOMÍNIO	condominium, or gated community
CONQUISTADOR	conqueror
COOPERANTE	expatriate worker, particularly one who, in the 1980s, was operating in Angola under schemes of cooperation between the Angolan government and Northern European and Eastern bloc countries
CUBATA	shack
DEGREDADO	convict
DONATÁRIO	land grantee
ECONOMIA PARALELA	parallel economy
ESTATUTO DO INDÍGENA (NATIVE STATUTE)	Law on Indigeneity
EXECUTIVO	Executive
FILHO DA TERRA	one born in Angola
FISCAL	tax inspector
FRONTEIRA DO ASFALTO	asphalt frontier
ILHÉU	native of Ilha de Luanda
KALÚ	diminutive for Kaluanda, or Caluanda, the natives of Luanda
KIANDA	the spirit of the water
KINGUILA	"a person who waits," literally describing the person's waiting on the street for customers
LANGA	see retornado
LEI DA SUPERFÍCIE	Law of Surface Rights
LOJA DO POVO	People's Store
MICATE	cakes fried in oil, a very popular Congolese dish
MORADOR	resident
MUSSEQUE	from sand, for the houses built on sand
ORDENAMENTO DO TERRITÓRIO	land management
PAÇO APOSTÓLICO	Archbishop's House

PODER POPULAR	people's power
PORTAS DA CIDADE	City's Gate
PORTAS DO MAR	Sea's Gate
QUINTAL	yard or backyard
RESERVA	reserve
RETORNADO	returnee, a term for Angolans who had been refugees in Democratic Republic of the Congo (DRC)
REVOLUÇÃO DOS CRAVOS	Carnation Revolution
SENADO DA CÂMARA	Senate
SESMARIA	land grant
SOBRADO	townhouse
SUBÚRBIO	periurban areas in the city of Maputo
TAIPA	rammed earth
URBANIZAÇÃO	urbanization
ZAZA	*see* retornado
ZIMBO	the currency used in the heyday of the Kingdom of Congo
ZUNGUEIRA	female street trader

Introduction

1 For a critique of such a trend in anthropological urban studies, see Low, "Anthropology of Cities."

2 António Olé, personal communication, December 2009.

3 The term *musseque*, etymologically, refers to the red sand that characterizes much of the soil in Luanda. During colonial times the term came to signify the "residential configuration typical of Luanda's peripheries" (Carvalho, *A câmara, a escrita*, 133). For a sociological and historical discussion of *musseques*, particularly in relation to the formation of Angolan urban culture, see Moorman, *Intonations*, especially chapter 1, 28–55.

4 Some of the metamorphoses in the work of Ole have arisen through its exhibition in various parts of the world, including Chicago (2001), Venice (2003), Düsseldorf (2004), and Washington (2009), and under titles such as *Township Wall*, *The Structure of Survival*, *Limit Zone*, *Domestic Landscapes*, and *Personalities Revisited*. For an account of Ole's artistic trajectory, see Siegert, *Na pela da cidade*.

5 Pereira, "A cidade visível," 182.

6 Oliveira and Tomás, *1961*.

7 In the 1920s, Le Corbusier suggested mass production as the solution to the housing shortages in Europe. He advocated that houses should be produced in the same way as any other industrial item. See, for instance, Le Corbusier, *Towards a New Architecture*.

8 Vieira, *A fronteira de asfalto*. Vieira's "frontier" has both social and morphological implications. On the one hand, it indicates how colonial society was marked by racial and class divisions. On the other, it refers to the physical difference between the formal, built-up historical city and the sprawling and unplanned slums of the *musseques*. For an understanding of how the *musseques* were discussed under late colonialism, see Monteiro, *A família nos musseques*; for a more contemporary discussion of the enduring consequences of colonial urbanism, see Amaral, "Luanda e os seus 'muceques.'"

9 See Andersen, Jenkins, and Nielsen, "Who Plans the African City," 336.

10 For a comprehensive discussion of how the colonial state came to use these categorizations, see the seminal work of Mamdani, *Citizen and Subject*. For a more specific

discussion of Portuguese colonialism regarding this issue, focused on Mozambique but also applicable to Angola, see O'Laughlin, "Class and the Customary."

11 Vieira, *A cidade e a infância*, 40.

12 See Home, *Of Planting and Planning*.

13 Pullan, "Frontier Urbanism," 17.

14 Donà, Comparone, and Righi, "Immunity and Negation," 58.

15 It is not a coincidence that city making in the colonies used several medical metaphors, such as the cordon sanitaire. For a relationship between immunology and city making in Africa, see Bigon, "History of Urban Planning."

16 For illustrative examples, based on less theorized African cities such as Kinsasha, see de Boeck and Plissart, *Kinshasa*; Devish, "'Pillaging Jesus.'" See also Abu-Lughod, "Tale of Two Cities."

17 Morton, *Age of Concrete*, 13.

18 Morton, *Age of Concrete*, 13.

19 Roque, "*Cidade* and *Bairro*."

20 Mamdani, *Citizen and Subject*.

21 The various Facebook conversations I had with the Angolan urban planner Miguel Dias were fundamental to understanding this point. Dias, personal communications, June–July 2020.

22 See, for instance, Dear and Dishman, *From Chicago to LA*; Wachsmuth, "City as Ideology"; Abbott, "Of Time and Space."

23 See Pieterse, "Cityness and African Urban Development."

24 Brenner and Schmid, "Toward a New Epistemology," 166.

25 Brenner, "Debating Planetary Urbanization," 571.

26 Brenner, "Debating Planetary Urbanization," 571.

27 Dear and Dishman, *From Chicago to LA*.

28 Deleuze and Guattari, *Thousand Plateaus*, 223.

29 See Schmid et al., "Towards a New Vocabulary."

30 Myers, "African Problem." See also Robinson, *Ordinary Cities*.

31 Wachsmuth, "City as Ideology," 77.

32 Derrida, "Structure, Sign and Play in the Discourse of Human Sciences," in *Writing and Difference*, 351–71.

33 Alexander, *City Is Not a Tree*.

34 Karatani, *Architecture as Metaphor*, 29.

35 Karatani, *Architecture as Metaphor*, 37.

36 Even though Max Weber made the "ideal type" an ubiquitous concept with his seminal book *Economy and Society*, his apt elaboration on it appears in the essay "The Objectivity of Knowledge in Social Science and Social Policy." He writes: "It [an ideal type] is obtained by means of a one-sided *accentuation* of *one* or *a number* of viewpoints and through the synthesis of a great many diffuse and discrete *individual* phenomena (more present in one place, fewer in another, and occasionally completely absent), which are in conformity with those one sided, accentuated viewpoints, into an internally consistent mental image" (Weber, "Objectivity of Knowledge," in *Collected Methodological Writings*, 125; author's italics). My contention

here is simply that contemporary urban theory is still critically infused with this sort of Weberian idealism. See Weber, *Economy and Society*; Weber, *Collected Methodological Writings*.

37 Fernandes, "Constructing the 'Right to the City,'" 202.

38 Fernandes, "Constructing the 'Right to the City,'" 202.

39 Gastrow, "Cement Citizenship, Housing, Demolition," 10; see also Gastrow, "Negotiated Settlements."

40 Davis, *Planet of Slums*.

41 Roque, "*Cidade* and *Bairro*," 340.

42 Croese, "Inside the Government."

43 Boeri, "Italian Landscape."

44 Even though Boeri is particularly interested in European cities, I find his approach useful for explaining Luanda. See Boeri, "Eclectic Atlases," n.p.

45 Benjamin, *One-Way Street*, 252.

46 Rabinow, *Anthropos Today*.

47 I am indebted to Michael Taussig for the courses he taught on Walter Benjamin at Columbia University, and for his guidance in helping me understand the mausoleum and the embalming of Agostinho Neto's body in light of Benjamin's writings.

48 Cvoro, "Dialectical Image Today," 92.

49 See, for instance, Narayan, "How Native," and Panourgiá, *Fragments of Death*.

50 Latour, *Reassembling the Social*, 5.

51 There is a considerable body of literature that addresses urban transformation after the removal of Roque Santeiro. These works will be discussed in subsequent chapters.

52 Aureli, *Possibility of an Absolute Architecture*.

Chapter I. Un-building History to Build the Present

1 Joseph Calder Miller describes *sobrados* as "large multistoried townhouses." According to Miller, *sobrados* "became symbol[s] of local aristocratic pretentions at Luanda. Some Luso-Africans lived with their families on the second stories of the *sobrados* in the upper part of the city, where large balconied windows opened on the sea and brought a measure of comfort and, it was fondly but vainly assumed, also of health from onshore daytime breezes that lessened the oppressiveness of the humidity." See Miller, *Way of Death*, 295.

2 As famously discussed by Marcel Mauss. See, Mauss, *Gift*, 7–8.

3 Abbas, "Building on Disappearance," 443.

4 Miller, *Way of Death*. See also David Eltis, who writes: "Although Whydah, on the Slave Coast, was once considered the busiest African slaving port on the continent, it now appears that it was surpassed by Luanda, in West Central Africa, and by Bonny, in the Bight of Biafra. Luanda alone dispatched some 1.3 million slaves, and these three most active ports together accounted for 2.2 million slave departures." Eltis, "African Side of the Trade." https://www.slavevoyages.org/voyage /essays#interpretation/a-brief-overview-of-the-trans-atlantic-slave-trade/the -african-side-of-the-trade/5/en/.

5   For slaves shipped from Angola and other ports, see Cândido, *African Slaving Port*. For a more qualitative perspective, see also Slave Voyages, https://www.slavevoyages.org/assessment/estimates. According to this platform, Portugal and Brazil managed to extract from Angola more than 5 million of the approximately 12 million Africans who arrived enslaved in the New World. The Portuguese and Brazilians were obviously active in other parts of the African continent, but they had almost exclusively dominated for centuries the trading of slaves in the various ports of Angola.

6   This did not mean that enslaved people did not attempt flight. Curto and Gervay, "Population History of Luanda," 37.

7   Boxer, *Portuguese Seaborne Empire*, 102.

8   Batalha, *Angola*, 145.

9   Despite its colloquial name, the Ilha is not an island in the proper sense of the word. Originally, this narrow strip of land was separated from the mainland. The first bridge, of wood and iron, was built in the late 1900s; only in the 1930s was it replaced by a more permanent stone bridge.

10 The origin of the term Loanda has been widely debated. Some authors argue that *luanda* may also mean "tribute," referring to the zimbu shells on Ilha de Luanda that the locals used to pay tribute to the king of Congo. See Cruz e Silva, *Luanda e seus lugares*, 5. Contrary to what has been written, the city only changed its name to São Paulo Assumpção de Loanda (or the shortened form, São Paulo de Loanda) when the Portuguese reconquered the city from the Dutch in 1648. As the word Loanda was too close in pronunciation to Holanda, the Portuguese name for the Netherlands, it was colloquially changed to Luanda. This spelling only became the official spelling of the name in 1927. See Couto, "Considerações."

11 See Coates, "Depósito de Degredados."

12 Just as in Bahia, Brazil, the Senado do Câmara followed the Ordenações do Reino, the document that comprised the legislation of Portugal and Brazil during the time of empire. See Boxer, *Portuguese Society in the Tropics*, 112.

13 Santos, *Das origens dos municípios portugueses*, 24–25.

14 At least three times in the city's history (in 1667, 1702, and 1732) the Senado da Câmara took on the administration of the city. Santos, *Das origens dos municípios portugueses*, 23.

15 Mourão, *Continuidades e descontinuidades*, 81.

16 Cardoso, *São Paulo assumpção de Luanda*, 15.

17 Cardoso, *São Paulo assumpção de Luanda*, 16.

18 The number of churches built at that time was immense, but it is worth referring to these: the Church of the Jesuits, the Igreja de Misericordia (Church of Mercy) with its hospital, the Igreja de São João dos Militares (Church of Saint John the Soldier), the Catedral de Nossa Senhora da Conceição (Cathedral of Our Lady of the Conception), the Igreja de Rosário (Church of the Rosary), and the Convento de São José (Convent of Saint Joseph), located at the gates of the city, where it is today the main buildings of the Central Hospital D. Maria Pia. See Santos, *Luanda d'outros tempos*, 84.

19 By this time, Pernambuco, Bahia, and Rio de Janeiro "were supplying almost all of the sugar consumed in Europe, and almost all the slaves producing it were African." See Eltis, "Early Slaving Voyages."

20 The early historiography of Luanda takes particular care to describe the Dutch occupation. See Rego, *A reconquista de Luanda*. For the implications of the Dutch occupation of Brazil and its repercussions in Angola, see Boxer, *Portuguese Seaborne Empire*.

21 See Santos, *Das origens dos municípios portugueses*, 30.

22 A well-established accusation in the literature is that the Dutch destroyed buildings and the city's archive, making reconstruction of Luanda's early days of difficult. Boxer records that "the Dutch invaders of 1641 intercepted the convoy which was carrying the municipal archives and some refugees up the river Bengo from the city, and they threw all the documents into the river after killing most of the inoffensive fugitives." See Boxer, *Portuguese Society in the Tropics*, 111. On burning churches, more specifically see, Cardoso, *São Paulo da Assumpção de Luanda*, 12.

23 Santos, *Luanda d'outros tempos*, 90.

24 Santos, *Luanda d'outros tempos*, 137.

25 Santos, *Luanda d'outros tempos*, 67.

26 Queiroz, *Luanda: Arquivo histórico*, 19

27 According to the 1781 census, the total population was about 9,755, of which 4,108 were male and 5,647 female. Most of them were enslaved, some were free, and only about 400 were whites. See Curto and Gervay, "Population History of Luanda."

28 Miller, *Way of Death*, 284.

29 Cardoso, *Luanda Antiga*, 19.

30 Oliveira, "Baskets, Stalls and Shops," 424.

31 J. Santos, *Luanda d'outros tempos*, 135.

32 J. Santos, *Luanda d'outros tempos*, 135.

33 M. Cardoso, *São Paulo da Assumpção de Luanda*, 14.

34 J. Santos, *Luanda d'outros tempos*, 118.

35 J. Santos, *Luanda d'outros tempos*, 118.

36 J. Santos, *Luanda d'outros tempos*, 118.

37 Bethel, "Independence of Brazil," 146.

38 See Cardonega, *História geral das guerras Angolanas*, 30.

39 Vanessa dos Santos Oliveira makes references to several women owners of arimos at that time. See Oliveira, "Donas, pretas livres," 450.

40 Boxer, *Portuguese Seaborne Empire*, 310.

41 Nascimento, "Das Ingombotas ao bairro operário."

42 Oliveira, "Baskets, Stalls and Shops," 422.

43 Loading heavy wood onto the ships was a technique frequently used at the time to prevent ships from sinking, given that the lighter they were, the more subject to the whims of the wind they would become.

44 Mingas, *Projecto de Pesquisa*.

45 For the implementation of cotton production in Angola, see Pitcher, "Sowing the Seed of Failure."

46 A slightly revised and augmented version of this piece was later on published in the book *Angola: História e arquitectura*. As the versions diverge, I will be quoting both of them to make sense of *Casa Luandense*. Batalha, *Angola*, 227.

47 For how the Estado Novo used Lusotropicalism to make the case for building multicultural societies in the tropics, see Castelo, "'O modo português.'"

48 Freyre, *Casa-grande e senzala*. An English translation of Freyre's text, *The Masters and the Slaves: A Study in the Development of Brazilian Civilization*, was published in 1970.

49 Batalha, *Uma casa setecentista de Luanda*, 12.

50 Batalha, *Uma casa setecentista de Luanda*, 9–10.

51 Batalha, *Uma casa setecentista de Luanda*, 6.

52 Batalha, Uma casa setecentista de Luanda, 5–6.

53 Batalha, *Uma casa setecentista de Luanda*, 6.

54 Batalha, *Angola*, 228.

55 Batalha, *Angola*, 229.

56 Ernesto Vilhena was the founder of the CDA and an art collector; he died in 1967.

57 Batalha, *Angola*, 230.

58 Batalha, *Angola*, 230.

59 Miller, *Way of Death*, 390.

60 Milheiro, *Nos trópicos sem Le Corbusier*, 64–65.

61 In fact, the first law to deal with cultural and material heritage was approved in 1976 and was more concerned with the nationalization of objects (rare and old books, photographs, museum and library collections) that otherwise could be taken out of the country. It only touches en passant on the question of the architectural legacy bestowed by colonialism. Decreto 80/76, October 14 (1976).

62 Despacho, August 31 (1981).

63 For the curators of the exhibition of monuments, these inclusions disqualify this building as a *sobrado*.

64 Ângela Mingas, personal communication, Luanda, July 2014.

65 "Kinaxixe O mercado."

66 Ângela Mingas, personal communication, Luanda, July 2014.

67 Part of this research was shared in an exhibition at Elinga Teatro. Mingas, "Sobrados."

68 Ângela Mingas, personal communication, Luanda, July 2014.

69 Pepetela, "Horror do vazio."

70 Cardoso, "Crude Urban Revolution," 4.

71 Angola's population is only 22 million people. See Cardoso, "Crude Urban Revolution," 11. According to the World Bank, "Oil dependence has been a lasting feature of the economy, and petroleum products have comprised between 87 and 98 per cent of total annual export since 1990." See World Bank Group, *Angola*, v.

72 Artists took the forefront in these battles. See Dias, "Angola."

73 Despacho, August 31 (1981).

74 Central Angola 7311, "Canibais na cultura." Rosa Cruz e Silva is a historian specializing in the slave trade and has authored at least one article on Luanda and its places of memory.

75 Despacho, August 31 (1981).

76 For the full discussion of how this project came about and the controversies it produced, see Croese, "Urban Governance."

77 Fonseca, "Emissão de 379 milhões de dólares."

78 "Angola's $7bn Project." See also Croese, "World-Class City Making."

79 For an understanding of the changes proposed to this section of the city, see Croese, "Global Urban Policymaking."

80 See, for instance, Abrantes, "Mal-estar teatral."

81 Châtelot, "Morte de um teatro."

82 Cited in Châtelot, "Morte de um teatro."

Chapter 2. Ordering Urban Expansion

1 Vieira da Costa, "Cidade Satélite no. 3," 14.

2 Nascimento, "Das Ingombotas ao bairro operário," 92.

3 Even though slavery would be replaced by many other forms of compulsion, and not only for labor purposes. In fact, according to Maria da Conceição Neto, slavery was only put to rest in 1910, with the establishment of the republic. See Neto, "A república no seu estado colonial."

4 Pereira, et al., *Projecto de uma companhia*, 7.

5 Pereira et al., *Projecto de uma companhia*. It was common during the Portuguese empire that convict labor powered the construction of infrustructure, particularly in Angola and Mozambique. On this issue, see Coates, *Convict Labor*.

6 For an exhaustive discussion of the process, costs, and difficulties involved in the construction of this railway, see Navarro, *Um império projectado*.

7 It was located on Rua José Rodrigues; the station was called Cidade Alta because it was used by the governor and other public authorities for their departures to the provinces.

8 Araújo, "A estação da Cidade Alta," 45.

9 Eça de Queiroz has been famously cited for his ironic comments on the incapacity of the Portuguese to colonize Africa. See Queiroz, *Uma campanha alegre*, 100–101.

10 The Portuguese empire had reached the conclusion that Angola and Mozambique were too large to be governed from Lisbon, so these colonies were allowed to govern themselves quite independently.

11 Cited in Fonte, "Urbanismo e arquitectura em Angola," 31.

12 For a discussion on Norton de Matos's struggle to end formal slavery in Angola, see Neto, "A república no seu estado colonial."

13 For an overview of Norton de Matos's tenure in Angola and the problems it elicited, such as corruption, see Smith, "António Salazar and the Reversal."

14 Obarrio, "Third Contact," 316.

15 For an authoritative discussion of the struggles to permanently eliminate enslavement practices in the early 1900s, and the implementation of the Native Statute, see Neto, "In Town and out of Town."

16 See Coquery-Vidrovitch, "From Residential Segregation."

17 Norton de Matos, *A província de Angola*, 12.

18 Norton de Matos, *A província de Angola*, 12.

19 Lugard, *Dual Mandate*.

20 Pélissier, *La colonie du minotaure*.

21 Fonte, "Urbanismo e arquitectura em Angola," 35.

22 Fonte, "Urbanismo e arquitectura em Angola," 35.

23 For the rationale that presided over the construction of Colonato da Cela, see, for instance, Castelo, "Reproducing Portuguese Villages in Africa."

24 Neto, "In Town and out of Town," 124.

25 Neto, "In Town and out of Town," 132.

26 Beevers, *Garden City Utopia*, 31.

27 For an understanding of the attempt at implementing the garden city model in colonial Africa, see Bigon, "Garden Cities in Colonial Africa"; "'Garden City' in the Tropics?"

28 For a discussion of various types of vessels and their particular features relating to their ability to approach the Bay of Luanda, see Miller, *Way of Death*, 369.

29 Amaral, *Luanda*, 27.

30 See Ciccantell and Bunker, *Space and Transport*.

31 Harvey, "Right to the City."

32 A civil engineer by profession, Perestrelo authored several small reports and the proposal for the works at Porto de Luanda in the 1940s. These documents provide important information about the envisioned development of the port and the techniques and materials employed, as well as the financial resources used for its construction. They concern not only the practicalities of the construction itself but also an interesting discussion of the linkage between the port and the future city. See Perestrelo, "As obras do Porto de Luanda"; "O Porto de Luanda."

33 I only partially agree with Milheiro, "O Gabinete de Urbanização Colonial."

34 The first link between Luanda and Ilha de Luanda was completed in the 1910s. Various interventions followed, the most recent being the one carried out by the Sociedade Baía de Luanda, in 2011. See Agência Angola Press, "Ponte que liga marginal."

35 For three years, from 1941 to 1944, Moreira da Silva and de Gröer worked on the master plan, traveling to Luanda a couple of times. The plan was submitted in November 1943 and presented at the Colonial Exhibition in Lisbon in November 1944.

36 Marques Pires, "O ateliê de arquitectura," 151.

37 Marques Pires, "O ateliê de arquitectura," 98.

38 The only proof that the Moreira da Silva and de Groër plan was concluded is a letter. See Marat-Mendes and Sampaio, "*Plano de urbanização*," 62.

39 Marques Pires, "Ateliê de arquitectura," 290.

40 Marques Pires, "Ateliê de arquitectura," 99.

41 Marques Pires, "Ateliê de Arquitectura," 290.

42 A common concern among European powers. For the case of Portugal, see Castelo, "'Village Portugal' in Africa."

43 Cooper, *Africa since 1940*, 91–92.

44 See Castelo, "'Village Portugal' in Africa."

45 Mourão, *Continuidades e descontinuidades*, 83.

46 See Tostões and Bonito, "Empire, Image and Power."

47 See Rosa, "Odam."

48 Cruz, "Memórias de um mercado tropical," 115.

49 Milheiro, *Nos trópicos sem Le Corbusier*.

50 This debate is evident in the polemic between the Swiss artist and designer Max Bill and Brazilian modernist architects, for instance. Aleca Le Blanc argues that European architects generally considered Brazilian modernist architecture to be characterized by a disjunction between aesthetic and function. Bill himself posited that modernist Brazilian architecture was running the risk of "being divorced from the praxis of quotidian life" owing to its focus on aesthetics. See Le Blanc, "Palmeiras and Pilotis," 104.

51 For examples of the work of colonial architects in other cities in Africa, see Tostões, *Modern Architecture in Africa*.

52 Fernandes is concerned with the participation of this generation in the design and construction of many other cities in Angola and Mozambique. See J. M. Fernandes, *Geração Africana*.

53 See Cruz, "Memórias de um mercado tropical," 58–59.

54 Nascimento, *Estudo da regularização*.

55 Nascimento, *Estudo da regularização*.

56 Mourão, *Continuidades e descontinuidades*, 314.

57 Cruz, "Memórias de um mercado tropical," 94.

58 See Oliveira and Tomás, *1961*.

59 The machete is considered the symbol of the uprisings of February 4, 1961, when a few dozen Angolan nationalists, armed with machetes, invaded colonial prisons to free other revolutionaries. The moment is celebrated in independent Angola as the beginning of the nationalist struggle. See Fortuna, "Entrevista com Simões Lopes de Carvalho," 105–22.

60 Decreto-Lei no. 40 333, October 14 (1955). This law concerned how to manage shared property, when various people share units in the same building.

61 For an overview of Norton de Matos's modernizing agenda in Angola, see deGrassi, *Provisional Reconstructions*.

62 Forced labor came to replace slavery through the promulgation of various pieces of colonial legislation, such as Código do Trabalho Indígena (Law of Native Labor), for Angola and Mozambique in 1928. In colonial legislation, labor was not a means through which a particular person takes part in the economy but was for the most part what defined the colonial subject itself. For an insightful discussion of labor-related questions in the context of Portuguese colonialism, see Cahen, "Seis teses sobre o trabalho forçado."

63 Mamdani, *Citizen and Subject*.

64 Gwendolyn Wright gives a powerful illustration of how this has played out in Africa. See Wright, *Politics of Design*. See also Bigon, *French Colonial Dakar*; Gandy, *Fabric of Space*.

65 Fry and Drew, *Tropical Architecture*.

66 See Birmingham, *Short History of Modern Angola*.

67 This is a shift that Mahmood Mamdani addresses in his oft-quoted book, *Citizen and Subject*.

68 Crowder, "Indirect Rule."

69 This is the origin of Luanda residents' attachment to their neighborhoods. See Moorman, *Intonations*.

70 These *bairros operários* built by the colonial government and, in particular, colonial companies were intended to house workers.

71 Liora Bigon might be hinting at this when she writes that "the aim of colonialism [was not] to improve African living standards, but to exploit the natural resources of the continent." See, Bigon, "Between Local and Colonial Perceptions," 57.

72 The influence of Auzelle is very clear in Carvalho's work. He was one of the creators of the *grands ensembles* (high-scale high-rise housing projects).

73 Fortuna, *Os lugares no espaço angolano*, 108.

74 He designed one of the most important modernist buildings in the city, which today houses the Radio National de Angola.

75 Carvalho, "Luanda do futuro," 29.

76 Carvalho explained this approach to Cláudio Fortuna in an interview he gave many years later. See Fortuna, *Os lugares no espaço angolano*, 114.

77 Cited in Magalhães and Gonçalves, *Moderno tropical*, 31.

78 Mourão, *Continuidades e descontinuidades*, 280–81.

79 For a discussion on the Native question in relation to power and law, see, for instance, Mamdani, *Citizen and Subject*.

80 The concept of immunity I have in mind comes from the work of Michel Foucault and Roberto Esposito. See, for instance, Foucault, *Society Must Be Defended*; Esposito, *Immunitas*.

81 See Cardoso, "Estação do Bungo."

82 There is a relationship between modernism and authoritarianism. Le Corbusier tried, unsuccessfully, to sell his projects to the Soviet Union. And, as has recently been demonstrated, he also connived with fascism. Even modernism in Brazil, as James Holston has abundantly demonstrated, only triumphed because it was supported by the undemocratic state. See de Jarcy, *Le Corbusier*; Holston, *Modernist City*.

Chapter 3. A Place to Dwell in Times of Change

1 An English translation, by Stephen Henighan, of *Os transparentes* was in fact published with the title *Transparent City*.

2 Or at least how invisibility tends to be used in urban studies in Africa. See de Boeck, *Kinshasa*.

3 For Scott's insightful and provocative discussion on the relationship between state and legibility, see, Scott, *Seeing Like a State*.

4 Fanon, *Wretched of the Earth*.

5 To this day independence is referred to as the end of the exploitation of man by man. See C. Santos, "A independência acabou."

6 Marcum, *Angolan Revolution*, 333.

7 Tomás, *Amílcar Cabral*.

8 Meijer and Birmingham, "Angola from Past to Present."

9 Rodrigues, *Regimes e impérios*, 210.

10   The unilateral proclamation of independence by Guinea-Bissau played an impor-
      tant role in bringing about the end of the colonial order, since it was in Guinea-
      Bissau that the movement of captains, the group of subaltern officials of the
      Portuguese army, was formed and later on overthrew the Estado Novo. See Tomás,
      O fazedor de utopias. For an understanding of the process behind the end of Estado
      Novo, see MacQueen, *Decolonization of Portuguese Empire*.

11   Canelas, *A hora da partida*.

12   Wolfers and Bergerol, *Angola in the Front Line*, 66.

13   For an understanding of the political conditions that brought about *poder popular*,
      see Mabeko-Tali, *Dissidências e poder de estado*.

14   The notion of *poder popular* gained traction, and the people's committees emerged
      on the very cusp of independence. They arose in the context of the void that ex-
      isted when centralized colonial power receded, and they filled the gap by perform-
      ing a number of tasks that the state was expected to attend to. The committees had
      to guarantee security in the *musseques,* for instance. For reasons that lie beyond the
      scope of this book, they identified with the MPLA, with members in some cases
      even becoming "fervent MPLA supporters"; see Mabeko-Tali, *Dissidências e poder de
      estado*.

15   Wolfers and Bergerol, *Angola in the Front Line*, 60.

16   Troufa Real, *Musseques of Luanda*, 58.

17   Troufa Real's study, *The Musseques of Luanda*, is the main source for this section.
      Troufa Real was in the Portuguese military and deployed to the Agrupamento de
      Engenharia de Angola (Engineering Group of Angola). Later, he became the direc-
      tor of the Planning Office of the Câmara Municipal de Luanda and chief of the
      Brigade for Projects of the Gabinete de Habitação de Angola (1975–76).

18   Troufa Real, *Musseques of Luanda,* 58.

19   Troufa Real, *Musseques of Luanda,* 58–59.

20   Troufa Real, *Musseques of Luanda,* 58.

21   Troufa Real, *Musseques of Luanda,* 58.

22   Troufa Real, *Musseques of Luanda,* 59.

23   Troufa Real, *Musseques of Luanda,* 61.

24   Troufa Real, *Musseques of Luanda,* 61.

25   Decreto-Lei no. 576/70, November 24 (1970).

26   Troufa Real, *Musseques of Luanda,* 62.

27   Decreto-Lei no. 576/70, November 24 (1970).

28   Troufa Real, *Musseques of Luanda,* 63

29   Troufa Real, *Musseques of Luanda,* 65.

30   Troufa Real, *Musseques of Luanda,* 102.

31   Troufa Real, *Musseques of Luanda,* 102.

32   Troufa Real, *Musseques of Luanda,* 8.

33   Troufa Real, *Musseques of Luanda,* 75.

34   Troufa Real, *Musseques of Luanda,* 75.

35   Troufa Real, *Musseques of Luanda,* 75.

36   Troufa Real, *Musseques of Luanda,* 76.

37 See Centro de Documentação 25 de Abril. "Direito das colónias à independência."
38 This was true even though the Portuguese had for the most part cleared the city of nationalists. The several dozen nationalists involved in the uprisings of 1961 were out of the picture back then. Some of them managed to flee and join the inchoate nationalist movement in the northern provinces, some were detained and spent years in prison, but the largest number were simply tortured and killed. See Pacheco, "A rebelião de um sacerdote."
39 Moorman, *Intonations*, 9.
40 Matos, *Há quarenta anos*.
41 See Canelas, *A hora da partida*, 73.
42 "Flight from Angola."
43 Kapuscinski, *Another Day of Life*, 13. For a critique of Kapuscinski's indulgence in poetic freedom, see Rushdie, *Imaginary Homelands*, 203.
44 Canelas, *A hora da partida*, 73.
45 For a discussion of Kapuscinski's knack for fabricating facts, see Rushdie, *Imaginary Homelands*, 203–8.
46 Kapuscinski, *Another Day of Life*, 6.
47 Matos, *Há quarenta anos*.
48 To give an idea of the scale of such flights, in September 1975 more than 4,000 people per day were arriving at Portugal's airports of Portela (in Lisbon) and Pedras Rubras (in Porto). See Matos, *Há quarenta anos*.
49 Canelas, *A hora da partida*, 77.
50 Kapuscinski, *Another Day of Life*, 2.
51 Esposito, cited in Swacha, "Book Review: Roberto Esposito." 199.
52 For an overview of the process of nationalization, see Ferreira, "Nacionalização e confisco."
53 Lei no. 3/76, March 3 (1976).
54 Lei no. 43/76, June 19 (1976).
55 Lei no. 43/76, June 19 (1976).
56 Lei no. 43/76, June 19 (1976).
57 Lei no. 43/76, June 19 (1976).
58 Lei no. 43/76, June 19 (1976).
59 Gastrow, "Negotiated Settlements," 53.
60 The real date of the arrival of the Cubans in Angola is one of the most serious controversies in the history of the country's independence. For many years, the Angolan authorities have denied that Cuban military forces were already operating in the country before the day of independence. Using Cuban archives, Piero Gleijeses has been able to argue that they were already in Angola by February 1975. See Gleijeses, *Conflicting Missions*.
61 Despacho, June 14, 1980.
62 Le Corbusier, *Towards a New Architecture*, 127.
63 This relation between the house and the urban is clear in Le Corbusier's most architectural project, *La ville Savoye*, which was fundamental in making the case for his International Style; see Scoffier, "Pour mieux comprendre la beauté."

64 Marcus, *Apartment Stories*, 17.

65 Murteira, "A economia colonial portuguesa," 33.

66 Muteira, "A economia colonial portuguesa," 36; Smith, "António Salazar and the Reversal," 666.

67 Murteira, "A economia colonial portuguesa," 37.

68 Murteira, "A economia colonial portuguesa,"48. See also Smith, "António Salazar and the Reversal" and Pimenta, *Angola, os brancos*.

69 Decreto-Lei no. 40 333, October 14 (1955).

70 Decreto-Lei no. 40 333, October 14 (1955).

71 Decreto-Lei no. 40 333, October 14 (1955).

72 Even though its headquarters were in Lisbon and its technicians only traveled to the colonies for short stays. See Milheiro and Dias, "Arquitectura em Bissau."

73 See Tostões, "How to Love Modern," 196.

74 Vieira da Costa, "Cidade Satélite no. 3," 11.

75 Even though after the 1960s the colonial population started to become more balanced, on account of families that were moving to the colonies. See Bhagavan, *Angola*, 9.

76 Cited in Ingold, *Making*, 48.

77 Simone, "People as Infrastructure."

78 This is the setting for one of the most widely read novels in Angola, Rui's *Quem me dera ser onda*.

79 Murray, *Taming the Disorderly City*.

80 Lefebvre, *Production of Space*, 86.

81 In terms of Angolan writers who have explored these topics, see, for instance, Pepetela, *O desejo de Kianda*; Ondjaki, *Os transparentes*; and Agualusa, *Barroco tropical*.

82 Cited in Buck-Morss, *Dialectics of Seeing*, 24.

83 See Benjamin, *Arcades Project*.

84 Marcus, *Apartment Stories*, 2.

Chapter 4. A City Decentered

1 Clapson, *Social History of Milton Keynes*, 17. See also Garreau, *Edge City*.

2 Gastrow, "Negotiated Settlements," 62.

3 Jameson, *Postmodernism*, 50.

4 Jameson makes this point through the deconstruction of the Bonaventure building. See Jameson, *Postmodernism*, 39.

5 See Palonen, "Building a New City."

6 This has been true of the South African case, for instance. The importance of the process of renaming places and sites in the aftermath of historical changes cannot be overstated. James Duminy has pointed out, in relation to South Africa, that "renaming has provided a platform for the redress of painful memories of racial exclusion, as well as the enactment of new territorial imaginaries and visions of South African history and culture." See Duminy, "Street Naming, Symbolic Capital," 311.

7 This is for, instance, what Brian Larkin has called, using Kant's category, the "colonial sublime." See Larkin, *Signal and Noise*, 35ff.

8　See Jacob, "A toponímia de Luanda."

9　Such an onomastic cartography must also seem familiar to those inhabitants of the postcolonial era who benefited from colonial education. African and Angolan history was not an academic subject, and students were more familiar with historical figures and toponomies of Portugal (they had to learn the train stations of continental Portugal by heart) than of Angola.

10　These names included many fabrications: some of them referred to people killed in foul play, or even to heroes who had never existed. Gleijeses's descriptions of the various failed attempts by MPLA guerrillas to enter Angolan territory through Zaire provide a good example; see Gleijeses, *Conflicting Missions*, 178–83.

11　Even though the Methodist church, properly speaking, is not on Missão Street. It is, curiously, located in Our Lady of Muxima Street.

12　Ângela Mingas, personal communication, Luanda, July 2014.

13　In some instances, only the statues were removed, and the pedestals left behind. For an artistic treatment of this practice, see the work of Kiluanji Kia Henda. See "Focus."

14　"Nomes das ruas."

15　"Nomes das ruas."

16　This would be a city that comúlies with what Lynch calls legibility. See Lynch, *Image of the City*.

17　Bigon and Njoh, "Toponymic Inscription Problematic," 26.

18　Bigon and Njoh, "Toponymic Inscription Problematic," 28.

19　As Frantz Fanon has so famously described. See Fanon, *Wretched of the Earth*.

20　Brooke, "Adam Smith Crowds Marx."

21　Appadurai, *Social Life of Things*, 16.

22　Development Workshop, "Informal Trading in Luanda's Markets," 7.

23　For a succinct description of the 1977 events, see Pawson, *In the Name of the People*.

24　Redvers, "Angolan Traders Mourn Loss."

25　Nascimento, "No Roque Santeiro."

26　Castro, Reschilian, and Zanetti, "Os candongueiros," 11.

27　The difficulties *musseque* dwellers had in finding a taxi willing to take them home are well expressed in a popular song from the late 1950s in Angola by Luiz Visconde, "Chofer de Praça." See Moorman, *Intonations*, 34.

28　See also Lopes, "Luanda cidade informal?," 105.

29　See also Lopes, "Candongueiros, kinguilas, roboteiros."

30　Lopes, "Dinâmicas do associativismo."

31　See Farley et al., "Continued Residential Segregation."

32　One such warning came from Simões de Carvalho, as discussed in chapter 2. See, Carvalho, "Luanda do futuro."

33　Fernandes and Hurst, *Angola Cinemas*.

34　See the canonical Anderson, *On Streets*.

35　See Pitcher and Graham, "Cars Are Killing Luanda."

36　Teresa Caldeira has pointed out the same issue in Brazilian cities: "As the elite retreat to their enclaves and abandon public places to the homeless and the poor, the number of places for public encounters between different social groups shrinks considerably." See Caldeira, *City of Walls*, 297.

37 Specter, "Extreme City."
38 Anderson, *On Streets.*
39 They were discharged as a consequence of the two peace agreements signed between the government and UNITA, in 1991 (in Bicesse, Portugal) and in 1994 (in Lusaka, Zambia). See Anstee, *Orphan of the Cold War.*
40 Development Workshop, "Informal Trading in Luanda's Markets."
41 Luandan street trader, personal communication, Luanda, July 3, 2015.
42 Lopes, "Dinâmicas do associativismo."

Chapter 5. Reversing (Urban) Composition

1 The same project that prompted the emergence of Associação Kalú, as discussed in chapter 1.
2 To be fair, the whole João Pedro enterprise not only had a business-oriented component, it also had a nostalgic component. The particular building was the first in Marginal to be erected, and since João Pedro was a white man who was born in Angola, a son of settlers who left the country in 1975, he wanted to bring the building back to its past glory. João Pedro, Personal communication, 2013.
3 Larkin, *Poetics and Politics of Infrastructure*, 328.
4 Rodgers, "Disembedding the City," 120
5 Roy, "What Is Urban?," 813.
6 Roy, "What Is Urban?," 817. For other important exceptions, see Nielsen, Sumich, and Bertelsen, "Enclaving."
7 A report on the sanitation crisis in Luanda states that the city could go two or three days without running water, and even when there was running water, it was available for only certain hours of the day. See Organização da Mulher Angolana et al., *Projecto de emergência.*
8 Lei no. 19/91, May 25 (1991).
9 Cardoso, "Crude Urban Revolution," 5.
10 Ferguson, "Seeing Like an Oil Company," 378.
11 Ferguson, "Seeing Like an Oil Company," 378.
12 See Appel, "Walls and White Elephants."
13 Gomes, "Entrevista com José Cerqueira," 18.
14 Ferguson, "Seeing Like an Oil Company," 378.
15 Specter, "Extreme City." This scheme, championed by oil companies, became the framework for hiring a mostly expatriate labor force in almost every sector of the economy, in which the hiring party was expected to provide housing or meet the costs of housing.
16 Specter, "Extreme City."
17 Decreto-Lei no. 40 333, October 14 (1955).
18 Lei no. 19/91, May 25 (1991).
19 See Tomás, "Mutuality from Above."
20 Frias and Udelsmann Rodrigues, "Private Condominiums in Luanda," 341.

21 Bureau Politico do Comité Central do MPLA, "Comunicado," September 1979.

22 Moreira, "This Neighbourhood," 43.

23 For a thorough description of this process, see Soares de Oliveira, *Magnificent and Beggar Land.*

24 Mbembe, *On the Postcolony,* 78.

25 Mbembe, *On the Postcolony,* 78.

26 Or structures of power that sometimes rival the state itself. See Nordstrom, "Shadows and Sovereigns."

27 See Soares de Oliveira, *Magnificent and Beggar Land.*

28 To the extent that the members of the clique "based on the presidential grounds" were called the Futunguistas. See Sogge, "Angola."

29 Pombalino was an architectural style that was used to renovate a number of buildings in Lisbon after the earthquake of 1755. Some elements of this style were used in the renovation of the governor's palace, particularly the façades.

30 Martins, "Luanda," 207.

31 Martins, "Luanda."

32 Nhuca Junior, personal communication, 2019.

33 Moreira, "This Neighbourhood."

34 The move was probably sealed with the conversion of dos Santos to Catholicism and his wedding ceremony at the Catholic church beside the palace, Igreja de Jesus. The ceremony was conducted by the archbishop himself, Dom Alexandre do Nascimento. One wonders if such an act did not also aim to bring back the political and religious dyad from colonial times. See chapter 1.

35 Decreto no. 57/01, September 21 (2001).

36 Decreto no. 24/98, August 7 (1998).

37 Decreto no. 57/01, September 21 (2001).

38 Decreto no. 57/01, September 21 (2001).

39 Croese, "Rebuilding by Demolishing."

40 Decreto no. 57/01, September 21 (2001).

41 Dar Al-Handasah, *Integrated Plans,* 50–51.

42 Alves, *Banco de Angola,* 22. Structurally, the National Assembly was constructed of reinforced concrete at a total cost of around 50,000 contos (equivalent to approximately US\$2 million today)—a small fortune at the time.

43 Alves, *Discurso do governador,* 22.

44 Ângela Mingas, personal communication, Luanda, July 2014.

45 Duarte, "Edifício sede da assembleia nacional."

46 Duarte, "Edifício sede da assembleia nacional."

47 One of the projects Odebrecht took part in was the construction of the massive Capanda Hydroelectric Dam, at the invitation of the Soviet construction company Technopromexport, on the Kwanza River in Malanje province, 400 kilometers (249 miles) from Luanda, from 1987–2007. This infrastructural project was sold to the Angolans as the solution to the electricity constraints in Luanda. However, the supply of electricity in Angola has never been constant.

48 Cardoso, "Crude Urban Revolution."

49 Jenkins, Robson, and Cain, "Luanda City Profile," 10.

50 Resolução no. 30/94, November 10 (1994).

51 Resolução no. 30/94, November 10 (1994).

52 Decreto no. 46-A/92, September 9 (1992).

53 Resolução no. 30/94, November 10 (1994).

54 The Brazilian construction firm Prado Valladares, founded by the engineer Lourenço Prado Valladares, was part of the initial deal and took control of the more technical aspects of the project. The firm, having arrived in Angola in 1994, won the confidence of the presidential circle on the basis of the development plan it tabled, titled "O plano estratégico para a infrastructuração da expansão sul da cidade" (Strategic infrastructure plan for the southward expansion of the city). Resolução no. 30/94, November 10, 1994, "Aprova o contrato para o desenvolvimento urbano e autofinanciado, celebrado ente o Governo da Província de Luanda e a Odebrecht Serviços no Exterior LTD" (It approves the contract for the urban ad self-financed development between the Provincial Government of Luanda and Odebrecht Serviços no Exterior LTD).

55 Jenkins, Robson, and Cain, "Luanda City Profile," 10.

56 Unless any mineral resources were found, in which case ownership would revert to the state.

57 Resolução no. 30/94, November 10 (1994).

58 Jenkins, Robson, and Cain, "Luanda City Profile," 10.

59 Cain and Development Workshop Angola, "Private Housing Sector."

60 Jenkins, Robson, and Cain, "Luanda City Profile," 10.

61 Jenkins, Robson, and Cain, "Luanda City Profile," 10.

62 As the investigative journalist Rafael Marques established, the manager of Sakus Empreendimentos e Participações was Mirko Martins, stepson of the then vice president of Angola, Manuel Vicente. See Morais, "O poço de água da Chevron."

63 "Odebrecht investe mais de mil milhões de dólares."

64 "Odebrecht investe mais de mil milhões de dólares."

65 Leaving aside the fact that interest rates can reach up to 25 percent, we can say that only 0.5 percent of the monetary amount that circulates through the Angolan banking system is in the form of loans. Thus, Deloitte Angola reported in 2007 that, with 15 commercial banks operating on the Angolan market, bank credit in 2006 accounted for just 0.5 per cent of the country's GDP. See Deloitte Angola, "Angolan Financial System in the Service of Development," 9.

66 This is what Ricardo Cardoso calls *confusão* planning. See Cardoso, "Crude Urban Revolution."

67 Decreto Presidencial no. 59/11, April 1 (2011).

Chapter 6. The Urban Yet to Come

1 For the existence of the Igreja de Nossa Senhora do Cabo, which was the first parish founded in Luanda in 1575, allegedly by the Portuguese who resided on the island before moving to the mainland, see Angop, "Data da realização das Festas da

Ilha do Cabo poderá ser alterada." See, Agência Angola Press (ANGOP), "Data da realização."

2 Vemba, "Vidas ao relento," 17.
3 Croese, "Post-war State-Led Development," 154. At least 600 families from Ilha de Luanda were still in tents as of January 2019. See "Moradores da Prédio."
4 Gomes, "A cidade é para os ricos."
5 Shatkin, for example, "Coping with Actually Existing Urbanism," 81; Marvin and Graham, *Splintering Urbanism*, 33; and Murray, *Urbanism of Exception*, xii.
6 Agência Angola Press, "Programa habitacional."
7 Agência Angola Press, "Acto central."
8 See Chatterjee, *Politics of the Governed*. For a sharp and incisive application of Chatterjee's concept to Luanda, particularly around some topics I discuss in this chapter, see Croese, "He Will Know How to Explain."
9 Some of these strategies fell under the Umbrella of the Belt and Road initiative. See Wang and Zhao, *Belt and Road Initiative*.
10 Corkin, *Uncovering African Agency*, 84.
11 Corkin, *Uncovering African Agency*, 135.
12 "Angola: Gabinete de Reconstrução Nacional."
13 Lei no. 9/04, "Lei das Terras de Angola" (Land Act of Angola).
14 Lei no. 9/04, "Lei das Terras de Angola" (Land Act of Angola).
15 See also Croese, "Post-war State-Led Development," 113.
16 Lei no. 9/04, "Lei das Terras de Angola" (Land Act of Angola).
17 Mamdani, *Citizen and Subject*.
18 For the various regimes of land ownership and housing related to the evictions from the city center to Zango, see also Croese, "Post-war State-Led Development."
19 Croese, "He Will Know How to Explain," 40.
20 Macrotrends, "Luanda, Angola Metro Area Population."
21 See Satgé and Watson, *Urban Planning*, 3. For other perspectives on the difficulty of implementing planning directives in Africa, see also Awal and Paller, *Who Really Governs Urban Ghana?*; Berrisford, Why It Is Difficult to Change?; and Goodfellow, "Planning and Development Regulation."
22 Dar Al-Handasah, *Integrated Plans*, vol. 1, chap. 3, 4.
23 Dar Al-Handasah, *Integrated Plans*, vol. 1, chap. 3, 37.
24 Dar Al-Handasah, *Integrated Plans*, vol. 1, chap. 8, 10.
25 Dar Al-Handasah, *Integrated Plans*, vol. 1, chap. 3, 41.
26 Dar Al-Handasah, *Integrated Plans*, vol. 1, chap. 3, 38.
27 Dar Al-Handasah, *Integrated Plans*, vol. 2, chaps. 3 and 20.
28 Dar Al-Handasah, *Integrated Plans*, vol. 2, chaps. 3 and 20.
29 Resolução no. 27/00, May 19 (2000). See Croese, "Post-war State-Led Development," 99.
30 Cardoso, "Crude Urban Revolution," 70.
31 Macedo, "Fernando Macedo: Um dia vamos rever a actual Constituição"; "Angola: Constituição—Omissões e Rectificações;" "Rafael Marques."
32 Dar Al-Handasah, *Integrated Plans*, vol. 1, chap. 6, 12.

33   MPLA, "PR cria grupo técnico."

34   Through, for instance, delimiting the scope of the prerogatives of the provincial governor. See "Carlos Feijó esclarece funções."

35   I am particularly referring to the ways in which Vanessa Watson has described the notion of urban fantasies in Africa. See Watson, "African Urban Fantasies."

36   Provincial Government of Luanda, *Plano Director Geral Metropolitano de Luanda*, 1:35.

37   Provincial Government of Luanda, *Plano Director Geral Metropolitano de Luanda*, 1:35.

38   Provincial Government of Luanda, *Plano Director Geral Metropolitano de Luanda*, 2:220.

39   Provincial Government of Luanda, *Plano Director Geral Metropolitano de Luanda*, 2:289.

40   Provincial Government of Luanda, *Plano Director Geral Metropolitano de Luanda*, 2:220.

41   As I have heard many ruling party officials say in informal conversations, using as the example the Partido Revolucionario Institucional, in Mexico (Institutional Revolutionary Party), which governed uninterruptedly for seventy-one years, from 1929 to 2000.

42   Provincial Government of Luanda, *Plano Director Geral Metropolitano de Luanda*, 2:147.

43   *Angola Strategy 2025* is a study commissioned by the Angolan government from the Brazilian Joaquim Nabuco Foundation that details the policies the state should implement to develop the country. It puts forward a set of long-term strategies to guide the government's actions in several key areas, such as development, employment, infrastructure, finance, and national cohesion. See Republic of Angola, Ministério do Planeamento (Ministry for Planning), *Angola 2025*.

44   Provincial Government of Luanda, *Plano Director Geral Metropolitano de Luanda*, 1:71.

45   Dar Al-Handasah, *Integrated Plans*, vol. 1, chap. 6, 2.

46   Provincial Government of Luanda, *Plano Director Geral Metropolitano de Luanda*, 1:105.

47   Provincial Government of Luanda, *Plano Director Geral Metropolitano de Luanda*, 1:128.

48   Provincial Government of Luanda, *Plano Director Geral Metropolitano de Luanda*, 2:255.

49   Goldman, "Speculative Urbanism."

50   Watson, "African Urban Fantasies."

51   Watson, "African Urban Fantasies," 224.

52   Watson, "African Urban Fantasies," 230.

53   More cynically, one can argue that these plans are not produced in order to be implemented. To put it differently, the plan is the goal itself, for the kind of effects it produces even without any implementation. For the PDGML, the Angolan state disbursed US$15 million. Furthermore, Isabel dos Santos and her associates have already managed to get several important contracts with the state. For instance, Urbinvest Projectos Imobiliários, alongside the Dutch company Van Oord Dredging and Marine Contractors BV, were given a contract of US$615 million for "dredging, and coast protection of the marginal da Corimba, in Southern Luanda." Furthermore, the concession, signed and turned into a presidential decree by the former president, involves other construction projects—namely, construction and rehabilitation for access to Corimba's Marginal, to be implemented by the consortium formed by the Landscape and China Road and Bridge Corporation Angola,

on the value US$690.1 million Some of these projects were later on annulled, when João Lourenço replaced Dos Santos as the President of the Republic in 2017. See "Isabel dos Santos promove Luanda"; "Isabel dos Santos ganha obra."

54 See Cain and Development Workshop Angola, "Private Housing Sector," 6ff. See also Lara and Bekker, "Resident Satisfaction."

55 Cain and Development Workshop Angola, "Private Housing Sector," 6.

56 The location was not far from Viana, the satellite city created by the Portuguese in an attempt to form an urban settlement that would take advantage of the existing northern railway and the administrative district of Calumbo. See, for instance, Croese, "Post-war State-Led Development," 2; see also, Fonte, "Urbanismo e arquitectura," 299.

57 I have shown the enactment of these principles in chapter 3, with the upgrading of Golfe; later on, in the 1980s, the government produced formal guidelines on autoconstruction: "the construction of individual or collective dwellings by the masses through their own initiative, using locally available materials and under the guidance of the state." In much of these intentions, there was the understanding that authorities should be tasked with providing the plans and the plots to be used for construction, as well as infrastructure and services, whereas the residents would pay for the construction of the house itself. In some cases, the state-owned bank BNA could provide loans for the beneficiaries of the program. Decreto 188/80, *Diário da República*, November 17, 1982, 1005.

58 Croese, "Post-war State-Led Development," 100.

59 Croese, "Post-war State-Led Development," 100.

60 For the Lei do Fomento Habitacional (Law for Promotion of Housing), see *Diário da República*, no. 3, September 3, 2007.

61 Croese, "Post-war State-Led Development," 104.

62 *Angonotícias*, "Ex-moradores do prédio Cuca satisfeitos com as novas moradias."

63 Decreto Presidencial no. 59/11, April 1 (2011).

64 For a discussion on how the construction of Kilamba was caught up in competing ideologies, see Pitcher and Moorman, "City-Building."

65 Viegas, *Luanda*.

66 "Presidente angolano mandou baixar preços."

67 Decreto Executivo Conjunto no. 142/13, May 17 (2013).

68 At the time, the exchange rate was US$1 to 10 kwanzas.

69 Buire, "Views of Suburban Luanda."

70 Sérgio, "Apartamentos do Kilamba."

71 Luamba, "Obras Chinesas em Angola," n.p.

72 De Soto, *Mystery of Capital*.

Coda. Is Luanda Not Paris?

1 Critical in this literature is the work of Michel de Certeau; see Certeau, *Practice of Everyday Life*.

2 Prendergast, *Paris and the Nineteenth Century*, 3.

3 Hence the need to move beyond the "orthodoxies of urban comparative research." See McFarlane and Robinson, "Introduction."

4 Robinson has done quite substantial work in trying to expand the vocabularies used for urban comparison. See, for instance, "Cities in a World," "Thinking Cities," and *Ordinary Cities*.

5 Malinowski, *Argonauts of the Western Pacific*, 4.

6 Of note here is the charitable gesture of Ash Amin and Nigel Thrift, who try to encompass dysfunctionality into a single theory of infrastructure. See Amin and Thrift, *Seeing Like a City*.

7 See Mumford, *City in History* and *Culture of Cities*.

8 Scott and Storper, "Nature of Cities," 1.

9 See de Boeck and Plissart, *Kinshasa*, and de Boeck and Baloji, *Suturing the City*.

10 Quayson, *Oxford Street, Accra*, 240.

11 Calvino, *Invisible Cities*, 78.

12 For an example of this, see Ward, "Diffusion Planning."

13 Pinkney, *Napoleon III and the Rebuilding of Paris*, 220.

14 Toledano, "Uncommon Resilience of Parisian Street Life."

15 Sutcliffe, *Autumn of Central Paris*, 321.

16 See Davis, *Planet of Slums*.

17 Pinkney, *Napoleon III*, 9.

18 Harvey, *Paris, Capital of Modernity*, 146.

19 Harvey, *Paris, Capital of Modernity*, 48.

20 Pinkney, *Napoleon III*, 70.

21 Sutcliffe, *Autumn of Central Paris*, 184.

22 Sutcliffe, *Autumn of Central Paris*, 185.

23 Nuttall and Mbembe, *Johannesburg*.

24 Watts, "Baudelaire over Berea?" For Nuttall and Mbembe's response, see their "A Blasé Attitude."

25 Jacobs, *Death and Life*.

26 Benjamin, *Arcades Project*.

27 Ondjaki, *Os transparentes*.

28 Aureli, *Possibility of an Absolute Architecture*.

29 Caldeira, *City of Walls*.

Books, Journals, and Periodicals

Abbas, Ackbar. "Building on Disappearance: Hong Kong Architecture and the City." *Public Culture* 6, no. 3 (1994): 441–64.

Abbott, Andrew. "Of Time and Space: The Contemporary Relevance of the Chicago School." *Social Forces* 75, no. 4 (1997): 1149–82.

Abrantes, José Mena. "Mal-estar teatral." *Redeangola Opinião*, May 24, 2014. http://www .redeangola.info/opiniao/mal-estar-teatral/.

Abu-Lughod, Janet. "A Tale of Two Cities: The Origins of Modern Cairo." *Comparative Studies in Society and History* 7 no. 4 (1965): 429–57.

Agência Angola Press. "Acto central do Dia Mundial do Habitat." Agência Angola Press, June 10, 2008. https://web.archive.org/web/20171104180858/http://www.angop.ao/ angola/pt_pt/portal/discursos-do-presidente/discursos/2013/7/34/Acto-central -Dia-Mundial-Habitat,88067694-0366-4920-af85-3d592640f5a2.html.

Agência Angola Press. "Angola: Data realizacão das Festas Ilha Cabo podera ser alterada." Agência Angola Press, October 27, 2016. https://cdn2.portalangop.co.ao/angola/pt_pt /noticias/sociedade/2016/9/43/Angola-Data-realizacao-das-Festas-Ilha-Cabo-podera -ser-alterada,f1a956db-76a9-45b4-9d1f-7bbfada7c6ad.html.

Agência Angola Press. "Ex-moradores da Ilha de Luanda identificam famílias benefi- ciadas com casa." *Portal de Angola*, January 25, 2019. https://www.portaldeangola.com /2019/01/25/ex-moradores-da-ilha-de-luanda-identificam-familias-beneficiadas-com -casas/.

Agência Angola Press. "Ponte que liga marginal à Ilha de Luanda será inaugurada sexta- feira." Agência Angola Press, May 25, 2011. http://www.angop.ao/angola/pt_pt/noticias /sociedade/2011/4/21/Ponte-que-liga-marginal-Ilha-Luanda-sera-inaugurada-sexta -feira,a1d9b44f-765f-45d6-8d15-b6033d566f41.html.

Agência Angola Press. "Programa habitacional pode ultrapassar um milhao de casas ate 2012." Agência Angola Press. Accessed July 13, 2020. http://www.angonoticias.com /Artigos/item/24538/programa-habitacional-pode-ultrapassar-um-milhao-de-casas-ate -2012.

Agualusa, José Eduardo. *Barroco tropical*. Lisbon: Dom Quixote, 2009.

Alexander, Christopher. "A City Is Not a Tree." *Architectural Forum* 122, no. 1 (1965): 58–62.

Alves, Comodoro Vasco Lopes. *Banco de Angola: O novo edifício de Luanda*. Lisbon: Oficinas da Litografia de Portugal, 1957.

Amaral, Ilídio Melo Peres do. "Luanda e os seus 'muceques', problemas de geografia urbana." *Finisterra* 18, no. 36 (1983): 293–325.

Amaral, Ilídio Melo Peres do. *Luanda: Estudo de geografia urbana*. Lisbon: Junta de Investigação do Ultramar, 1968.

Amin, Ash, and Nigel Thrift. *Seeing Like a City*. Cambridge: Polity Press, 2017.

Andersen, Jørgen Eskimose, Paul Jenkins, and Morten Nielsen. "Who Plans the African City? A Case Study of Maputo: Part 1—The Structural Context." *International Development Planning Review* 37, no. 3 (2015): 331–52.

Anderson, Stanford. *On Streets*. Cambridge, MA: MIT Press, 1978.

André, Bráulio. "Políticas habitacionais em Angola: O caso do programa Novas Centralidades em Luanda." MA thesis, Universisdade Federal do Rio de Janeiro, 2019.

"Angola: Gabinete de Reconstrução Nacional devia apresentar contas e fechar as portas." Voice of America Portuguese, March 20, 2011. https://www.voaportugues.com/a/article-03-18-11-angola-saturday-118256494/1259808.html.

"Angola: Constituição—Omissões e Rectificações." Voice of America Portuguese, February 22, 2010. https://www.voaportugues.com/a/a-38-2010-02-02-voa7-92260309/1258054.html

"Angola's $7bn Project Stalks Hilton Hotels." *Business Report*, June 6, 2014. https://www.iol.co.za/business-report/international/angolas-7bn-project-stalks-hilton-hotels-1699874.

Anstee, Margaret. *Orphan of the Cold War: The Inside Story of the Collapse of the Angolan Peace Process, 1992–93*. Basingstoke, UK: Palgrave Macmillan, 1996.

Appadurai, Arjun. *The Social Life of Things: Commodities in Cultural Perspective*. Cambridge: Cambridge University Press, 1986.

Appel, Hannah. "Walls and White Elephants: Oil Extraction, Responsibility, and Infrastructural Violence in Equatorial Guinea." *Ethnography* 13 no. 4 (2012): 439–65.

Araújo, Sara Laíde Pinto. "A estação da Cidade Alta e a linha de Ambaca: Comparação com situações semelhantes em Portugal." MA thesis, Lusíada University, Lisbon, 2017.

Aureli, Pier Vittorio. *The Possibility of an Absolute Architecture*. Cambridge, MA: MIT Press, 2011.

Awal, Mohammed, and Jeffrey Paller. "Who Really Governs Urban Ghana?" Africa *Research Institute*, January 27 2016. https://media. Africaportal.org/documents/ARI-CP-WhoReallyGovernsUrbanGhana-download.pdf.

Baptista, Idalina. "Practices of Exception in Urban Governance: Reconfiguring Power inside the State." *Urban Studies* 50, no. 1 (2013): 39–54.

Batalha, Fernando. *Angola: Arquitectura e história*. Lisbon: Vega, 2006.

Batalha, Fernando. *Uma casa setecentista de Luanda*. Luanda: Edições Spal, 1966.

Beevers, Robert. *Garden City Utopia: A Critical Biography of Ebenezer Howard*. Basingstoke, UK: Macmillan, 1988.

Benjamin, Walter. *The Arcades Project*. Cambridge, MA: Harvard University Press, 1999.

Benjamin, Walter. *One-Way Street, and Other Writings*. London: Penguin, 2009.

Berrisford, Stephen. "Why It Is Difficult to Change Urban Planning Laws in African Countries." *Urban Forum* 22 (2011): 209–28.

Bethel, Leslie. "The Independence of Brazil and the Abolition of the Brazilian Slave Trade: Anglo-Brazilian Relations, 1822-1826." *Journal of Latin American Studies* 1, no. 2 (1969): 115-47.

Bhagavan, M. R. *Angola: Prospects for Socialist Industrialization.* Uppsala, Sweden: Scandinavian Institute of African Studies, 1980.

Bigon, Liora. "Between Local and Colonial Perceptions: The History of Slum Clearances in Lagos (Nigeria), 1924-1960." *African and Asian Studies* 7, no. 1 (2008): 49-76.

Bigon, Liora. *French Colonial Dakar: The Morphogenesis of an African Regional Capital.* Manchester, UK: Manchester University Press, 2016.

Bigon, Liora. "'Garden City' in the Tropics? French Dakar in Comparative Perspective." *Journal of Historical Geography* 38, no. 1 (2012): 35-44.

Bigon, Liora. "Garden Cities in Colonial Africa: A Note on Historiography." *Planning Perspectives* 28, no. 3 (2013): 477-85.

Bigon, Liora. "A History of Urban Planning and Infectious Diseases: Colonial Senegal in the Early Twentieth Century." *Urban Studies Research* 2012 (2012): 1–12. https://doi.org/10.1155/2012/589758.

Bigon, Liora, and Ambe J. Njoh. "The Toponymic Inscription Problematic in Urban Sub-Saharan Africa: From Colonial to Postcolonial Times." *Journal of Asian and African Studies* 50, no. 1 (2015): 25-40.

Birmingham, David. *A Short History of Modern Angola.* Oxford: Oxford University Press, 2015.

Boeri, Stefano. "Ecletic Atlases." *Urban Media Lab Traffic.* Accessed June 18, 2020. https://urbanmedialabtraffic.files.wordpress.com/2012/04/boeri_eclectic_atlases.pdf.

Boxer, Charles Ralph. *The Portuguese Seaborne Empire, 1415-1825.* London: Hutchinson, 1969.

Boxer, Charles Ralph. *Portuguese Society in the Tropics: The Municipal Councils of Goa, Macao, Bahia, and Luanda, 1510-1800.* Madison: University of Wisconsin Press, 1965.

Brenner, Neil. "Debating Planetary Urbanization: Towards an Engaged Pluralism." *Environment and Planning D: Society and Space* 36, no. 3 (2018): 570-90.

Brenner, Neil, and Christian Schmid. "Toward a New Epistemology of the Urban?" *City* 19, nos. 2-3 (2015): 151-82.

Brooke, James. "Adam Smith Crowds Marx in Angola." *New York Times,* December 29, 1987.

Buck-Morss, Susan. *The Dialectics of Seeing: Walter Benjamin and the Arcades Project.* Cambridge, MA: MIT Press, 1990.

Buire, Chloé. "Views of Suburban Luanda: Banishing the Ghosts from Kilamba." Africa Research Institute, September 2, 2015. https://www.africaresearchinstitute.org/newsite/blog/views-of-suburban-luanda-banishing-the-ghosts-from-kilamba/.

Bureau Politico do Comité Central do MPLA. "Comunicado." September 1979.

Cahen, Michel. "Seis teses sobre o trabalho forçado no império português continental em África." *África,* no. 35 (2015): 129-55.

Cain, Allan, and Development Workshop Angola. "The Private Housing Sector in Angola: Angola's Tentative Development of a Private Real-Estate Market." *Centre for Affordable Housing Finance in Africa,* February 10, 2017. https://www.researchgate.net/publication/334625073_Private_Housing_Sector_in_Angola_Angola's_tentative_development_of_a_private_real-estate_market.

Caldeira, Teresa Pires do Rio. *City of Walls: Crime, Segregation, and Citizenship in São Paulo*. Berkeley: University of California Press, 2000.

Calvino, Italo. *Invisible Cities*. London: Vintage Books, 1997.

Cândido, Mariana Pinho. *An African Slaving Port and the Atlantic World*. Cambridge: Cambridge University Press, 2013.

Canelas, Catarina. *A hora da partida: Angola, 1974–1975*. Lisbon: Verso de Kapa, 2017.

Cardonega, António de Oliveira. *História geral das guerras Angolanas*. Lisbon: Agência-Geral do Ultramar, 1940.

Cardoso, Manuel da Costa Lobo. *Luanda Antiga*. Luanda: Museu de Angola, 1951.

Cardoso, Manuel da Costa Lobo. *São Paulo assumpção de Luanda: Apontamentos para a sua história, subsídios para a história de Luanda*. Luanda: Museo de Angola, 1954.

Cardoso, Pedro. "Estação do Bungo." *Rede Angola*, August 20, 2015. http://www.redeangola.info/roteiros/estacao-do-bungo/.

Cardoso, Ricardo V. "The Crude Urban Revolution: Land Markets, Planning Forms, and the Making of New Luanda." PhD diss., University of California, Berkeley, 2015.

"Carlos Feijó esclarece funções do governador de Luanda." *Folha 8*, September 22, 2014. https://jornalf8.net/2014/carlos-feijo-esclarece-funcoes-governador-de-luanda/.

Castelo, Cláudia. "*O modo português de estar no mundo*": *O luso-tropicalismo e a ideologia colonial poortuguesa (1933–1961)*. Lisbon: Edições Afrontamento, 1999.

Castelo, Cláudia. "Reproducing Portuguese Villages in Africa: Agricultural Science, Ideology and Empire." *Journal of Southern African Studies* 42, no. 2 (2016): 267–81.

Carvalho, Fernão Simões de. "Luanda do futuro." *Ronda pelo ultramar* 2 (1963): 27–29.

Carvalho, Ruy Duarte de. A câmera, a escrita e a coisa dita . . . : Fitas, textos e palestras. Lisbon; Cotovia, 2008.

Castelo, Cláudia. "'Village Portugal' in Africa: Discourses of Differentiation and Hierarchisation of Settlers, 1950s–1974." In *Rethinking White Societies in Southern Africa*, edited by Duncan Money and Danelle van Zyl-Hermann, 115–33. London: Routledge, 2000.

Castro, José Caléia, Paulo Romano Reschilian, and Valéria Zanetti. "Os candongueiros e a 'desordem' urbana de Luanda: Uma análise sobre a representação social dos transportes informais." *Revista Brasileira de Gestão Urbana* 10, no. 1 (2018): 7–21.

Cerqueira, José. "Entrevista José Cerqueira [Interview with José Cerqueira]: 'A saída da crise passa por encarar de frente a luta contra a inflação.'" *Novo Jornal*, July 4, 2020: 18–19.

Certeau, Michel de. *The Practice of Everyday Life*. Translated by Steven Rendell. Berkeley: University of California Press, 1984.

Châtelot, Christophe. "Morte de um teatro em Luanda, vítima dos promotores—Elinga." *Buala*, September 28, 2012. http://www.buala.org/pt/cidade/morte-de-um-teatro-em-luanda-vitima-dos promotores-elinga.

Chatterjee Partha. *The Politics of the Governed: Reflections on Popular Politics in Most of the World*. New York: Columbia University Press, 2006.

Ciccantell, Paul S., and Stephen G. Bunker. *Space and Transport in the World-System*. Westport, CT: Greenwood, 1998.

Clapson, Mark. *A Social History of Milton Keynes: Middle England/Edge City*. London: Routledge, 2004.

Coates, Timothy. *Convict Labor in the Portuguese Empire, 1740–1932: Redefining the Empire with Forced Labor and New Imperialism.* Leiden: Brill, 2014.

Coates, Timothy. "The Depósito de Degredados in Luanda, Angola: Binding and Building the Portuguese Empire with Convict Labor, 1880s to 1932." *International Review of Social History* 63 (2018): 151–67.

Cooper, Frederick. *Africa since 1940: Capitalism, Empire, Nation-State.* Cambridge, MA: Harvard University Press, 2014.

Coquery-Vidrovitch, "From Residential Segregation to African Urban Centres: City Planning and the Modalities of Change in Africa South of the Sahara." *Journal of Contemporary African Studies* 32, no 1. (2014): 1–12.

Corkin, Lucy. *Uncovering African Agency: Angola's Management of China's Credit Lines.* London: Routledge, 2016.

Couto, Carlos. "Considerações em torno do vocâbulo 'Luanda.'" *Estudos Históricos* 13–14 (1975): 171–82.

"Criada comissão para gerir as reservas fundiárias ocupadas ilegalmente." *Rede Angola,* May 27, 2016. http://www.redeangola.info/governo-estuda-destino-das-reservas-fundiarias-ocupadas-ilegalmente/.

Croese, Sylvia. "Global Urban Policymaking in Africa: A View from Angola through the Redevelopment of the Bay of Luanda." *International Journal of Urban and Regional Research* 42, no. 2 (2018): 198–209.

Croese, Sylvia. "He Will Know How to Explain: Everyday Politics in Postwar Urban Angola." *Comparative Studies of South Asia, Africa and the Middle East* 39, no. 1 (2019): 37–48.

Croese, Sylvia. "Inside the Government, but Outside the Law: Residents' Committees, Public Authority and Twilight Governance in Post-war Angola." *Journal of Southern African Studies* 41, no. 2: 405–17.

Croese, Sylvia. "Post-war State-Led Development at Work in Angola: The Zango Housing Project in Luanda as a Case Study." PhD diss., Stellenbosch University, 2013.

Croese, Sylvia. "Rebuilding by Demolishing: The Politics of National Reconstruction." *Pambazuka,* March 25, 2010. https://www.pambazuka.org/governance/angola-rebuilding-demolishing.

Croese, Sylvia. "Urban Governance and Turning African Cities Around: Luanda Case Study." Partnership for African Social and Governance Research Group, Paper No. 018. Nairobi, 2016.

Croese, Sylvia. "World-Class City Making in Africa—A View from Angola through the Redevelopment of the Bay of Luanda." Paper presented at the African Centre for Cities, University of Cape Town, Cape Town, February 24, 2016. Accessed February 17, 2019. https://www.africancentreforcities.net/event/world-class-city-making-in-africa-a-view-from-angola-through-the-redevelopment-of-the-bay-of-luanda-2/.

Crowder, Michael. "Indirect Rule, French and British Style." *Africa: Journal of the International African Institute* 34, no. 3 (1964): 197–205.

Cruz, Diogo Alexandre Pedrosa Amaral da. "Memórias de um mercado tropical: Mercado do Kinaxixe e Vasco Vieira da Costa." MA thesis, University of Coimbra, 2012.

Cruz e Silva, Rosa. *Luanda e seus lugares de memória: Texto da palestra alusivo às comemorações da fundação da cidade de Luanda.* Luanda: Governo da Província de Luanda/Direcção Provincial da Cultura, 2009.

Curto José C., and Raymond R. Gervay. "The Population History of Luanda during the Late Atlantic Slave Trade, 1781–1844." *African Economic History* 29 (2001): 1–59.

Cvoro, Uros. "Dialectical Image Today." *Continuum: Journal of Media and Cultural Studies* 22, no. 1 (2008): 89–98.

Dar Al-Handasah. *Integrated Plans of Urban and Infrastructure Expansion of Luanda/Bengo.* 8 vols. Luanda: Ministry of Urbanism and Housing, 2009.

Davis, Mike. *Planet of Slums.* London: Verso, 2006.

Dear, Michael, and Dallas Dishman, eds. *From Chicago to LA: Making Sense of Urban Theory.* Thousand Oaks, CA: Sage Publications, 2001.

de Boeck, Filip, and Sammy Baloji. *Suturing the City: Living Together in Congo's Urban Worlds.* London: Autograph ABP, 2016.

de Boeck, Filip, and Marie-Françoise Plissart. *Kinshasa: Tales of the Invisible City.* Leuven, Belgium: Leuven University Press, 2004.

deGrassi, Aaron. "Provisional Reconstructions: Geo-histories of Infrastructure and Agrarian Configuration in Malanje, Angola." PhD diss., University of California, Berkeley, 2015.

de Jarcy, Xavier. *Le Corbusier, un fascisme français.* Paris: Albin Michel, 2015.

Deleuze, Gilles, and Félix Guattari. *A Thousand Plateaus: Capitalism and Schizophrenia.* Minneapolis: University of Minnesota Press, 1987.

Deloitte. *Banca em Análise: Angola 2007.* Lisbon: Editando, 2007.

Derrida, Jacques. *Writing and Difference.* London: Routledge, 2002.

de Soto, Hernando. *The Mystery of Capital: Why Capitalism Triumphs in the West and Fails Everywhere Else.* New York: Basic Books, 2007.

Development Workshop. "Dossier Habitação Janeiro Dezembro 2016." *Extratos da imprensa Angolana sobre questões sociais e de desenvolvimento,* January–December 2016. http://housingfinanceafrica.org/app/uploads/DW-Angola_CAHF_Dossier-Habitacao -2016-Jan-Dezembro.pdf.

Development Workshop. "Informal Trading in Luanda's Markets, Streets and at Home." Report submitted to International Centre for Development Research (IDRC), Luanda, June 2009. https://idl-bnc-idrc.dspacedirect.org/bitstream/handle/10625/40346/128835.pdf.

Development Workshop. "Projecto de emergência de saneamento base pelo musseque de Luanda/Emergency Sanitation for Luanda's Musseques." Report prepared for Organização da Mulher Angolana, Gabinete de Renovação e Reabilitação dos Musseques, Instituto Nacional de Saúde Pública, Luanda, 1989.

Devish, René. "'Pillaging Jesus': Healing Churches and the Villagisation of Kinshasa." *Africa* 66, no. 4 (1996): 555–86.

Dias, Pedro. "Angola: Artistas opõem-se à destruição de edifícios históricos." VOA Portuguese, June 22, 2014. https://www.voaportugues.com/a/angola-artistas-op%C3%B5em-se-%C3%A0o -destrui%C3%A7%C3%A3o-de-edif%C3%ADcios-hist%C3%B3ricos-/1941688.html.

Donà, Massimo, Loredana Comparone, and Andrea Righi. "Immunity and Negation: On Possible Developments of the Theses Outlined in Roberto Esposito's 'Immunitas.'" *Diacritics* 36, no. 2 (2006): 57–69.

Duarte, Teixeira. "Edifício sede da assembleia nacional de Angola." *Teixeira Duarte.* Accessed October 17, 2018. http://teixeiraduarte.com.br/construcao/edificio-sede-da -assembleia-nacional-de-angola/.

Duminy, James. "Street Renaming, Symbolic Capital, and Resistance in Durban, South Africa." *Environment and Planning D: Society and Space* 32, no. 2 (2014): 310–28.

Eltis, David. "The African Side of the Trade." *Slave Voyages.* Accessed April 22, 2020. https://www.slavevoyages.org/voyage/essays#interpretation/a-brief-overview-of-the -trans-atlantic-slave-trade/the-african-side-of-the-trade/5/en/.

Eltis, David. "A Brief Overview of the Trans-atlantic Slave Trade." *Slave Voyages.* Accessed April 22, 2020. https://www.slavevoyages.org/voyage/essays#interpretation/a-brief -overview-of-the-trans-atlantic-slave-trade/introduction/0/en/.

Eltis, David. "Early Slaving Voyages." Slave Voyages. Accessed April 22, 2020. ttps://www .slavevoyages.org/voyage/essays#interpretation/a-brief-overview-of-the-trans-atlantic -slave-trade/early-slaving-voyages/3/en/

Esposito, Roberto. *Immunitas: The Negation and Protection of Life.* Cambridge: Polity Press, 2011.

"The Fall of Africa's Richest Woman." *Business Report,* August 9, 2018. https://www.iol.co .za/business-report/international/the-fall-of-africas-richest-woman-isabel-dos-santos -16335869.

Fanon, Frantz. *The Wretched of the Earth.* Translated by Constance Farrington. New York: Grove Press, 1963.

Farley, Reynolds, Charlotte Steeh, Tara Jackson, Maria Krysan, and Keith Reeves. "Continued Racial Residential Segregation in Detroit: 'Chocolate City, Vanilla Suburbs' Revisited." *Journal of Housing Research* 4, no. 1 (1993): 1–38.

Ferguson, James. "Seeing Like an Oil Company: Space, Security, and Global Capital in Neoliberal Africa." *American Anthropologist* 107 no. 3 (2005): 377–82.

Fernandes, Edésio. "Constructing the 'Right to the City' in Brazil." *Social and Legal Studies* 16, no. 2 (2007): 201–19.

Fernandes, José Manuel. *Geração Africana: Arquitectura e cidades em Angola e Moçambique, 1925–1975.* Lisbon: Livros Horizonte, 2002.

Fernandes, Walter, and Miguel Hurst. *Angola cinemas.* Göttingen, Germany: Steidl, 2015.

Ferreira, Manuel Ennes. "Nacionalização e confisco do capital português na indústria transformadora de Angola (1975–1990)." *Análise Social* 37, no. 162 (2002): 47–90.

"Flight from Angola." *Economist,* August 26, 1975. https://www.economist.com/middle -east-and-africa/1975/08/16/flight-from-angola.

"Focus: Kiluanji Kia Henda." *Frieze.com,* October 1, 2012. https://frieze.com/article/focus -kiluanji-kia-henda.

Fonseca, Bruno. "Emissão de 379 milhões de dólares de dívida pública para 'salvar' Baía de Luanda." *Rádio Observador,* May 10, 2017. https://observador.pt/2017/05/10/emissao -de-379-milhoes-de-dolares-de-divida-publica-para-salvar-baia-de-luanda/.

Fonte, Maria Manuela Afonso da. "Urbanismo e arquitectura em Angola: De Norton de Matos à revolução." PhD diss., Universidade Técnica de Lisboa, 2006.

Fortuna, Cláudio. "Entrevista com Simões Lopes de Carvalho: O plano director Não serve para das lugar a construção." *Acrimar,* August 3, 2017. http://acrimararquitectura .blogspot.co.za/2015/03/entrevista-com-simoes-lopes-de-carvalho.html.

Fortuna, Cláudio. *Os lugares no espaço angolano*. Luanda: TM Editora, 2015.

Foucault, Michel. *Society Must Be Defended*. New York: Picador, 2003.

Freyre, Gilberto. *Casa-Grande e Ssenzala: Formação da família brasileira sob o regime da economia patriarcal*. São Paulo: Livraria José Olympo Editora, 1933.

Freyre, Gilberto. *The Masters and the Slaves: A Study in the Development of Brazilian Civilization*. Translated by Simon Putnam. New York: Knopf, 1970.

Frias, Sónia, and Cristina Udelsmann Rodrigues. "Private Condominiums in Luanda: More Than Just the Safety of Walls, a New Way of Living." *Social Dynamics* 44, no. 2 (2018): 341-58.

Fry, Maxwell, and Jane Drew. *Tropical Architecture in the Humid Zone*. New York: Reinhold, 1964.

Gandy, Matthew. *The Fabric of Space: Water, Modernity, and the Urban Imagination*. Cambridge, MA: MIT Press, 2014.

Garreau, Joel. *Edge City: Life on the New Frontier*. New York: Anchor, 2011.

Garrido, Marco. "The Ideology of the Dual City: The Modernist Ethic in the Corporate Development of Makati City, Metro Manila." *International Journal of Urban and Regional Research* 37, no. 1 (2013): 165-85.

Gastrow, Claudia. "Cement Citizenship, Housing, Demolition and Political Belonging in Angola." *Citizenship Studies* 21, no. 2 (2017): 1-16.

Gastrow, Claudia. "Negotiated Settlements: Housing and the Aesthetics of Citizenship in Luanda, Angola." PhD diss., University of Chicago, 2014.

Gleijeses, Piero. *Conflicting Missions: Havana, Washington, and Africa, 1959-1976*. Chapel Hill: University of North Carolina Press, 2002.

Goldman, Michael. "Speculative Urbanism and the Making of the Next World City." *International Journal of Urban and Regional Research* 35, no. 3 (2010): 555-81.

Gomes, Miguel. "A cidade é para os ricos." *Redeangola*, December 19, 2016. http://www.redeangola.info/especiais/cidade-e-para-os-ricos/.

Goodfellow, Tom. "Planning and Development Regulation amid Rapid Urban Growth: Explaining Divergent Trajectories in Africa." *Geoforum* 22 (2013): 83-93.

Graham, Stephen, and Simon Marvin. *Splintering Urbanism: Networked Infrastructures, Technological Mobilities and the Urban Condition*. London: Routledge, 2001.

Grant, Richard. "Sustainable African Urban Futures: Stocktaking and Critical Reflection on Proposed Urban Projects." *American Behavioral Scientist* 59, no. 3 (2015): 294-310.

Harvey, David. *Paris, Capital of Modernity*. New York: Routledge, 2004.

Harvey, David. "The Right to the City." *New Left Review* 15 (Sept.–Oct. 2008): n.p. https://newleftreview.org/issues/II53/articles/david-harvey-the-right-to-the-city.

Holston, James. *The Modernist City: An Anthropological Critique of Brasília*. Chicago: University of Chicago Press, 1989.

Home, Robert. *Of Planting and Planning: The Making of British Colonial Cities*. London: Routledge, 1997.

Hon, Tracy, Johanna Jansson, Garth Shelton, Liu Haifang, Christopher Burke, and Carine Kiala. "Evaluating China's FOFAC Commitments to Africa and Mapping the Way Ahead." Report prepared by the Centre for Chinese Studies for the Rockefeller Foundation, January 2010. https://scholar.sun.ac.za/handle/10019.1/21173.

Human Rights Watch. "'They Pushed Down the Houses': Forced Evictions and Insecure Land Tenure for Luanda's Urban Poor." *Human Rights Watch* 19, no. 7(A) (May 2007). https://www.hrw.org/reports/2007/angola0507/.

Ingold, Tim. *Making: Anthropology, Archaeology, Art and Architecture*. London: Routledge, 2013.

Jacob, Berta Maria Oliveira. "A toponímia de Luanda: Das memórias coloniais às pós-coloniais." MA thesis, Universidade Aberta, Lisbon, 2011.

Jacobs, Jane. *The Death and Life of Great American Cities*. New York: Knopf, 2016.

Jameson, Fredric. *Postmodernism, or, The Cultural Logic of Late Capitalism*. Durham, NC: Duke University Press, 1991.

Jenkins, Paul, Paul Robson, and Allan Cain. "Luanda City Profile." *BibliotecaTerra*, January 1, 2003. http://bibliotecaterra.angonet.org/sites/default/files/luanda_city_profile.pdf

Kapuscinski, Ryszard. *Another Day of Life*. London: Picador, 1987.

Karatani, Kojin. *Architecture as Metaphor: Language, Number, Money*. Cambridge, MA: MIT Press, 1995.

"Kinaxixe O mercado que era um símbolo de Luanda já não existe." *Público*, September 22, 2008. https://www.publico.pt/2008/09/22/jornal/kinaxixe-o-mercado-que-era-um-simbolo-de-luanda-ja-nao-existe-276979.

Lara, Tchiloia, and Michiel C. Bekker. "Resident Satisfaction as a Project Quality Measure: The Case of Nova Vida Housing Project." *Journal of Contemporary Management* 9 (2012): 364–81.

Larkin, Brian. "The Politics and Poetics of Infrastructure." *Annual Review of Anthropology* 42 (2013): 327–43.

Larkin, Brian. *Signal and Noise: Media, Infrastructure, and Urban Culture in Nigeria*. Durham, NC: Duke University Press, 2008.

Latour, Bruno. *Reassembling the Social*. Oxford: Oxford University Press, 2005.

Le Blanc, Aleca. "Palmeiras and Pilotis: Promoting Brazil with Modern Architecture." *Third Text* 26, no. 1 (2012): 103–16.

Le Corbusier. *The Athens Charter*. New York: Grossman Publishers, 1973.

Le Corbusier. *Towards a New Architecture*. New York: Dover Publications, 1986.

Lefebvre, Henri. *The Production of Space*. Cambridge: Wiley-Blackwell, 1992.

Lopes, Carlos. "Candongueiros, kinguilas, roboteiros e zungueiras." *OpenEdition Journals* 13, no. 1 (2006): 163–83. https://journals.openedition.org/lusotopie/1505.

Lopes, Carlos. "Dinâmicas do associativismo na economiainformal: Os transportes de passageiros em Angola." *Análise social* 45, no. 195 (2010): 367–91.

Lopes, Carlos. "Luanda cidade informal? Estudo de caso sobre o bairro Rocha Pinto." *Estudos de Desenvolvimento no. 6: Urbanização acelerada em Luanda e Maputo—Impacto da guerra e das transformações socioeconómicas (décadas 80 e 90) textos preliminares*. Lisbon: Centro de Estudos sobre África e do Desenvolvimento, 2001.

Low, Setha M. "The Anthropology of Cities: Imagining and Theorizing the City." *Annual Review of Anthropology* 25 (1996): 383–409.

Luamba, Manuel. "Obras Chinesas em Angola são sinónimo de má qualidade." *Deutsche Welle*, August 8, 2018. https://www.dw.com/pt-002/obras-chinesas-em-angola-s%C3%A3o-sin%C3%B3nimo-de-m%C3%A1-qualidade/a-44995560.

Lugard, Frederick J. D. *The Dual Mandate in British Tropical Africa*. Edinburgh: Blackwood, 1922.

Lunga, Mario. "Canibais na cultura: O comportamento animalesco e acultural da Ministra da cultura Rosa Cruz e Silva." *Central Angola 7311*, April 22, 2014. https:// centralangola7311.net/2014/04/22/canibais-na-cultura-o-comportamento-animalesco-e -acultural-da-ministra-da-cultura-rosa-cruz-e-silva/.

Lynch, Kevin. *The Image of the City*. Cambridge, MA: MIT Press, 1960.

Mabeko-Tali, Jean-Michel. *Dissidências e poder de estado: 1962–1974*. Vol. 3. Luanda: Editorial Nzila, 2001.

Macedo, Fernando. "Fernando Macedo: Um dia vamos rever a actual Constituição e pôr fim à forma de eleição do Presidente da República." *Club-k*, August 11, 2015. https:// www.club-k.net/index.php?option=com_content&view=article&id=21883:fernando -macedo-um-dia-vamos-rever-a-actual-constituicao-e-por-fim-a-forma-de-eleicao-do -presidente-da-republica&catid=14&Itemid=1090&lang=pt;.

MacQueen, Norrie. *The Decolonization of Portuguese Africa: Metropolitan Revolution and the Dissolution of Empire*. Harlow, UK: Longman, 1997.

Macrotrends. "Luanda, Angola Metro Area Population." *Macrotrends*. Accessed December 5, 2020. https://www.macrotrends.net/cities/20049/luanda/population.

Magalhães, Ana, and Inês Gonçalves. *Moderno tropical: A arquitectura portuguesa em Angola e Moçambique, 1948–1975*. Lisbon: Tinta-da-China, 2009.

Malinowski, Bronisław. *Argonauts of the Western Pacific*. London: Routledge and Kegan Paul, 1922.

Mamdani, Mahmood. *Citizen and Subject: Contemporary Africa and the Legacy of Late Colonialism*. Princeton, NJ: Princeton University Press, 1996.

Marat-Mendes, Teresa, and Mafalda Teixeira de Sampaio. "The *plano de urbanização de cidade de Luanda* by Étienne de Groër and David Moreira da Silva (1941–1943)." In *Urban Planning in Lusophone African Countries*, edited by Carlos Nunes Silva, 57–77. Farnham, UK: Ashgate, 2015.

Marcum, John. *The Angolan Revolution: The Anatomy of an Explosion*. Vol. 1. Cambridge, MA: MIT Press, 1969.

Marcus, Sharon. *Apartment Stories: City and Home in Nineteenth-Century Paris and London*. Berkeley: University of California Press, 1999.

Marques Pires, Maria do Carmo. "O ateliê de arquitectura/urbanismo de David Moreira da Silva e Maria José Marques da Silva Martins: Visibilidade da memória." PhD diss., University of Porto, 2012.

Martins, Isabel. "Luanda: A cidade e arquitectura." PhD diss., University of Porto, 2000.

Matos, Helena. "Há quarenta anos o desespero dos retornados: Tirem-nos daqui." *Observador*, September 19, 2015. https://observador.pt/especiais/tirem-nos-daqui/.

Mauss, Marcel. *The Gift: Form and Functions of Exchange in Archaic Societies*. London: Routledge, 2001.

Mbembe, Achille. *On the Postcolony*. Berkeley: University of California Press, 2001.

McFarlane, Colin, and Jennifer Robinson. "Introduction: Experiments in Comparative Urbanism." *Urban Geography* 33, no. 6 (2012): 765–73.

Meijer, Guus, and David Birmingham. "Angola from Past to Present." *Conciliation Resources Accord*, no. 15 (Oct. 2004): n.p. https://www.c-r.org/accord/angola/angola-past -present.

Milheiro, Ana Vaz. *Nos tropicos sem Le Corbusier: Arquitectura luso-africana no Estado Novo.* Lisbon: Relógio d'Água, 2012.

Milheiro, Ana Vaz. "O Gabinete de Urbanização Colonial e o traçado das cidades luso-africanas na última fase do período colonial português." *Urbe Revista Brasileira de Gestão Urbana* 2, no. 4 (2012): 215-32.

Milheiro, Ana Vaz, and Eduardo Costa Dias. "Arquitectura em Bissau e os gabinetes de urbanização colonial (1944-1974)." *arq.urb*, no. 2 (2010): 80-114. https://revistaarqurb .com.br/arqurb/article/view/104.

Miller, Joseph Calder. *Way of Death: Merchant Capitalism and the Angolan Slave Trade, 1730-1830.* Madison: University of Wisconsin Press, 1997.

Mingas, Ângela, coord. *Projecto de pesquisa: Património cultural imóvel de Luanda.* Luanda: CEICA, Universidade Lusíada de Angola, 2019.

Mingas, Ângela, ed. *Sobrados: Dia International dos Monumentos e Sítios, UNESCO.* Centro de Estudos e Investigação Científica de Arquitectura—Universidade Lusíada de Angola. Luanda, 2019.

Ministério do Planeamento (Ministry of Planning). *Angola: 2025: Angola, Um país com future-sustentabilidade, equidade, modernidade: Estratégias de desenvolvimento a longo prazo para Angola (2025), Volumes I-II [Angola 2025: Angola a country with future-sustainability, equity, modernity: Long-term development strategy for Angola (2025).* Luanda, 2007.

Monteiro, Ramiro L. *A família nos musseques de Luanda: subsídios para o seu estudo.* Luanda: Fundo de Acção Social no Trabalho em Angola, 1973.

Moorman, Marissa J. *Intonations: A Social History of Music and Nation in Luanda, Angola, from 1945 to Recent Times.* Athens: Ohio University Press, 2008.

"Moradores do Prédio da Cuca realojados no projecto Zango de Viana." *Angola Xyami*, December 8, 2010. https://angolaxyami.blogspot.com/2010/12/moradores-do-predio-da -cuca-realojados.html.

Morais, Rafael Marques de. "O poço de água da Chevron e a elite do Talatona." *Maka Angola*, December 18, 2012. https://www.makaangola.org/2012/12/o-poco-de-agua-da -chevron-e-a-elite-do-talatona/.

Moreira, Paulo. "This Neighbourhood Is an Endangered Species: Investigating Urban Conflict and Reciprocity between Chicala and Luanda, Angola." PhD diss., London Metropolitan University, 2018.

Morton, David. *Age of Concrete: Housing and the Shape of Aspiration in the Capital of Mozambique.* Athens: Ohio University Press, 2019.

Mourão, Fernando Augusto Albuquerque. *Continuidades e descontinuidades de um processo colonial através de uma leitura de Luanda: Uma interpretação do desenho urbano.* São Paulo: Terceira Margem, 2006.

MPLA, "PR cria gabinete técnico para projectos da capital angolana." MPLA. Accessed August 13, 2020. http://www.mpla.ao/imprensa.52/noticias.55/pr-cria-gabinete-tecnico -para-projectos-da-capital-angolana-.a1451.html.

Mumford, Lewis. *The City in History: Its Origins, Its Transformations, and Its Prospects.* New York: MJF Books, 1989.

Mumford, Lewis, *The Culture of Cities.* London: Secker and Warburg, 1946.

Murray, Martin J. *City of Extremes: The Spatial Politics of Johannesburg.* Durham, NC: Duke University Press, 2011.

Murray, Martin J. *Taming the Disorderly City: The Spatial Landscape of Johannesburg after Apartheid.* Ithaca, NY: Cornell University Press, 2008.

Murray, Martin J. *Urbanism of Exception: Dynamics of Global City Building in the Twenty-First Century.* Cambridge: Cambridge University Press, 2019.

Murteira, Mário. "A economia colonial Portuguesa em África (1930–1975)." *Economia Global e Gestão* 2, no. 2 (1997): 31–63.

Myers, Garth. "The Africa Problem of Global Urban Theory: Re-conceptualising Planetary Urbanisation." *International Development Policy*, no. 10 (2008): 231–53. https://journals.openedition.org/poldev/2739

Narayan, Kirin. "How Native Is a 'Native' Anthropologist?" *American Anthropologist* 95, no. 3 (1993): 671–86.

Nascimento, Saymon. "No Roque Santeiro." *Angola Drops*, January 24, 2009. http://angoladrops.blogspot.com/2009/01/no-roquesanteiro.html.

Nascimento, Úlpio. *Estudo da regularização e protecção das barrocas de Luanda.* Lisbon: Laboratório Nacional de Engenharia Civil, 1952.

Nascimento, Washington Santos. "Das ingombotas ao bairro operário: Políticas metropolitanas, trânsitos e memórias no espaço urbano luandense (Angola 1940–1960)." *Locus: Revista de História, Juiz de Fora* 20, no. 2 (2015): 79–101.

Navarro, Bruno. *Um império projectado pelo "silvo da locomotiva": O papel da engenharia portuguesa na apropriação do espaço colonial africano: Angola e Moçambique (1869–1930).* Lisbon: Edições Colibri, 2018.

Neto, Maria da Conceição. "In Town and out of Town: A Social History of Huambo (Angola), 1902–1961." PhD diss., School of Oriental and African Studies, University of London, 2012.

Neto, Maria da Conceição. "A república no seu estado colonial: combater a escravatura, establecer o 'indigenato.'" *Ler História*, no. 59 (2010) 205–25.

Nielsen, Morten, Joson Sumich, and Bjørn Enge Bertelsen. "Enclaving: Spatial Detachment as an Aesthetics of Imagination in an Urban Sub-Saharan African Context." *Urban Studies* 58, no. 5 (2020): 881–902.

"Nomes das ruas de Luanda moram na clandestinidade." *Angonotícias*, March 29, 2009. http://www.angonoticias.com/Artigos/item/21765/nomes-das-ruas-de-luanda-moram-na-clandestinidade.

Nordstrom, Carolyn. "Shadows and Sovereigns." *Theory, Culture and Society* 17, no. 4 (2000): 35–54.

Norton de Matos, José Maria. *A província de Angola.* Porto, Portugal: Maranus, 1926.

Nuttall, Sarah, and Achille Mbembe. "A Blasé Attitude: A Response to Michael Watts." *Public Culture* 17, no. 1 (2005): 193–202.

Nuttall, Sarah, and Achille Mbembe. *Johannesburg: The Elusive Metropolis.* Durham, NC: Duke University Press, 2008.

O'Laughlin, Bridget. "Class and the Customary: The Ambiguous Legacy of the Indigenato in Mozambique." *African Affairs* 99, no. 394 (2000): 5–42.

Obarrio, Juan. "Third Contact: Invisibility of the Customary in Northern Mozambique." In *The Politics of Custom: Chiefship, Capital, and the State in Contemporary Africa*, edited by John L. Comaroff and Jean Comaroff, 305–35. Chicago: University of Chicago Press, 2018.

"Odebrecht investe mais de mil milhões de dólares em casas de luxo em Luanda." *Angonotícias*, June 16, 2011. http://www.angonoticias.com/Artigos/item/30528/odebrecht -investe-mais-de-mil-milhoes-de-dolares-em-casas-de-luxo-em-luanda.

Oliveira, Pedro Aires, and António Tomás. *1961, Portugal: Uma retrospectiva, 4*. Lisbon: Tinta-da-China, 2019.

Oliveira, Vanessa dos Santos. "Baskets, Stalls and Shops: Experiences and Strategies of Women in Retail Sales in Nineteenth-Century Luanda." *Canadian Journal of African Studies/Revue Canadienne des études africaines* 54, no. 3 (2020): 419–36.

Oliveira, Vanessa dos Santos. "Donas, pretas livres e escravas em Luanda (Séc. XIX)." *Estudos Ibero-Americanos* 44, no. 3 (2018): 447–56.

Ondjaki. *Transparent City*. Translated by Stephen Henighan. London: Europa Editions, 2021.

Ondjaki. *Os transparentes*. Luanda: Editoral Caminho, 2012.

Pacheco, Carlos. "A rebelião de um sacerdote." *Público*, May 3, 2006. https://www.publico .pt/2006/05/03/jornal/a-rebeliao-de-um-sacerdote-76643.

Palonen, Emilia. "Building a New City through a New Discourse: Street Naming Revolutions in Budapest." In *The Political Life of Urban Streetscape: Naming, Politics, and Place*, edited by Reuben Rose-Redwood, Derek Alderman, and Maoz Azaryahu, 98–113. Abingdon, UK: Routledge, 2017.

Panourgiá, Neni. *Fragments of Death, Fables of Identity: An Athenian Anthropography*. Madison: University of Wisconsin Press, 1995.

Pawson, Lara. *In the Name of the People: Angola's Forgotten Massacre*. London: I. B. Tauris, 2014.

Pélissier, René. *La colonie du minotaure: Nationalismes et révoltes en Angola, 1926–1961*. Vol. 2. Orgeval, France: Pélissier, 1978.

Pepetela. *O desejo de Kianda*. Lisbon: Dom Quixote, 1995.

Pepetela. "Horror do vazio." Esquerda.net. May 9, 2009. https://www.esquerda.net /content/horror-do-vazio-um-texto-de-pepetela-sobre-luanda.

Pereira, Silvano F. L., Arcénio P. P. de Carpo, V. R. Schut, and E. Eduardo G. Possolo. *Projecto d'uma companhia para o melhoramento do commércio, agricultura e indústria na Província de Angola: Que se deve estabelecer na cidade de São Paolo d'Assumpção de Loanda, e da qual são fundadores Silvano F. L. Pereira, de Londres, Arcénio P. P. de Carpo, de Loanda, A. Y. R. Shut, D'Hamburgo, eE Eduardo G. Possolo*. Lisbon: Typ da Revolução de Setembro, 1848.

Pereira, Teresa Matos. "A cidade visível e a cidade tangível: A paisagem urbana como palimpsesto na obra de António Ole." *Revista: Estúdio Artistas Sobre Outras Obras* 4, no. 8 (2013): 181–87.

Perestrelo, Afonso Cid. "As obras do Porto de Luanda." In *Separata da Técnica: Revista de Engenharia dos Alunos do I.S.T.*, 1–10. Lisboa: Instituto Superior Técnico, 1941.

Perestrelo, Afonso Cid. "O porto de Luanda." In *Separata da técnica: Revista de engenharia dos alunos do I.S.T.*, 1–16. Lisboa: Instituto Superior Técnico, 1945.

Pieterse, Edgar. "Cityness and African Urban Development." *Urban Forum*, no. 21 (2010): 205–19.

Pimenta, Fernando Tavares. *Angola, os brancos e a independência*. Porto: Afrontamento, 2009.

Pinkney, David H. *Napoleon III and the Rebuilding of Paris*. Princeton, NJ: Princeton University Press, 2019.

Pitcher, M. Anne. "Sowing the Seed of Failure: Early Portuguese Cotton Cultivation in Angola and Mozambique, 1820–1926." *Journal of Southern African Studies* 17, no. 1 (2011): 43–70.

Pitcher, M. Anne, and Aubrey Graham, "Cars Are Killing Luanda: Cronyism, Consumerism, and Other Assaults on Angola's Postwar, Capital City." In *Cities in Contemporary Africa*, edited by M. J. Murray and G. A. Myers, 173–99. New York: Palgrave Macmillan, 2006.

Pitcher, M. Anne, and Marissa Moorman. "City-Building in Post-socialist and Post-conflict Luanda: Burying the Past with Phantasmagorias of the Future." In *African Cities Reader III: Land, Property and Value*, edited by Ntone Edjabe and Edgar Pieterse, 123–34. Cape Town: African Centre for Cities and Chimurenga, 2015.

Prendergast, Christopher. *Paris and the Nineteenth Century*. New York: Willey, 1995.

"Presidente angolano mandou baixar preços das casas na nova cidade de Kilamba." *Jornal de Notícias*, November 9, 2012. https://www.jn.pt/mundo/palops/interior/presidente -angolano-mandou-baixar-precos-das-casas-na-nova-cidade-de-kilamba-2877511.html.

Provincial Government of Luanda. *Plano Director Geral Metropolitano de Luanda*. Luanda: Provincial Government of Luanda, July 2005.

Pullan, Wendy. "Frontier Urbanism: The Periphery at the Centre of Contested Cities." *Journal of Architecture* 16, no. 1 (2001): 15–35.

Quayson, Ato. *Oxford Street, Accra: City Life and the Itineraries of Transnationalism*. Durham, NC: Duke University Press, 2014.

Queiroz, Artur. *Luanda: Arquivo histórico: séc. XVI–séc. XXI*. Luanda: Colecção Novembro, 2014.

Queiroz, Eça de. *Uma Ccampanha Aalegre, "Farpas."* Lisbon: Livros do Brasil, 2001.

Rabinow, Paul. *Anthropos Today: Reflections on Modern Equipment*. Princeton, NJ: Princeton University Press, 2003.

Rádio e Televisão de Portugal. "Revolução de Abril: A declaração de Spínola do 27 de Julho de 1974". *Rádio e Televisão de Portugal*. Accessed November 30, 2019. http://media .rtp.pt/descolonizacaoportuguesa/pecas/a-dec142/cao-de-spinola-de-27-de-julho-de -1974/.

"Rafael Marques: Angola tem de alterar 'Constituição bonapartista' para ser uma democracia." *Observador*, November 6, 2018. https://observador.pt/2018/11/06/rafael-marques -angola-tem-de-alterar-constituicao-bonapartista-para-ser-uma-democracia/.

Redvers, Louise. "Angolan Traders Mourn Loss of Roque Santeiro Market." BBC Radio, September 18, 2010. http://news.bbc.co.uk/2/hi/programmes/from_our_own _correspondent/9008930.stm

Rego, A. da Silva. *A reconquista de Luanda em 1648 e alguns por problemas por ela levantados.* Lisbon: Universidade Técnica de Lisboa, 1964.

Robinson, Jennifer. "Cities in a World of Cities: The Comparative Gesture." *International Journal of Urban and Regional Research* 35, no. 1 (2011): 1–23.

Robinson, Jennifer. *Ordinary Cities: Between Modernity and Development.* London: Routledge, 2013.

Robinson, Jennifer. "Thinking Cities through Elsewhere: Comparative Tactics for a More Global Urban Studies." *Progress in Human Geography* 40, no. 1 (February 1, 2016): 3–29.

Rodgers, Dennis. "Disembedding the City: Crime, Insecurity and Spatial Organization in Managua, Nicaragua." *Environment and Urbanization* 16, no. 2 (2004): 113–24.

Rodrigues, Luís Nuno, ed. Regimes e impérios: as relações luso-americanas no século XX. Lisbon: FLAD, 2006.

Roque, Sandra. "*Cidade* and *Bairro*: Classification, Constitution and Experience of Urban Space in Angola." *Social Dynamics* 37, no. 3 (2011): 332–48.

Rosa, Edite Maria Figueiredo e. "Odam—A construção do moderno em Portugal: Entre o universal e o singular." *Proyecto, Progreso, Arquitectura*, no. 11 (2014): 26–39.

Roy, Ananya. "What Is Urban about Critical Urban Theory?" *Urban Geography* 37, no. 6 (2015): 810–23.

Rui, Manuel. *Quem me dera ser onda.* Lisbon: Edições Cotovia, 1991.

Rushdie, Salman. *Imaginary Homelands: Essays and Criticism, 1981–1991.* London: Granta Books, 1991.

Santos, Cristina. "A independência acabou com a exploração do homem pelo homem." *FatimaMissionaria*, November 7, 2011. https://www.fatimamissionaria.pt/artigo.php ?cod=21175&sec=8.

Santos, José de Almeida. *Das origens dos municípios portugueses aos primeiros tempos da Câmara Municipal de Luanda.* Luanda: Centro de Informação e Turismo de Angola, 1965.

Santos, José de Almeida. *Luanda d'outros tempos.* Luanda: Centro de Informação e Turismo de Angola, 1965.

Satgé, Richard, and Vanessa Wilson. *Urban Planning in the Global South: Conflicting Rationalities in Contested Urban Space.* Cham, Switzerland: Palgrave Macmillan, 2018.

Schmid, Christian, Ozan Karaman, Naomi C. Hanakata, Pascal Kallenberger, Anne Kockelkorn Lindsay Sawyer, Monika Streule, and Kit Ping Wong. "Towards a New Vocabulary of Urbanisation Processes: A Comparative Approach." *Urban Studies* 55, no. 1 (2018): 19–52.

Scoffier, Richard. "Pour mieux comprendre la beauté d'aujourd'hui en architecture." *Le Portique: Revue de Philosophie et de Sciences Humaines*, no. 28 (2012): 3–9.

Scott, Allen J., and Michael Storper. "The Nature of Cities: The Scope and Limits of Urban Theory." *International Journal of Urban and Regional Research* 39, no. 1 (2015): 1–15.

Scott, James C. *Seeing Like a State: How Certain Schemes to Improve the Human Condition Have Failed.* New Haven, CT: Yale University Press, 2008.

Sérgio, Paulo. "Apartamentos do Kilamba baixam de preço." *Portal de Angola.* Accessed June 15, 2013. https://www.portaldeangola.com/2013/06/apartamentos-do-kilamba -baixam-de-preco/.

Shatkin Gavin. "Coping with Actually Existing Urbanisms: The Real Politics of Planning in the Global Era." *Planning Theory* 10, no. 1 (2011): 79–87.

Sheller, Mimi, and John Urry. "The City and the Car." *International Journal of Urban and Regional Research* 24, no. 4 (2000): 737–57.

Sidaway, James D. "Enclave Space? A New Metageography of Development?" *Area* 39, no. 3 (2007): 331–39.

Siegert, Nadine. *Na pele da cidade / In the Skin of the City.* Luanda: Instituto Camões, 2009.

Simone, AbdouMaliq. *For the City Yet to Come: Changing African Life in Four Cities.* Durham, NC: Duke University Press, 2004.

Simone, AbdouMaliq. "People as Infrastructure: Intersecting Fragments in Johannesburg." *Public Culture* 16, no. 3 (2004): 407–29.

Smith, Alan K. "António Salazar and the Reversal of Portuguese Colonial Policy." *Journal of African History* 15, no. 4 (1974): 653–67.

Soares de Oliveira, Ricardo. *Magnificent and Beggar Land: Angola since the Civil War.* London: Hurst, 2015.

Sogge, David. "Angola: The Client Who Came in from the Cold." Transnational Institute, October 1, 2000. https://www.tni.org/en/article/angola-the-client-who-came-in -from-the-cold.

Specter, Michael. "Extreme City: The Severe Inequality of the Angolan Oil Boom." *New Yorker*, June 1, 2015. http://www.newyorker.com/magazine/2015/06/01/extreme-city-specter.

Stern, Michael A., and William M. Marsh. "Editors' Introduction: The Decentered City—Edge City and the Expanding Metropolis." *Landscape and Urban Planning* 36, no. 4 (1997): 243–46.

Sutcliffe, Anthony. *The Autumn of Central Paris: The Defeat of Town Planning, 1850–1970.* London: Arnold, 1970.

Swacha, Michael. "Book Review: Roberto Esposito, *Immunitas—The Protection and Negation of Life.*" *Polygraph: An International Journal of Culture and Politics*, nos. 23–24 (2013): 197–203.

Toledano, Alex. "The Uncommon Resilience of Parisian Street Life." *New York Times Magazine*, November 16, 2015. https://www.nytimes.com/2015/11/16/magazine/the -uncommon-resilience-of-parisian-street-life.html?smid=fb-nytimes&smtyp=cur&_r =2&referer=http://m.facebook.com/.

Tomás, António. *Amílcar Cabral: The Life of a Reluctant Nationalist.* London: Hurst, 2021.

Tomás, António. *O Ffazedor de utopias: Uma biografia de Amílcar Cabral.* Lisbon: Tinta-da-China, 2008.

Tomás, António. "Mutuality from Above: Urban Crisis, the State and the Work of Comissão de Moradores in Luanda." *Anthropology Southern Africa* 37, nos. 3–4 (2014): 175–86.

Tostões, Ana. "How to Love Modern [Post-]colonial Architecture: Rethinking Memory in Angola and Mozambique Cities." *Architectural Theory Review* 21, no. 2 (2017): 196–217.

Tostões, Ana, ed. *Modern Architecture in Africa: Angola and Mozambique.* Lisbon: ICIST, Técnico, 2013.

Tostões, Ana, and Jessica Bonito. "Empire, Image and Power during the Estado Novo Period: Colonial Urban Planning in Angola and Mozambique." In *Urban Planning in Lusophone African Countries*, edited by Carlos Nunes Silva, 43–56. Farnham, UK: Ashgate, 2015.

Troufa Real, Nuno. "O Arquitecto que gostava de ser marinheiro." *Ukuma: Fundação Troufa Real*, December 22, 2016. http://www.ukuma.net/wp/2016/12/22/troufa-real-o-arquitecto-que-gostava-de-ser-marinheiro/.

Troufa Real, José. *The Musseques of Luanda: Housing in Angola, a New Neighbourhood "Golfe."* Óbidos: Sinapis, 2011.

Vemba, Sebastião. "Vidas ao relento." *Novo Jornal*, April 24, 2009.

Viegas, Sílvia Leiria. *Luanda: Cidade (im)previsível? Governação e transformação urbana e habitacional: Paradigmas de intervenção e resistências no novo milénio.* PhD diss., Universidade de Lisboa, 2015.

Vieira, Luandino. *A Cidade e a infância.* Lisbon: Casa dos Estudantes do Império, 1960.

Vieira da Costa, Vasco. "Cidade Satélite no. 3: Ante-projecto de uma Cidade Satélite para Luanda." MA thesis, Universidade do Porto, 1948. https://repositorio-tematico.up.pt/handle/10405/48347.

Wachsmuth, David. "City as Ideology: Reconciling the Explosion of the City Form with the Tenacity of the City Concept." *Environment and Planning D: Society and Space* 32, no. 1 (2014): 75–90.

Wang Linggui and Jianglin Zhao, eds. *The Belt and Road Initiative in the Global Context.* New Jersey: World Scientific, 2019.

Ward, Stephen V. "Diffusion Planning: Agents, Mechanisms, Networks and Theories." In *The Routledge Handbook of Planning History*, edited by Carola Hein, 90–114. New York: Routledge, 2018.

Watson, Vanessa. "African Urban Fantasies: Dreams or Nightmares?" *Environment and Urbanization* 26, no. 1 (2005): 215–31.

Watts, Michael. "Baudelaire over Berea, Simmel over Sandton?" *Public Culture* 17, no. 1 (2005): 181–92.

Weber, Max. *Collected Methodological Writings.* Translated by Hans Henrik Brunn. Edited by Hans Henrik Brunn and Sam Whimster. London: Routledge, 2012.

Wolfers, Michael, and Jane Bergerol. *Angola in the Front Line.* London: Zed Books, 1983.

World Bank Group. *Angola: Systematic Country Diagnostic—Creating Assets for the Poor.* Washington, DC: World Bank Group, December 2018.

Wright, Gwendolyn. *The Politics of Design in French Colonial Urbanism.* Chicago: University of Chicago Press, 1991.

Legal Documents

Acordão no. 484, June 27, Tribunal Constitucional (Constitutional Tribunal), "Recurso Ordinário de Inconstitucionalidade Interposto por Sociedade Comercial Mota e Irmãos, sobre o Acórdão do Plenário do Tribunal Supremo" (Ordinary unconstitutionality appeal presented by Sociedade Comercial Mota e Irmãos on decision of the plenary of the Supreme Tribunal), *Diário da República*, 2018. https://jurisprudencia.tribunalconstitucional.ao/jurisprudencia/acordao-n-0-484-2018/.

Centro de Documentação 25 de Abril. "Direito das colónias à independência: Lei no. 7/74, de 27 de julho 1." Centro de Documentação, 25 de Abril (accessed November 22, 2019). http://www1.ci.uc.pt/cd25a/wikka.php?wakka=descono3.

Decreto 188/80, November 17, Conselho de Ministros (Council of Ministers), "Lei da Autoconstrução" (Law on autoconstruction), *Diário da República*, I Série, no. 271: 1005-6.

Decreto Executivo Conjunto no 142/13, May 17, Ministry of Finance and Ministry of Urbanism, "Fixa as condições de commercialização das Habitações do Fundo de Fomento Habitacional nas Centralidades do Kilamba e Cacuaco" (Set the conditions for sale of housing belonging to Fund of Housing Development in the Centralidades do Kilamba e Cacuaco), *Diário da República*, I Série, no. 92, 2013: 1142-43.

Decreto-Lei no. 6/04, October 22, Conselho de Ministros (Council of Ministries), "Cria na dependência do Presidente da República, na sua qualidade de Chefe do Governo, o Gabinete de Reconstrução Nacional" (It creates under the dependency of the presidente of the republic, as head of the government, the Office of National Reconstruction), *Diário da República*, I Série, no. 85, 2004: 1994-95.

Decreto-Lei no. 40 333, October 14, Gabinete do Ministro (Minister's Office), "Estabelece o regime de propriedade horizontal" (It establishes the regime of horizontal property), *Diário da República*, I Série, no. 223, 1955: 879-86.

Decreto-Lei no. 576/70, November 24, Presidência do Conselho (Presidential Council), "Define a política dos solos tendente a diminuir o custo de terrenos para construção" (It defines the policy of urban land in order to decrease the cost of tracts of land for construction), *Diário da República*, I Série, no. 273, 1970: 1749-56.

Decreto no. 24/98, August 7, Conselho de Ministros (Council of Ministers), Cria o Gabinete de Obras Especiais, abreviadamente (G.O.E.) sob dependência directa do Presidente da República" (It creates the Office of Special Works, abbreviated G.O.E. under the direct dependency of the President of the Republic), *Diário da República*, I Série, no. 34, 1998: 435-36.

Decreto no. 46-A/92, September 9, Conselho de Ministros (Council of Ministries), "Determina que governos provinciais podem constituir o direito de superfície sobre terrenos de que sejam proprietários, a favor de pessoas singulares e colectivas" (It determines that provincial governments may constitute surface rights on tracts of land of their on in favor of private and legal persons), *Diário da República*, I Série, no 36, 1992: 468.

Decreto no. 57/01, September 21, Conselho de Ministros (Council of Ministers), "Aprova o estatuto orgânico do Gabinete de Obras Especiais" (It approves the organic statute of the Office of Special Works), *Diário da República*, I Série, no. 43, 2001: 778-84.

Decreto no. 80/76, October 14, Presidência da República (Presidency of the Republic), "Que determina a forma de conservação e proteção do património histórico e cultural do povo angolano" (On the determination of the form of conservation and protection of the Angolan's people historical and cultural heritage), *Diário da República*, I Série, no. 244, 1976: 797-99.

Decreto Presidencial no. 59/11 April 1, Presidência da República (Presidency of the Republic), "Estabelece as Bases dos Planos Integrados de Expansão urbana e Infra-Estruturas do Luanda e Bengo" (It establishes the bases for the Integrated Plans of Urban Expansion and Infrastructure of Luanda and Bengo," *Diário da República*, I Série, no. 62, 2011: 1-1557.

Despacho, June 14 1980, Ministério da Construção e Habitação (Ministry of Construction and Habitation), "Intervenciona o prédio pertencente a Fânia Prado de Oliveira"

(It takes over the building belonging to Fânia Prado de Oliveira), *Diário da República*, I Série, no. 140: 1021.

Despacho, August 31, Secretaria de Estado da Cultura—Gabinete do Secretário de Estado (State Secretary of Culture—Office of the State Secretary), Determina a classificação como monumentos históricos (It determines classification as a historical monument), *Diário da República*, I Série, no. 2015, 1981: 729-30.

Lei no. 03/07, September 3, Assembleia Nacional (National Assembly), "Lei de bases do fomento habitacional" (Basic law for promotion of housing), *Diário da República*, I Serie, no. 3, 2007: 1590-96.

Lei no. 3/76, March 3, Conselho da Revolução (Council of the Revolution), "Lei das Nacionalizações e Confiscos" (Law of nationalizations and confiscations), *Diário da República*, I Série, no. 52, 1976: 131-37.

Lei no. 9/04, November 9, Assembleia Nacional (National Assembly), "Lei das Terras de Angola" (Land act of Angola), *Diário da República*, I Série, no. 90, 2004: 2118-36.

Lei no. 19/91, May 25, Assembleia do Povo (People's Assembly), "Lei Sobre a Venda do Patrimonio Habitacional do Estado" (Sale of state housing property act), *Diário da República*, I Série, no. 22, 1991: 288-91.

Lei no. 21-C/1992, August 28, Comissão Permanente da Assembleia do Povo (Permanent Commission of the People's Assembly), "Sobre a concessão de titularidade do uso e aproveitamento da terra" (on the granting of entitlement of land use), *Diário da República*, I Série, no. 32: 392 (610-67).

Lei no. 43/76, June 19, Conselho da Revolução (Council of the Revolution), "Lei sobre o confisco de imóveis" (Law on the confiscation of buildings), *Diário da República*, I Série, no. 144, 1976: 543.

Resolução no 27/00, November 24, Comissão permanente do conselho de ministros (Permanent commission of the council of ministries), "Aprova plano de gestão do crescimento urbano de Luanda" (It approves the plan for the management urban growth of Luanda), *Diário da República*, no. 50, I Série, 2000: 265-978.

Resolução no. 30/94, November 10, Concelho de Ministros (Council of Ministries), "Aprova o contrato para o desenvolvimento urbano e autofinanciado, celebrado ente o Governo da Província de Luanda e a Odebrecht Serviços no Exterior LTD" (It approves the contract for the urban and self-financed development between the Provincial Government of Luanda and Odebrecht Serviços no Exterior LTD), *Diário da República*, I Série, no. 50, 1994: 570-71.

Brazil, 39; Dutch occupation of, 36, 223n20; modernism in, 228n82; modernist architecture in, 74; Ordenações do Reino and, 222n12; Portuguese explorers in, 33; right to the city and, 13; transport of slaves to, 40, 62, 222n5
Bungo, 79–80

Cabral, Amílcar, 94, 124–25
Cacuaco, 18, 71, 82, 109, 120, 188
Caetano, Marcelo, 24, 94–95, 110
Caldeira, Teresa, 21, 213, 232n36
candongueiros, 134–36, 138, 143
Cape Verde, 33, 125
capitalism, 212; flâneur and, 208; oil sector and, 155; surplus society and, 181–82; transition to, 156; urban planning and, 168
Cardoso, Ricardo, 50, 154, 168, 189, 235n67
Carnation Revolution (Revolução dos Cravos), 94–96, 102, 115, 123
Carvalho, Fernão Simões de, 76, 81–82, 228n72, 228n76, 232n32
Casa Luandense, 31–32, 43, 45–46, 56, 78, 86, 203, 223n46
Cazenga, 98, 185
cement city (*cidade de cimento*), 7, 11, 18
centralidades (centralities/urban growth areas), 6, 9, 11, 14, 144, 180, 195–96, 202; gated communities and, 151. *See also* Kilamba; Zango
Chicala, 159, 163
China, 16, 183, 186, 189, 196, 198–99; Kilamba and, 198–200; loans from 16, 183, 186, 189
centralization, 128, 144, 160
Centro Político Administrativo, 159, 163–65
Cidade Alta, 20, 25, 34–35, 52f, 75, 161–67, 190, 193; Bairro dos Ministérios and, 80; Caminhos de Ferro de Luanda (CFL) and, 63; perimetization of, 151, 163, 174; Roque Santeiro and, 160; Station, 85, 225n7
citizenship, 13–14, 186, 202; Angolan, 102; performance of, 9; urban, 4
city making, 95, 208, 220n15; colonial, 6, 23, 127; Luanda's, 81, 135
cityness, 9, 12, 208
civil war (Angola), 102, 115, 144; displacement and, 48, 92; end of, 25, 50, 163, 181–82, 186, 190, 201; reconstruction and, 178
class, 7, 31, 56, 61, 116; diversity, 123; divisions, 219n8; separation, 78, 83, 128; status, 84

Colonato da Cela, 66, 226n23
colonial city-making, 6, 127, 220n15
colonialism, 4, 8, 47, 96, 228n71; architectural legacy of, 224n61; Carnation Revolution and, 102; developmental, 108; end of, 137; late, 80, 121, 219n8; Portuguese, 44, 60, 105, 220n10, 227n62; squatting and, 87; topographic references and, 123; urban life and, 115
colonization, 3, 47, 65, 85; modern, 22, 37; white, 38
comités populares (people's committees), 96–99, 229n14
Companhia de Desenvolvimento Urbano (EDURB), 169–71
Companhia de Diamantes de Angola (Angolan Diamond Company; CDA), 43, 45–47, 55, 224n56
concrete city, 60, 92, 130, 172
condominiums, 151, 158, 167–68, 170–74, 181. *See also* gated communities
consolidated urban core (Luanda), 8, 60, 76, 85, 111, 128–29
constitution of 2010 (Angola), 189, 192, 198
Coqueiros, 46, 78–79
Creole society, 41, 79
crime, 21, 150–51
Croese, Sylvia, 15, 186
Cruz e Silva, Rosa, 51, 224n74
Cubans in Angola, 106–7, 113, 230n60

Dar Al-Handasah (Dar Group), 165, 187–90, 193–95, 198
Davis, Mike, 14, 209
De Boeck, Filip, 21, 207
decentralization, 144, 202
De Gröer, Étienne, 69–72, 75, 120, 196, 208, 226n35, 226n38. *See also* Moreira da Silva, David
degredados (convicts), 34, 62, 73
discontinuity, 195, 211
Dos Santos, José Eduardo, 25, 54–55, 126, 162, 181–83, 189–92, 194, 199–201, 238n53; authoritarianism of, 14; conversion to Catholicism of, 234n34

Elinga Teatro, 20, 22, 29–33, 41, 50–56
enslaved people, 14, 22, 34–40, 68, 79, 221–22nn4–6, 223n27; *bairros* and, 80; in

urban fragmentation, 24–25, 114, 143, 156, 195, 211; in the Global South, 208; in Luanda, 15, 84, 136, 144, 150–51, 167, 173, 205

urban grid, 116, 178; expansion of, 3–4, 14, 20, 22, 25, 60, 86–87, 121, 149, 151, 172

urbanism, 95, 97, 178, 195; bifurcated, 180; colonial, 117, 142, 150, 219n8; fantasy, 192; French, 70; frontier, 5; in Luanda, 25, 154; Northern understandings of, 11; Southern, 10, 25, 121, 206

urbanists, 4, 48, 75, 79–80, 85, 110; colonial, 119, 128, 137; European, 74; Southern, 9–10; Soviet, 162. *See also* Vieira da Costa, Vasco

urbanizations (*urbanizaçoes*), 3, 6, 14, 65, 95, 151, 168–72, 180, 202; colonial, 7, 178; of Luanda 17, 22, 34, 43, 187; modern, 11; planetary, 9–10; slums and, 211. *See also* centralidades; Kilamba; Projecto Nova Vida; Zango

urban theory, 12, 16, 20–21, 206–208, 211, 213; classical, 9–10, 120; contemporary, 120, 150, 221n36; critical, 121, 195

urban transformation, 19, 50, 76–77, 143, 150, 179, 191–92, 195; bifurcation of the urban and, 182; Cidade Alta and, 163, 191; Dos Santos and, 25, 201; Luanda Sul program and, 170; petrodollars and, 154; presidential palace and, 151, 174; Roque Santeiro and, 17, 221n51; scale of, 9

Urbinvest, 191–92, 237n53

Viana, 71, 82, 109, 188, 238n56

Viegas, Sílvia, 13, 199

Vieira, Luandino, 1, 5, 219n8

Vieira da Costa, Vasco, 48, 59–61, 72, 74–76, 81, 83–85, 110, 208

violence, 100, 102–3, 139–40, 151–52; urban, 158

Watson, Vanessa, 187, 195, 237n35

Weber, Max, 12, 220n36

Zaire, 134–35, 232n10

Zambia, 66, 101, 233n39

Zango, 19, 25, 178, 180, 186, 196–98, 200, 202, 236n18

zoning, 67, 70, 82, 119, 128; enforcement of, 75; laws, 205; regulations, 81, 107